The King of the Norse

JM Harrington

Table of Contents

Appendix 1 - Place Names

Asgard~Land of the Norse Gods

Byzantine~Istanbul

Coll~Hebridean island

Corfe Gate~Corfe Castle

Dyflin~Dublin

Danemark~Denmark

Ennor~Main Scilly Island

Escanceaster~Exeter

Faeroes~Faroe Islands

The Fylde ~(Scandinavian: "field") is a coastal plain in Lancashire

Gardarike~Kiev

Gipeswic~Ipswich

Hlidarendi~Gunnar's home

Jorvik~York

Kernow~Cornwell

Leirvik~Lerwick

Liddyford~Ford across the River Lyd

Lloegr~England (the lost lands of the British)

Lund~Lund, Southern Sweden

Lundey~Lundy

Murchaddun~Maldon

Manu~Isle of Man

Novgorod~Russia

Osilia~Estonia

Porth Kernow~Porthcurno

Prydain~Britain

Scania~Skane southern county of Sweden, previously Danish

Sceapige~Sheppey

Svea~Swedes

Swanwich~Swanage

Syllingar~Scilly Islands

Temese~Thames

Tinganese~Torshavn, capital of the Faeroes

Vendland~North Poland

Wincanceaster~ Winchester

Ynys Mon~Anglesey

Appendix 2 - People

Aethelbald~Earl of Devon

Aethelflaed~Brihtnoth's wife

Aethelgar~Archbishop of Canterbury 988-990

Aethelred~Saxon king of England

Aelfstan~Bishop of Rochester

Aelthryth~King Aethelred's mother

Aethelwine~Brihtnoth's nephew and leader of his housecarls

Aethelwold~dead bishop of Wiltshire

Aldred~Slave of Kernow

Alfred~Bishop of Rochester's scribe.

Alfric~Ealdorman of Hampshire

Alfvine~leader of the Jomsviking rebels

Amlaib~Previous King of Dublin

Arnguda~Gunnar's sister

Baldr~Longship captain for King Ivar

Berg~Alfvine's lieutenant

Bergporar~Njal's wife and cousin of Freyja.

Bjarni~Slave ship captain

Bjornsson~rich but bitter Icelandic merchant

Brian Boru~High King Ireland

Brihtnoth~Earl of the East Saxons

Brynjolf~Olaf's lieutenant

Cadoc~Cornish King

Edgard~Earl of Kent

Elfgar~son of Alfric

Erik Ericsson~Old friend of Gull and Gunnar.

Eyjolf~Lawyer and opponent of Njal.

Flosi~Harald's man

Freyja~Gunnar's wife

Gilli~Jarl of the Hebrides

Glum~Harald's man

Greta~Harald Sveinsson's wife.

Godwin~Earl of Wiltshire

Grim~second son of Njal

Gull~killed in Lund, brother of Harald

Gunnar~our hero

Gustav~Brother of Gull and Harald.

Guthmund~Danish Jarl loyal to Svein

Gyda~Wife of Olaf Trygvasson

Harald~oldest of the sons of Svein

Helga~Berg's wife, Gyda's woman

Helgi~Harald's man

Hild-Yxa~wife of Bjorn Bjornsson

Hjort~Gunnar's youngest brother

Hroar~husband of Arnguda

Hrut~Harald's man

Ivar ~Norse king of Waterford

Jarn~King of Dublin

Justin~Danish Jarl loyal to Svein

Kari~Olaf's lieutenant

Kent~Ragnal's captain

Ketil~Alfvine's lieutenant

Kjarten~Olaf's lieutenant

Kolskegg~Gunnar's brother

Litta~Slave ship worker

Maban~bastard son of king Cadoc

Mael Sechnaill~King of Mide Ireland

Mawgan~Cornish Seer

Mort~Olaf's right hand man.

Njal~The greatest lawyer of Iceland

Olaf Trygvasson~Viking lord and future King of Norway

Ragnal~Prince of Dublin

Saint Oswald~Archbishop of Worcester

Sigeric~Bishop of Ramsbury

Sigurdthe Stout~Jarl of Orkney

Sihtric~Ivar's son

Skarphedin~oldest son of Njal

Soren Guldhuvud~Bjorn's farm manager

Styrbjorn~Leader of the Jomsviking

Sweyn Forkbeard~King of the Danes

Thorgils~Harbour master in Iceland

Thorod~Mercian Lord

Thorstein~Njal's farm manager

Tristan~The Kings son

Ulf Rottskagg~Alfvine's man

Wulfgar~Brihtnoth's Saxon champion

Wulfsige~abbot of Ramsey

Appendix 3 - Information

1 hand~4 inches

Althing~Scandinavian meeting place

Atgeir~Pole Spear

Bludgeld~reparation to the family of a murdered individual.

Burgh~Defended town

Ceorls~Saxon soldier, house guard

Dal Riata~Irish kingdom in Wales

Faering~small boat with two sets of oars and a sail about 10 feet long (30 hands)

Fyrd~The peasant army raised to fight large battles

Garn~Bits of wool and yarn

Grimnir~one of Odin's names

Groda~Frog

Holmgang~old Scandinavian duel

Huscurls~Viking soldier, house guard

Jarl~Lord/Earl

Jarv~Wolverine

Jomsviking~legendary company of Viking mercenaries of the 10th century

Jord~Goddess of the earth, Odin's wife

Karv~short haul boat about 17 feet long

Loki~God of the underworld and of mischief

Mjolnir~Thor's hammer

Odin~King of the Norse Gods

Odjur~Beast

Orm~Snake

Ragnarok~End of times for the Norse Gods

Sais~Welsh for English, Saxon

Seax~small knife worn in the belt.

Seidr~Old Norse form of sorcery.

Sichel~sickle, small scythe

Skei~Large longship, 30m long

Skit~shit

Skraeling~Norse word for Native American

Thegn~District leader

Thor~God of war

Thralls~Slaves

Varangian~Viking Guard of the Western Roman Emperor at Byzantium

Witan~The Saxon Royal court

Yggdrasil~The tree of life, Odin's horse

There was a man whose name was Gunnar. He was one of Unna's kinsmen, and his mother's name was Rannveig. Gunnar's father was named Hamond.

He was a tall and strong man - best skilled in arms of all men. He could cut, thrust or shoot, if he chose, as well with his left as with his right hand, and he hewed so swiftly with his sword, that three swords seemed to flash through the air at once. He was the best shot with the bow of all men, and never missed his mark. He could leap more than his own height, with all his war-gear, and as far backwards as forwards. He could swim like a seal; and so it has been said that no man was his match.

He was handsome of feature and fair skinned. He was blue-eyed, ruddy-cheeked and his hair was thick, and of good hue. The most courteous of men was he, of sturdy frame and strong will, wealthy in goods, a fast friend, but hard to please when making them.
(Njal's Saga. Part 1: Section 19)

Prologue

September 984

I know this is a dream but I do not wake, it is the dream that I often have. I am back in Scania again re-living the worst day of my life. I am face down in the sticky cold blood of my friend. Lying on the floor of this animal building, the blood and dust is stuck to my face and I remember the pain in my head. I am thankful it is only a memory as I always find it hard to remember pain. In this dream I open my eyes and see Gull dead next to me. He is lying face up with his throat ripped open, as if Hugin himself were the size of a goat and had clawed at Gull's neck with his talons.

Why always this dream? I do not want to be here, I do not want to witness the death of my closest friend again. But it is too late, Gull is dead and soon I will be accused of his murder again. Why can I never remember the moment of Gull's death, why does the memory only start here?

We had argued the night before while drunk, and I recall being very angry with Gull. Again, I can never remember the details from the previous night. I can see Erik Ericsson put his hand on my chest and tell me that if I wanted to fight Gull I would have to fight him too. Then it was more drinking, ale, mead and some evil drink from Vendland.

I have a lump on my head and that contributes to me feeling groggy and slow to get up. That was when I heard the men at the doorway.

"Odins breath!"

It is Erik Ericsson and Gull's older brother, Harald.

"YOU son of a thrall, what have you done." Erik shouts at me.

I look blankly back at the two men, still in a state of shock, and hungover.

Harald coldly walks over to me and grabs a handful of my hair saying, "Gunnar, you big ugly bastard, you will pay for this."

Erik moves toward me and starts to draw his sword from its scabbard. "He will pay with his life, NOW," says Erik. I notice his face is shiny with the sweat of a hangover, and I notice every piece of dust floating in the sunlight, shining through the doorway.

"No Erik," interrupts Harald, "get the men, let everyone know what he has done and then we will hang the bastard."

13

Erik slams his sword back into the scabbard, stands staring at me for a moment, before marching out of the barn. I hear Erik shouting to rouse the crowd.

*

I look up at Harald and he does something that I do not expect, he smiles.

My mind is racing, Erik is waking the men, this will give me a chance, and one chance is all I need. I grab for Harald's scrotum and squeeze as hard as I can. I have hands like spades, hands that are used to life as a Viking, rowing long distances, using a sword and using an axe on trees and men.

The smile drops from Harald's lips, he crumbles in the grip, hands trying to pull my fingers away, I squeeze with all my strength, tears drip from his eyes and a small, high pitched shriek leaves his lips. He falls down into a ball whimpering, dropping his weapon.

As he hits the floor, I release my grip and I am out the door of the barn and running for my life.

I run beside the hall, passing hung-over and sleeping Danes. I run down the hill as fast as I can in the rough direction of the quay, not knowing where to go or what to do. At the foot of the hill I see a horse by a tree. I attempt to mount the horse in one leap and my luck holds. The horse half bolts but I have a strong hold on its mane and manage to turn it in the direction of the quay. Uppakra Lund quay is about a league west and I pray that I will make it. There is smoke due west and I head straight for it.

As I near the quay, I see three longships pulled up on land and warriors fighting their way up the pier. They are killing anyone stupid enough to try and stop them, the Viking have arrived in Lund...

Chapter 1

Spring 988

Olaf Trygvasson stands in the middle of his longboat, unconsciously rocking with the movement, and looking at the island in the distance. The raven on board was making some noise as it could see land and had had enough of this sea journey. The sea spray hits him in the face and wind ruffles his clothes. To his right is the land of Kernow, a land of savages and wild men, a place that even the Saxon have never properly conquered.

He looks into his heart and believes that at last the grief has left him. It took many raids, after that attack on Lund, to sate his hunger for revenge, but eventually his thirst was quenched.

Revenge was finally his. He smiles to himself, revenge against whom? Odin, Thor, Loki or the Christian god? Are any of them to blame for the loss of his wife, or was he, in some way, to blame?

He has sworn never to return to the kingdom of Vendland after his loss. He also swore he would never lay with another woman, what a foolish thing to swear, a man needs a wife, or he is never complete.

"Jarl Olaf, are we stopping at the island?"

Mort's words bring him back from his thoughts.

"No Mort, find somewhere quiet along the coast of Kernow. Let's hope for a peaceful landing, we need food, water and dry land."

"We also need women and ale," Mort quips, and the crew cheer.

Olaf smiles, "ale we can trade for, women might need some persuading."

The crew put their backs into rowing a little quicker with the reminder of what may be on offer. Olaf returns to his thoughts.

He had heard that an Althing had been called by Queen Gyda, sister of the King of Dyflin, King Jarn, the only fully Norse Kingdom in all of Ireland. The rumour was that the Queen needed a husband. All worthy men across the northern world would seek her hand, as reports said that she was a fine looking, intelligent woman, powerful and very wealthy. Olaf Trygvasson was determined to be her husband; he was young, wealthy and strong, plus he had a claim to the throne of Norway.

Yes, Olaf thinks, a man needs a wife but a Jarl needs a wife, wealth and allies.

Looking along the coast, Olaf can see they are being watched, although he feels no trepidation. There are almost sixty battle hardened Vikings on his longboat, and behind him are two further boats of sixty. However, Olaf is not complacent; his men know their drill and are scrupulous about every landing on unfriendly soil. No chances are taken; caution and strength are the order of the day.

When they are secure on the beach, and the locals have drifted away at the show of strength from the horde, Olaf sits alone, looks out to sea and contemplates his life.

Born in Orkney after his mother, Astrid, fled the killers of his father, murdered because he was the son of the deposed king. Olaf and his mother then set off for Gardarike, where Astrid's brother Sigurd was in the service of King Valdemar. Olaf was only three years old when they set sail for Novgorod. The journey was not successful. When they reached the Baltic Sea they were captured by Osilian Vikings and the people aboard were either killed or taken as slaves. He was sold into slavery until, years later; he came under the protection of Queen Allogia, of Vendland. As Olaf grew older, Valdemar made him chief over his men-at-arms, but later the king became unhappy with how popular he was with the king's soldiers. Fearing he might be a threat to the safety of his reign, Valdemar stopped treating Olaf as a friend. As Olaf's wife, Geira, had died, he had nothing more to keep him in Vendland, so he decided to go Viking.

How the norns have weaved his life, descended from Norse kings, to slavery, a general in Valdemar's army, and now a Viking Jarl.

Olaf thinks if he can secure this marriage to Queen Gyda then, and only then, can he think about his birth right.

"Lord," it is Mort, "we have visitors." Mort gestured up the beach and Olaf notices a welcome party of very nervous men from Kernow.

In the centre there was an elaborately dressed old man, walking with a large staff, most likely for balance, Olaf thought. Alongside him were two warriors as big as Olaf, at least nineteen hands high. The main group were flanked by more warriors, that, Olaf noted, had all their weapons sheathed but on display, ready to use if things turn sour. Olaf could see that behind the chief were three men, each carrying a boar and a cart with barrels loaded. The cart kept getting stuck in the sand and Olaf hoped there was ale inside. Olaf could hear the men, who were closer to the welcoming group, start whooping with delight. Olaf looked closer and could make out a group of women with ropes around their necks; thralls, Saxon slaves of the men of Kernow.

A man, who was similarly roped up, was brought up next to the chief. In accented Danish he shouts out, "Are you Danes, enemies of the Sais?"

Olaf turns to Mort, "stay near, I need you to listen closely" for Mort was gifted in language and knew some of the British tongue, and all there was to know of the Saxon.

"We are no friend of the Saxon," Olaf shouts, remembering the Celtic word for Saxon.

"Come closer friends, so that we can talk more comfortably." Olaf smiles as he says this, trying to put the locals at ease. The approaching group are bearing gifts but they must be well aware that one hundred and eighty fighting Danes could take almost anything they want. Olaf is not a stupid man and it is easier and less costly to accept the gifts, enjoy them, and then move on to Dyflin.

Aldred, dressed as a monk, translated. He started by telling Olaf and his chief men how he was captured by the men of Kernow during a push by King Aethelred to subdue the tiny country at the edge of his realm. Aldred explained that he trained as a monk but enjoyed drinking and fighting too much for that boring life, apparently he was going to hell so he may as well enjoy himself while he was on God's earth, not that slavery was much fun, although still better than being a monk.

Olaf looked at him. He was withered and emaciated like some of the Christian holy men in Vendland, but he had the hands of a warrior and his eyes missed nothing.

He continued that this two bit king at the edge of the world was called Cadoc, and claimed to be the King of all Kernow and the rightful King of Lloegr, Aethelred's Saxon lands. Cadoc wanted to befriend a Danish Lord and recapture the east of his kingdom, hence the gifts.

Olaf thought this was a believable enough story but he suspected Cadoc preferred to offer gifts than be raided by another strong foe.

Cadoc said something unintelligible to Aldred, and one of his personal guard smacked Aldred around the head.

"They are making sure I tell you what they want me to, although the stupid bastards have no idea what we are saying," Aldred grinned and seemed unfazed by the strike.

17

Cadoc had a fat, red, pock marked and scowling face. Olaf could not work out if this minor king was constantly angry or constantly drinking; he decided it could be both.

Next to Cadoc his son Tristan started to speak, he was a good looking man of fifteen hands with pale white skin and jet black hair. He must completely take after his mother, thought Olaf. Aldred translated his words.

"My father, the honourable King of all Kernow, hopes you and your men enjoy his gifts. However, he has one gift left that he offers to your lord only. In our kingdom we have the most famous seer of all Prydain and he is devoted to King Cadoc and Kernow, tomorrow he will tell your future. My bastard brother, Maban, will take you to Mawgan the sage. With this final gift we hope to seal our alliance."

As this was being translated one of the big warriors, who stood by King Cadoc, came over and stood beside Aldred. Olaf looked to Mort and Mort nodded, Aldred was translating almost word for word.

*

The three Viking ships and one small local boat left Porth Kernow and headed west the next morning. Most of Olaf's men had sore heads from the Kernish ale but enough had stayed sober to thwart any ambush from the primitive locals.

Olaf had promised nothing and suggested everything with regard to an alliance. If he was to marry Queen Gyda he may need some allies against the Saxon king.

Olaf made himself comfortable as they would take the morning to reach the island of Ennor.

*

At Corfe, in the Purbeck hills, King Aethelred talks with his advisor, Saint Oswald, Archbishop of Worcester, and his mother Aelthryth.

"At times like this I wonder what my father would have done and wish I had the counsel of my friend Bishop Aethelwold," the King stood a little distraught.

"Most honourable King, unfortunately dear brother Aethelwold is now with God and we must advise you of the threat to your kingdom. God will guide your hand.

"First we have the devils Vikings raiding along your southern and eastern coasts and second that fat fool, Cadoc, seems to be preparing for war in the valleys of Kernow.

"Now I have intelligence that a Viking horde has met with Cadoc and it seems he now has allies." Saint Oswald, the most honourable, left this information hanging for the King to digest.

Aethelred stood up and spoke, "so far I have no news from Northumbria so I must assume no bad news from that quarter, also Mercia is quite peaceful but as always Wessex seems to take the brunt of all abuses. I have had enough of that drunken, sweaty Kernish fool. It is time to rid ourselves of that louse so that we can be free to deal with the threat of the pagan Norsemen."

"Well said, son, you will be remembered as a great King, like your father, a man who protected England through the dark days."

"Thank you, mother." The King turned to the local thegn, "Alwin, call my lords to council so we can plan the cleaning of Kernow."

Aethelred paced the hall while waiting for the Saxon lords to attend the Witan. He had had a difficult time as king and still was not sure how much he could trust England's Earls.

Not for the first time he wished Aethelwold had lived longer, as far as the king was concerned his old bishop was the only man he could really trust and would give wise council.

"Mother, if you were king, what action would you take?"

"Son, I would never be king as I am only a woman, but if I were queen and tasked with protecting my husband's realm, I would crush Cadoc quickly and concentrate on protecting my people from the pagan Norse."

"Thank you mother, you are a better man than many in my kingdom."

Alwin ran out of the great hall at the top of the mound and down to the town to gather the lords attending the king. Luckily for Alwin, Thegn of Purbeck, all the main men were drinking Saxon beer together, and in good spirits.

Aethelbald, Earl of Devon, Thorod a trusted Mercian Lord, Edgard Earl of Kent, Ealdorman Brihtnoth of Essex and Godwin Earl of Wiltshire all were ready to attend the king's wishes.

A little out of breath Alwin spoke, "My lords, the King wishes to hold council with you in the great hall of Corfe."

Thorod laughed loudly at this as he thought it just a small back water compared to the prosperous town of Tamworth.

"Now Thorod be polite and remember your King chose this location," Godwin chided his old friend with a smile. With this comment all the men walked up the hill toward the hall to meet their King.

The men made light talk about the weather and women, and Thorod thought they all tried very hard not to venture into politics. He knew too well what had happened that day years ago to the king's older brother at Corfe. The whole thing planned and executed by men such as these.

"But, my lord, surely we can ignore a parasite like Cadoc and focus our strengths against the Viking's that claim a kingdom in England. I am speaking of the lands of Dyflin that border Mercia and Northumbria at the Fylde." Thorod sat down and gave the floor back to the King.

Aethelred stood. "Thank you, Lord Thorod for your counsel, but the Fylde is an established stronghold of the Danes, whereas Cadoc is offering them a new foothold in our kingdom. We all know that Cadoc and his Welsh followers still dream of their own kingdom and will look for any alliance to try and achieve that. They also have a deep hatred for the kingdom of England and will always be a parasite on our backs. I suggest we take a very strong army into Kernow and crush them finally, this will leave us free to defend ourselves from Norse or Dane."

"I agree with our king," Godwin sat quickly after showing his support.

"You make a strong argument my lord, but this Mercian is troubled by the strong Norse presence in our kingdom. We have many who are descended from Danes and I cannot vouch for their loyalty. I will offer you as many men as I can spare, but I plead with my Lord King for assistance in Mercia on the morrow." Thorod, having had his say, offered the floor to Aethelbald of Devon.

"My lord, I would be eternally grateful if we can stop the men of Kernow raiding my farms. They do not have a large army but their fyrd will contain women and children who will fight to their last breath." Aethelbald sat down and everyone looked toward Edgard, Earl of Kent, so that he could have his say.

"My dear King and faithful friends, your plan is a good one but can I ask that no men from Kent are used in the destruction of Kernow? We are daily protecting the border from the threat of invasion."

At this Ealdorman Brihtnoth stood up. He was by far the eldest of the king's loyal Earls, being two and sixty years of age. He was a wise and brave man with many years' experience of repelling the northern invaders from his shore.

"My Lord King, the East Saxons also have a constant threat of invasion from Dane and Norse, but I believe we can offer some assistance. However, Kernow is another country on the far side of the kingdom and I would suggest we could help more by sending some men to man the Burghs in the absence of the valiant warriors of Wessex and Mercia." The Earl of Essex now sat and the King stood.

"I thank my loyal advisors for your support and I assure Earl Thorod that once Cadoc of Kernow is dead and his ambitions crushed, we can then look to the threat within Mercia."

At the end of the discussion it was decided that men of Devon, the house guards and the fyrd, would be supported by the king's own guard, with five hundred men of Wiltshire and a thousand men from Mercia. The Earl of Kent was excused the strain of supplying men as they all knew he kept them safe from raiding Vikings. Although with a proposed strength of four thousand this would be a force strong enough to crush the false kingdom of Kernow.

*

On returning to King Cadoc, Aldred expected to be killed, but the monks' habit he wore seemed to scare them from killing a holy man. Not that any of them were Christian, or anything like what he would have called Christian, but they were very much in awe of all holy men. Besides, one of the warriors had heard that monks knew how to brew ale, so as long as Aldred could make them ale he could stay alive. Unfortunately, Aldred knew almost nothing about making ale and he had killed a monk to get this habit.

*

The Saxon army gathered outside Escanceaster and waited for the king to arrive. The Earls were due at Aethelbald's hall in preparation for the long march. Aethelbald was pacing up and down, impatient to get on with the job of protecting his border.

"Where the hell is Thorod?" Nobody answered Aethelbald, as they had already discussed Thorod's habit of drinking with his men when on campaign. The person they were all really waiting for was the King himself.

Godwin toyed with his beer as he watched Aethelbald pace up and down. His impatient peer was likely to gain quite a chunk of land if the king really did crush the Kernish. Surely England's honourable prince would see the advantage he would hand the Earl of Devon and most likely claim the land of Kernow for himself. Although, as Godwin knew very well, when a king does you a favour he expects repayment twice over. Godwin's thoughts were broken by three horsemen riding toward the hall. The three men were challenged by the halls guards but it was only a formality as it was Thorod and two of his personnel.

Thorod was already talking as he climbed down from his horse, "I don't know why you two old women cannot have a drink with your men, how do you ever gauge their mood?" Thorod was shaking his head and trying to look serious but Godwin had been chided many times by his friend and knew it was his usual opening gambit when in the field.

Aethelbald started to mumble a reply to Thorod but Godwin had had enough of his whining and just spoke over him. "Well, Thorod, surely you did not ride all the way over here to abuse your friends. Have you news?"

"Ah, my old friend is impatient for the slaughter. Very well boys, here is the news this fine day. My scouts have spotted the King's advanced horsemen coming from the east. I have formulated some plans of my own but we will have to wait for our King and hopefully Aethelbald can give us some local knowledge."

The last great old roman road ended at Escanceaster so the marching army would have to use farmer's tracks as they headed west. Most of the journey toward the Tamar would be in Aethelbald's relatively safe earldom, although the land directly east of the Tamar suffered constant raids from Cadoc's men. The intelligence from the men of Devon estimated that Cadoc could muster up to eight hundred men plus the fyrd. The bulk of the army carried an air of confidence not shared by Godwin of Wiltshire. He was not an old man but he was by no means young and he had been fighting for England for nearly twenty years now. The one thing he knew about war was that it never ever turned out as you expected, weak or strong foe. King Cadoc was a weak man in spirit but his son Tristan organised their fighting men and knew very well that you could hide quite a few men in the valleys of Kernow.

Godwin felt that this would not be a straight forward fight of shield wall against shield wall, but with a lot of harrying and night attacks, advance and retreat. In fact he felt it would be a long, drawn out, and skit war.

*

Aldred was going to die. This did not surprise him in the least; he had many a brush with death and he almost welcomed it this time. He should have died after the Norseman Olaf left but he got a small stay of execution and now at last he would be found out. He had tried to make ale for Cadoc and Kernow but he was a novice and he had no master brewer to teach him the trade.

He stood still and said a little prayer to himself, and then he thought, 'who am I praying to? I don't believe in any gods.' At this he decided to pray to Mithras, hoping it would irritate the Christian god, if he was listening.

King Cadoc was on his way to try his latest and probably last brew. Even Aldred was surprised the men of Kernow had not killed him yet; he had brewed three ales already and each one was slightly less disgusting than the last. He had managed to convince them that a good brew required good ingredients and luckily for him they swallowed this excuse.

If only they had trusted him to drink ale rather than make it, they would have been most pleased. Still, the old woman he had spoken to had encouraged him to leave the slops for at least three weeks and maybe add some honey to feed the ale. This made him smile; he did not know that ale needed feeding.

Well this brew was his last hope; he actually thought that if they let him make at least twenty ales maybe the last one would be a little palatable. Still with the old woman's advice and some less rotten grains he felt that this one had something. He had tasted it and it was not too bad, not good, but not too bad. Perhaps if you had something strong to kill your taste buds then maybe this brew could be used in case you ran out of the other stuff.

Well, here came Cadoc with his entourage, Aldred noticed that Tristan and Maban were with him and Maban had his sword out ready for a fight, or an execution.

"Well Saxon, we are starting to think you do not know how to brew ale?"

Aldred ignored Tristan's remark and spoke up. "Dear King Cadoc, I believe you will enjoy this ale, as I have used your finest grain and some good quality honey from the king's own bees."

23

At this Aldred took a wooden cup, dipped it in the brew and held it toward the King. Maban stepped forward and took the cup and smelt it and then took a small sip.

King Cadoc and Tristan watched their bastard kin and waited. Then Maban tipped the contents of the cup down his neck and scooped up another cup and gave it to his father.

"Well Maban, you did not spit it out, is it drinkable?" The King looked surprised.

"Try it father, I think the Saxon has been lucky today, by pure chance he has made a decent drink."

Cadoc first smelt the brew and then took a mouthful, which he spat out. Aldred could not believe it, surely Maban had at least tolerated his drink, and he watched the King closely. Then Cadoc smiled at him, showing only a few teeth. "Not bad Saxon, a little sour, but I like it sour."

Aldred finally relaxed. He felt light headed, he may just live another day.

Tristan stepped forward in an attempt to try some, although his father was reluctant to let go of the cup. "Well done Aldred, my father wanted to kill you after the last disaster but I am glad I convinced him to give you one more chance." Tristan then tried a small draught of the ale and smiled, "tonight we shall drink your ale and see how bad our heads feel in the morning."

It was a strange evening for Aldred, the locals were queuing for his beer and it was a very potent brew, and soon enough everyone was drunk. The poor Saxon slave girls were passed around any of the men that wanted them; he felt those poor creatures would be better off dead. He had tried to speak to them over the last months but they had lost their life spark, and answered most of his attempts with silence.

The most important thing he noticed was that those guarding him had been less and less intense, perhaps they thought he was a dead man, or if he ran he would not get far, he was not sure. He was sure that if the opportunity rose tonight he would make a run for it while the men of Kernow slept off their hangovers.

Chapter 2

Thou wilt become a renowned king, and do celebrated deeds. Many men wilt thou bring to faith and baptism, and both to thy own and others' good; and that thou mayst have no doubt of the truth of this answer, listen to these tokens. When thou conquer in thy ships many of thy people will conspire against thee, and then a battle will follow in which many of thy men will fall, and thou wilt be wounded almost to death, and carried upon a shield to thy ship; yet after seven days thou shalt be well of thy wounds, and immediately thou shalt let thyself be baptised.

Olaf could remember all that Mawgan the seer had said; he felt in shock as the words related to dreams he had been having for some time.

He stood at the back of the longship steering the boat into the oncoming waves and leaned hard on the rudder as the waves hit the prow, covering all the men in salty spray. Olaf did not care about the cold, the damp or the weather, as he was stunned by the news from Ennor. His dreams were haunted by a death in battle, but now he thought on it, he was always close to death when he awoke. So does this mean he will come close to dying, but survive? If he believes all that Mawgan has said then he will be cut down but recover after a week. But can the seer be believed? One thing that he has often thought about, but told no one, is his interest in the Christian god. If this prophecy is true then the Christian god must be the right path for a man?

Olaf shook his head against the spray; he must concentrate on getting his ships into a bay and let the storm pass. He thought back to when leaving Ennor and it amused him to think of Aldred the Saxon pleading to go with him as his interpreter. Of course he left the man with the men of Kernow, for if he were to sail with Olaf he would most likely cut their throats as they slept. Jarl Olaf had learnt you can never trust a Saxon.

The Viking longships pushed on through the storm, praying to Thor that they would survive his wrath. Maban, the Kernish king's bastard son, had told them there was an island a little to the east of north, they would know it by the copse of trees at the highest point, and Maban had given them a British name for it, although the Norse called it Lundey. If they needed to, he said there was a bay on the east side which would bring them shelter. This day Thor relented and the longships found their way around to the bay and survived the storm.

*

Njal was unhappy that he took on the case. At first it had seemed a straight forward business argument, but it had turned nasty and Bjorn would not compromise. Njal suspected his odious wife was egging him on, fuelled by her greed. Also the opponents Bjorn was taking on were rumoured to be bandits, or at least related to them. Njal sent a little thanks to Odin for allowing him to break through the stubborn head of Bjorn, allowing him to try and mediate in the dispute.

Njal and Bjorn were riding together across open country to try and negotiate with the sons of Ragnal. Njal had spent so long trying to get mediation in this dispute he even ignored advice from his friend Gunnar.

"Drop the case Njal, and drop Bjorn, he would do the same to you, you owe him no loyalty. He has already taken up more time than he will ever pay for. Sweyn and Jarv Ragnalsson will hold a grudge for life and will seek revenge until they are satisfied."

Njal was not stupid, he knew the words that Gunnar spoke were true, and deep in his heart he felt a little afraid.

"Do not think I will buckle easily Njal, I am the best merchant in all of Iceland and nobody can out negotiate me."

"Do not be a fool Bjorn, you must be willing to give up something and meet somewhere in the middle."

As they were talking they were riding their ponies along a track in a small valley. Ahead Njal could not be sure but he thought he could see some riders coming toward them.

"Bjorn, look ahead, my eyes are not as good as they were. Do you see riders in front?"

"Oh, skit!"

*

Yggdrasil was galloping as fast as I dared him to. I cursed myself for not telling Njal I would accompany him to see Sweyn and Jarv. They were not the type of men you had a dispute with, as they normally ended things with blood being spilt. They always seemed to live on the verge of being outlawed but always managed to bully somebody or pay them off.

26

The more I thought of them the more I wished I had brought with me more arrows, although I carried my long and short swords, too. Above the noise of my horse I heard a shout and decided to climb the nearest hill top to see if there was anything I could see.

"Look, Sweyn! It is the fat arsehole who sold us the rotten fish."

"It was not rotten; it was fresh the day you bought it."

Njal could not help admiring the fact that Bjorn stood up to these men, although they would surely kill them both soon. Njal had a short sword but he could see no weapon on Bjorn, perhaps he carried a knife. Although it did not matter, neither of them were fighting men and the sons of Ragnal were renowned for fighting.

The two brothers had four hardened bandits with them but Njal thought they could easily kill the lawyer and merchant without their help.

"Lawyer, we are disappointed in you. We heard you were a decent man but it seems you have bad taste in friends."

"Bjorn, now would be a good time to negotiate with the brothers."

"Shut up lawyer, there is never going to be any negotiating. The fat gris sold us rotten fish and he has to pay."

Sweyn approached Bjorn, holding his sword out.

"Kill him, brother, and kill the lawyer too. We can bury their corpses in the hills, nobody will know."

Sweyn cut at Bjorn with his sword and the merchant tried to defend his body with a thick leather bag of documents. The action ended with a damaged bag and Bjorn falling from his horse as Njal released his own sword.

"Look, the lawyer is going to fight us. Hey Njal are you sure you are holding the right end?"

Jarv rode toward Njal with his sword up screaming a war cry. About two horse lengths from the lawyer Jarv flew back off his horse and hit the ground hard; an arrow was buried deep in his chest.

"What the Hel is going on?"

Sweyn turned his horse around, looking for the source of the arrow. There was another thud and one of his henchmen hit the ground with an arrow in the head. Another arrow hit Sweyn's horse and he managed to jump free before he was thrown. Then out of the low Icelandic sun, riding down the hill was a big blonde warrior, fighting his mare to get to his prey as soon as he could.

"Turn and attack boys," the three men still on horseback turned to face their attacker, shields up and swords high.

*

I came down the hill with the sun at my back, hoping to gain any advantage I could. The hill was not big but the odds had improved with two dead and one off his horse. The three riders prepared for my attack and turned their horses toward me. I looked past them and saw Njal trying to engage Sweyn; Njal was no fighter but was holding his own. I gripped the back of my horse with my knees and unleashed both my swords. There was a gap between two of the riders and I tried to steer Yggdrasil at the gap with my knees. The man on my left was a little in front, I would go for his head and the throat of the one on my right. I hit the shield a little hard on my left and it put me off the stroke on my right, but luck was on my side. I missed the rider's throat but ran him straight through his shoulder, my sword came out his back and when it was almost all the way through it cut its way free, leaving him with only one good arm. The third rider was close behind and hacked at my midriff but it was a pathetic attempt and I dodged it easily. I was quickly a distance of over twenty paces away from the remaining two riders, so sheathed my swords and prepared my bow. I only had one arrow left and both riders had turned and were heading back toward me. I let loose my last arrow while asking for Thor's help. It flew true and garrotted the man to my right, burying the shaft deep in his throat. It had an effect on his friend as it was now one on one and he continued to come to me. I now had my favourite sword free and enjoyed the weight of it in my hand. The low sun glistened off the shaft, making the iron look like gold. Time had slowed as it always does in these moments, and I watched him approach with caution in his eyes. He held the shield up a little too high with his sword up ready to strike. He had the bearing of a man defending rather than attacking and I gambled. I waited for him to strike first and dodged back, receiving a cut across my arm. But I managed to stab upward at the right point and caught him under his arm, where there was no protection. He carried on beyond me before slipping off his horse and laying on the ground moaning.

I turned my horse to see a standoff between Njal and Sweyn. The bandit brother had his seax to the fat throat of my ungrateful neighbour, Bjorn. I trotted over and the thug addressed me.

"I have been telling the lawyer that you should both ride away and leave me with a healthy pony or I will kill the merchant."

Sweyn stood behind Bjorn with his seax hard against the merchant's neck, so much so that a little blood could be seen. Bjorn's eyes were bulging in fear and he tried not to gulp as it made the cut deeper. His life was now in my hands as much as Sweyn's and although he was a fool he did not deserve to die. Njal was stumped; he did not know what to do so I spoke for us all while Bjorn sweated.

"Sweyn, you are not a trustworthy man, how do we know you will not kill our favourite merchant as soon as we are gone?"

"You will just have to trust me Gunnar, oh and how is that pretty wife of yours?"

I did not like that arsehole speaking about Freyja and decided then what I would do, after all it was only Bjorn there and not Njal.

"Sweyn, never speak about my wife."

I flicked my sword over so I held the blade and threw it straight at Sweyn's head. I could throw my seax confidently into a tree from twenty paces but had never tried throwing my sword before. I did the whole thing on instinct and as it left my hand I felt like I had thrown well. Time seemed to slow as it does when you are excited or in battle, and I watched the blade turn end over end as it travelled toward the despicable outlaw. The low sun flashed off the blade every time it lay parallel with the horizon and as it neared Sweyn time righted itself. The point entered his left eye and came out of the back of his head. He folded to the floor, dead.

Bjorn was visibly shaking now and finally found the strength to speak up.

"I did not know you were so accurate at throwing, Gunnar."

"Nor did I Bjorn, I guess I was lucky I missed you."

*

King Cadoc and his subjects were laughing, singing and fighting; apart from those who were in a drink induced sleep.

Aldred was getting quite good at brewing and he had tried adding more honey to make the beer sweeter. It was a little sweeter but it was also much stronger, which gave even the poor thralls a break from the constant abuse they had to put up with.

The brew had been ready first thing and the drinking had started early. The King was fast asleep and looking even unhealthier; his face was closer to purple than red now, but he did have a smile on his comatose face.

Maban was wrestling his brother Tristan which consisted of them falling on top of each other and rolling about laughing.

The last brew that Aldred had made threw temptation in his path. However, he took a cautious approach to his escape and he was glad now that he had. At the end of that evening, when most of the local population were sleeping off the effects of his draught, Aldred wandered quietly to the edge of the Kernish conurbation. What he saw frightened him as he almost just ran for it earlier that evening. There was a whole troop of Cadoc's armed men the other side of the river; Aldred would have run straight into them.

Luckily for him the local troops had heard about his beer and tonight were being treated with a taste. Not everyone was here and he guessed that the fyrd was guarding the border with Devon.

He looked around and noticed that Maban had passed out and Tristan was chasing a young maid around. The girl looked like she wanted to be caught. Perhaps when Tristan was happily tupping, Aldred could drift to the edge of the camp and have a look around. He decided he must be a little brave today or he would forever have to brew beer for these stinking savages. He tried to watch Tristan while he dished out the remainder of the beer to the few that still wanted to drink.

Finally the prince took the pretty girl away for some privacy and that left nobody of authority around conscious.

Aldred walked off toward the remainder of the bread and cheese, meaning to collect some before diverting toward the piss hole so he had an alibi for leaving the brew. When he left the main part of the camp he then heard what sounded like a number of horsemen arriving from the east.

"Arseholes!" Aldred was never going to get a break; he would never escape with Cadoc's horsemen around. He glanced through the tree cover to watch their approach. A few of Cadoc's guards were standing in the middle of the camp and turned to see their comrades arrive. The horses raced through the shallow ford and into the camp on the dry plain. The first horse broke into the camp but did not slow down, it raced toward the men and the rider hacked his sword down and sliced into one of the drinking men. The injured man was cleaved between his neck and shoulder and a great spray of blood shot over his drinking partner. He had suffered his death blow and folded to the ground.

Aldred was shocked how silent it was for that second, but the screaming started soon after. Many horsemen arrived and they were all heavily armed and proceeded to chase down the Kernish. He saw Maban up and standing in the middle of three horsemen, swinging an axe around. He looked around for the old King and saw him lying peacefully with an axe buried in his chest. There was no sign of Tristan but Aldred was sure he would not be enjoying his tupping.

Now the important thing for Aldred was not to be mistaken for a local, but he was already worrying about his deception as a monk. He was sure the Saxons would not look kindly on his impersonation.

Most of the nearby men of Kernow had been killed or chased away and the Saxon horsemen were joined by foot soldiers that proceeded in rounding up the women. From some of the screams he heard the raping had started, it made him feel ashamed of his countrymen and himself. He remembered taking part in this orgy of destruction when he was younger and he could never forget the tears of the young girl he abused. He could never go back and help her but he could do something about the women here.

Aldred came out of his hiding place and made himself known to the Saxon who looked like he was directing things.

"Good Day, I am brother Aldred," he found himself trying to speak his best Saxon, after all these months of using the horrible British tongue.

"What is a dirty Saxon monk doing at the end of the world?" The man on horseback looked ready to strike him down, his sword still out and ready.

"I was captured the last time King Aethelred raided these lands."

"But I led those raids, and I know we took no monks with us."

Aldred looked closely at the man on the horse and he looked familiar but Aldred could not be sure, so he tried a new tactic, the truth.

"I rode with Earl Thorod and if I am not mistaken you are Earl Godwin of Wiltshire?"

31

"It is true that Thorod fought with us, but that was nearly two years ago. I still do not remember a monk in our party, so Aldred explain yourself or you will be just another dead man of Kernow."

"Lord have mercy, when we raided I was separated from my fellows and I had just defeated a fighting monk from Tamar. I took his clothes and tried to get back to the safe lands of Devon when I was captured at the river. Dressing as a monk saved my life for these two years."

Earl Godwin turned to one of his men. "Take this man to Earl Thorod, if he does not recognise this Aldred, kill him."

"Lord, thank you, but I came out to try and stop the rape of these poor women, they have done no harm."

"Aldred, you have gone soft in the head while you have been here. Some of the boys have been looking forward to this all week. Anyway these are not women, they are only savages, right leave us now so we can kill the rest of these scum."

"Come on monk, my name is Rand, just in case I have to kill you and you are a monk, you can give me forgiveness in the next life."

As Rand and Aldred rode off to find the Mercian troops, Godwin gathered his cavalry and infantry together to check survivors and wounded.

Earl Godwin's captain, Aelle, came over and discussed the battle.

"I think it is a success Lord, we have only lost three men and we have two who have bad injuries."

A screaming war cry came from beyond the copse; Godwin turned and saw men and horses melt out of the trees toward them. In the centre was a man on horseback in full war gear, some of it looked very old, possibly Roman?

Aelle, on foot, called out, "War formation, shield wall, NOW!"

At Liddyford, Prince Tristan of Kernow had come back to avenge his father's death.

On the left of the copse was an incline that sloped up to the height of a man and on the right was thick bracken. The new King of Kernow set up a shield wall in front of the copse with the natural barriers protecting his flanks. The Saxon army was drifting across the ford, but the water was too shallow to be any help for the young King.

He came down off his horse and joined the shield wall in the centre of the second row. On joining, his men gave out a loud cheer, and if Aldred had been there to advise Godwin he would have told him that Prince Tristan was greatly loved, unlike his dead father.

After getting over the surprise arrival, Godwin now concentrated his mind on defeating the main part of Cadoc's army. He felt pleased as he had no stomach for routing out rebels in isolated valleys and was more confident in his men's ability in a shield wall.

Aelle had organised the Saxon wall and it looked formidable. Godwin had about five hundred men at his disposal, fifty on horse and the rest on foot. They faced possibly one hundred and fifty men of Kernow and he could only see five horses.

Rinc and Selwyn, Aelle's seconds, took over the flanks and Aelle would stand in the centre with Godwin. Godwin leaned on his horse and spoke with Aelle, "can we get any troops to climb that small incline?"

"I will send a few men to have a look, but I think we can defeat this shield wall quickly, we have more than twice the men they have."

"Let's get on with it then Aelle, I want to get home to my wife and farm as early as possible."

As a cheer came across the void Aelle gave the order and the men at the front of the Saxon wall started to bang their swords on shields in rhythm as they started to approach their opponent's wall. The men in the second row held their broad-axes above their heads for the Kernish men to see.

The approach was not fast; they had to cover about one hundred and fifty roman yards but they did not run. No matter how brave you are you do not want to run to your potential death. Even the bravest took their time when facing their time in the shield wall.

Tristan was focused but nervous, he had Talek & Maban either side of him and usually that would instill him with confidence, but not today. Maban still looked a little green and Talek was swaying, as for him he could feel the start of a headache and his balls hurt as they had been promised a maiden and the job was interrupted.

Maban lent forward and vomited bile on the floor in front of him. The stench of the bile set off a few of the men in the front row who had drunk a belly full of Aldred's brew.

King Tristan of Kernow started to think that maybe Aldred had put something in their drink anticipating this attack. But Aldred would have had no idea his kin were to attack, and all of his beers had wicked after effects.

He decided that what they needed was a quick, but not too quick, end to this battle. He prayed to his father's spirit that his plan would work; he asked for silence and addressed his army.

"Men of Kernow, we are a small nation but a proud one. We are descended from Roman Generals and Celtic Warriors. We are the children of Arthur, Guinevere, Agricola and Merlin. We are the rightful people of Lloegr and the hated enemy of the Sais. Today the Sais has come into the last free part of Prydain and means to wipe us from the memory of this fine land.

So fight, men of Kernow, fight for your land, for your mothers, wives and daughters. Today we fight and we kill as many Sais as will come and men will sing of this day in a hundred years' time."

The men roared their approval and all the small army felt cheered, the less experienced believed they may just be successful today. Then the Saxon shields started to make noise and the young king looked across the gap and realised that this would be the very last stand against the enemy, and there would be nobody left to sing their song.

*

Aelle had moved to the front of the line leaving Godwin three rows back to direct the battle. He was a big, muscular and resilient man who had been cut down three times in front of his men to get up and continue fighting. The men did not necessarily like him but they trusted him, and they also believed he could not be killed.

He was used to fighting Norse, Dane and Irish so it was a new experience to be facing the Kernish shield wall, as he was defending the southern coast the last time they raided Kernow. His entire previous foe had had a reputation before the fight but less was known to him how the men of Kernow would perform in battle. By the look of them Aelle felt this would be an easier fight.

He halted the Saxon wall about ten paces from their opponents and the abuse between the two armies began. It was of little use, as no man from either side understood anything the other side said. Eventually one of Tristan's men stripped naked and ran out into the gap and screamed abuse at the Saxon wall. The man was very drunk and stumbled around. Aelle felt that his opponents were a pathetic bunch, up close only a hard core of them had good weapons and shields and the men at the flanks looked as if they had dug up their weapons from an ancient grave.

The pathetic berserker was now strutting up and down close to the Saxon wall, occasionally spitting at his foe. Aelle had had enough and stepped forward to face the man. The Saxon army from Wiltshire cheered as their hero faced up to the idiot. The naked man looked a little shocked and Aelle swung his sword hard at the fools' body. Even Aelle was shocked that he did not even raise his own weapon to defend himself, and the Saxon blade buried itself deep in his trunk. It was like chopping a dead pig as there was no resistance. Aelle pulled hard at his sword to remove it from the man's body and it was followed by a gush of blood. The man opened his mouth to scream but a cup load of blood spewed from his mouth. Aelle noticed that his penis had shrunk away to nothing and then the poor idiot fell down and started to fit. Aelle stood over him and stuck his sword in the dying man's head and ended his suffering. The Saxon Captain stepped back into the first row and his men cheered again.

Tristan shouted at his men, "Do not be disheartened, I will kill their champion and I will be dressed and sober."

But before he could step through his lines a great shout went up from the Saxon horde and a volley of small axes were thrown across the gap. This disrupted the men on the Kernish side and the Saxon shield wall crossed the last few yards and slammed into the Kernish line. Tristan was pushed back as the front row of fifty men took the full weight of the Sais push. At last the pushing started and the second row pushed the backs of the first row. Arms wrapped around two men in front and feet jammed hard into the ground to gain purchase. The stench of piss and faeces filled the air to be mixed with the smells of stale vomit. He heard a cry and saw a man in the front drop to the ground, his place was quickly filled by a man from the second row. Many broad-axes were being swung by the Saxon second row, meaning to catch the Kernish shields and pull them down, so the men in the front could stab with their short swords. Tristan had tried to train his troops but the lesser men were at the flanks and their second row had not raised their shields to protect their friends at the front. Carnage happened on his right, nearest the bracken. The front row had been exposed; Tristan took a full blow on his shield and glanced to his right again. He saw a broad-axe come down, time seemed to slow down as it scraped the side of a young fighters head; the weapon moved slowly down the flesh, peeling it away as if it were the skin of an apple. The young man screamed having lost his ear and all the hair and skin on his left side. But there was worse as the axe buried itself into the young man's shoulder as if it had been thrown and stuck in an old log. He went down and the man behind him froze, and was gifted with a Saxon sword across the throat. Tristan was mesmerised by the distance the blood sprayed, covering the first three rows of Saxon.

He focused on the fighting in front of him in time to see Talek stabbed in the mouth; the young prince saw the weapon exit at the back of Talek's head. Maban roared next to him and went into frenzy, he looked as if he had three swords and four arms as he hacked, slashed and cut through the front row of the Saxons, for his half-brother had lost his closest and dearest friend. He was eventually checked by the Saxon captain in the middle of the line. Maban and Aelle slugged it out within a small gap at the centre of the lines, Tristan did not think his bastard brother could keep it up and he sensed that he was weakening. Aelle saw the slight difference in Maban and pushed hard at him with blow after blow landing, Maban only just defending. Tristan leaned forward and grabbed his brother's jerkin and pulled him back, "Close Up!" The shields locked together, the pushing and stabbing resumed.

"Maban, how are you?"

"He caught me, brother, I am losing blood."

Maban had sustained three major cuts to his sword arm, but the blood was flowing slowly and Tristan felt this meant his brother would survive.

"Brother, go to the back of the lines and try and repair your wounds," Tristan had to shout this as the axes had started to come over again, clanging on the shields at the front.

*

Godwin was getting frustrated, but he knew he should be patient, the odds meant that his victory would be assured. The frustration was that only his front two rows could fight with the core of the opponents trained guard.

Selwyn was on the left flank and had turned the Kernish wall, but the bracken was a hard foe cutting at their legs. Rinc had finally managed to push forward with the right flank but there was a sheer incline that created a natural barrier for the opponent. Godwin needed to attack another flank and help came from a young soldier tasked with scouting the incline.

Drefan approached the Ealdorman directing the troops. "Lord Godwin, my scouts have found a track to access the top of the incline, if we could have one hundred men we could come down hard on the savages."

"Take one hundred men from the reserve, Drefan, and make sure you turn this battle."

Drefan dropped back with his troop and collected the extra men, scouting along the river until they were out of view. The scouts took them a circular route to the other side of the incline. Frene, the chief scout, came forward to Drefan, "we have to get through this deep thicket and then we can climb up the hill, then we must head in the direction of the river and we will come down on our foe."

"Good work Frene, we will be heroes today."

The thicket was filled with bush and bramble with young trees bursting through. It was a hard task to push through but it was only about ten yards across.

Drefan was excited, he loved war and got bored quickly when there was no fighting. He understood why the young Danes would become Vikings; they were lucky and would have adventure and excitement almost every day. Today could mean that he would become a more important warrior in the eyes of Ealdorman Godwin, and that would mean promotion and wealth. He would be boasting later how he led the troop that turned the battle and defeated the King of Kernow.

They made their way through the deep thicket, through the close trees and bramble. Drefan was impatient to get up the hill and ready an attack on Kernow; his keenness to join the battle almost became his downfall. He burst through the thicket followed by his closest allies and was confronted by the fyrd of Kernow.

The fyrd being made up of the fit and able population, usually male, all of them promised to support their lord in times of strife or war. There were hundreds of men and women with swords, axes, forks and farmer's sichels, they were unskilled in battle but they knew they were fighting for their lives. There was a brief silence as the fyrd looked at the Saxon troop as it continued to be ejected from the thicket.

Drefan turned to his nearest man and screamed, "Back, back now, RUN!"

As they scrambled back into the thicket a loud triumphant scream went up from behind and they heard the sound of hundreds of angry Celts moving toward them.

"Turn round go back and hell is coming," Drefan screamed while crashing into his men running hard through the thicket, as they tried to escape the oncoming horde. They might make it and he hoped the thicket would slow down the massive angry crowd behind. Whip like branches slapped against his face and brambles tore at his legs but he pushed on. What was a few scratches when only death by a frenzied mob was the alternative?

"Don't look back and run for your life." Drefan was through and ran back toward the army, not looking back for fear of capture.

*

Godwin had gathered all his horsemen together, as he was going to try a different tactic with the belligerent Prince. The shield wall would pull back on his order and then the cavalry of fifty would be used to further demoralise the enemy; this would give the Wiltshire shield wall a rest.

It was a pity as the left flank was having greater and greater success, but Godwin felt it would be a slower victory wrapping the opponent's wall on itself.

"Wiltshire HOLD, fall back," the front line stopped pushing against their enemy and stepped back with their colleagues. Both lines dropped their shields, visibily exhausted.

*

Tristan could now see clearly what the Sais were planning; all their horsemen were gathered behind the lines in one place and looked ready to pounce. He said a silent prayer to himself hoping that the fyrd would come now and save them from the oncoming attack. He was sure that his shield wall would break under a direct push from the cavalry. Maban was at the back of his small army with the rest of the wounded but any who could still stand and wield a weapon would be needed back and now. Tristan sent word to the rear.

*

Godwin had finished giving his instructions to his horsemen and had told them to wait on his order. He wanted to defeat the enemy but he did not want to run down his own men in the process.

He thought he heard someone calling his name from a distance and he turned to look beyond the incline.

"Earl Godwin, turn the wall, the FYRD IS COMING."

He then saw Drefan and his men running at full pelt back toward the safety of the Saxon militia.

"Turn the wall, turn the wall, the fyrd are behind us." Drefan was gasping as he tried to relay the urgency of his request.

Godwin was about to make the order when he saw the shield wall moving back and trying to face both the army in the copse and the oncoming threat from around the

38

incline. Aelle had pre-empted the order and had already acted. Drefan and his men, at least the ones who had managed to stay ahead of the fyrd, made it to the safety of the wall of shields. As they approached the shields opened up and swallowed them whole.

Godwin heard the fyrd before seeing them, he expected a large force but he did not fear it. His soldiers were professionals and he knew you only threw the fyrd in where you needed extra numbers or when you were desperate.

Ealdorman Godwin smiled to himself, mentally congratulating the young prince on his planning, and knew all of his own expertise on the battle field would be needed to win today.

Chapter 3

Brother will battle to bloody end
And sister's kin commit foul acts
There's woe in the world, wantonness rampant,
An axe age, a sword age, shields are sundered,
A storm age, a wolf age, before the world crumbles,
No mercy or quarter will give to man.
The sun grows dark, earth sinks in the sea,
The bright stars fall from the skies.
Flames rage and fires leap high,
Heaven itself is seared by heat.

Standing in the shield wall he can see the Saxons running and screaming, but oddly he can hear nothing. He focuses on the Saxon horde running forward, holding battle axe and sword high with shields up protecting their bodies. He can see the spittle spraying from screaming mouths, the piss stains on their jerkins and the mud splashing up their legs as feet slam down in the marsh, but still it is silent.

The feeling of trepidation around him is strong as he shouts to his men, "hold firm and lock shields, trust your brothers." His voice sounds to him like a hollow echo.

He is standing back in the third row, the Jarl of his men, his job to direct proceedings in the chaos of battle and to ensure victory.

As the Saxons approach they lower their shields and try to close the gap between them and his colleagues.

His men brace themselves and he feels, rather than hears, the crash as shield slams into shield. His body shudders as his whole group try and hold the attack. Axes fly down on his men and short swords stab through any gap. He sees men opening their mouths to scream and fall, but again hears nothing.

Olaf looks around and there is only one more line of men behind him. They are six men wide, across this strip of high ground in the marsh, and only four deep. He feels that the gods have deserted him, this is a suicide mission and surely all will die under the onslaught.

Next to him is his old friend Mort, who says something to him which he cannot hear, what has happened to his ears?

Mort laughs and slips his short sword into Olaf's belly although surprisingly he feels nothing. Looking down he sees his guts start to spill out, the blue snake of his guts swimming in a sea of blood. He tries pushing them back in when an axe crashes into his shoulder. He looks up as he crumbles and can see no Saxon, only his men turning on him and hacking at him with their weapons. He drops his sword and wonders if he will ever reach Valholl.

Then he screams…

Mort is there next to him.

"Jarl, what is it?"

Olaf sits up and rubs his hands over his face.

He manages to mumble to his friend, "A dream, Mort, just a dream," thank the gods, he thinks.

"It is ok Jarl Olaf; you did not shout too loud, I only heard as I could not sleep."

Olaf feels a sense of relief and shame; he is shaking slightly but thinks Mort hasn't noticed. Bad dreams are not a good omen, and men do not want to serve a lord that has bad luck hanging over him.

"Do you want to tell me of the dream?" Mort looks concerned.

"Don't worry Mort, it was the shield wall, last thing I remember is shouting as I cut a Saxon down." Why is he lying to his oldest friend?

Mort smiles, "I understand Olaf, some of these Saxon have very hard heads."

They both laugh and Mort fetches Olaf some ale.

"Well, how are your thoughts about today?"

One thing Olaf appreciates about Mort is that he is direct.

"I will do my best, and I think my best will be more than enough. The only man with a better case than me would be King Sweyn of Denmark.

I am young but not too young, not bad to look at, I have wealth, three longships, one hundred and eighty men who follow me and a legal claim to the throne of Norway."

"If you put it like that, I will marry you," Mort laughs at his own joke and gains a smile from his Jarl.

"Mort, this country, Dyflin, is a rich kingdom with a claim across the sea, within the Saxon lands. But this will be a big step up for me. I hope one of the gods is looking out for Olaf Trygvasson."

"Will we carry on our Viking adventure? I am beginning to enjoy the free money we get from the Saxons every time we growl at them."

"Of course, Mort, but first I must impress Queen Gyda and then we can meet somebody who needs a troop of Vikings."

"I think I am going to like Dyflin."

"Me too, Mort, me too."

Olaf and Mort walk down to the shore of Dyflin to buy some smoked fish for breakfast. Olaf's wearing his finest war gear minus his chain mail, he wants to impress everyone, not scare them. Mort had already had a bath and it was not even Saturday, or Lordag, the day of bathing.

"Mort you smell so good if Gyda does not want me I may take you up on your offer of marriage."

Mort was a little surprised by Olaf's merriment and laughed along with his friend and lord. Olaf could be a very serious man and had not had much to be happy about since the death of his wife in Vendland. Mort was pleased that he was at last relaxing a bit and thought that if his master could win Gyda's hand they would all profit. Mort liked Olaf a lot but he was sometimes scared by his friend's zeal and single mindedness, although he would want to be next to no other man in battle.

They bought some breakfast and weak ale and watched the longboats arriving in Dyflin. One boat was already spilling men on the quay and a group of Vikings, very much dressed for war, made their way into the town. As they approached Olaf and Mort the man at the front was shouting, "Make way, make way for Jarl Alfvine!"

There was plenty of room for the sixty odd men to get by but they started to jostle Olaf, Mort and any other bystanders in their way.

Mort stood in front of Olaf, and with his hand on his sword spoke, "You will walk around Jarl Olaf, and learn some manners"

A big red bearded Viking pushed Mort in the face and he crashed to the floor. "Move out the way aersling."

Olaf reached for his sword but red beard punched him hard in the chest and Olaf toppled back, falling in a pile of fish offal and mud.

A crowd of Vikings stood behind red beard as he spoke down at Olaf and Mort, "You skits are lucky you did not try pulling your weapon on Jarl Alfvine, as you would be dead now."

Olaf attempted to rise and confront him but the big man put his foot on Olaf's chest saying, "mind your temper, Jarl Fish-Guts, or it may get you killed."

Mort reached over and put his hand on Olaf's sword arm. "There will be time for vengeance, lord."

Red beard and his crew moved on laughing and throwing scorn at Olaf and Mort.

They got up and Olaf looked down at his fine war gear, "those whoresons Mort, I will make sure I get revenge for their insult. Look at my clothes! I stink of fish and skit, and we are due to be presented to Queen Gyda at noon!"

"We will think of something lord," although what, Mort did not know.

*

Ulf Rottskagg was laughing still as the Jomsviking set up camp. "Ketil, Berg, did you see the look on the face of that groda dressed up like a woman?"

Ketil smirked. "Yes Ulf, but he was more like a sea bird rooting around those fish guts."

"You both should show more discipline, are we not Jomsviking?" Berg was annoyed at their childish behaviour, "you don't even know who he is."

"Do I look like I care," growled Ulf.

"Now Ulf, you are my most gentle and caring servant, aren't you?" Alfvine asked.

Ulf's face was in a rage, no man could get away with insulting him in public, and he was disappointed that his own lord had done so, after the loyalty Ulf showed him so recently.

"Come on Ulf; don't look so upset, I am only joking with you. And don't look so upset, I promise you will soon have someone to fight." Alfvine smiled at his man and Ulf grunted in acknowledgment.

"We have to work hard as the Althing will start at noon and I mean to win this battle. I do not want to have to spend all my time wandering the seas of the world."

"We will be ready lord," Berg reassured his master.

Alfvine wondered how long he could still call his band of men Jomsviking; after all he had been thrown out of their stronghold at Jomsborg.

The problem for Alfvine was that as he grew older, all that the Jomsviking stood for meant less and less to him. He had started rebelling inside first and hated that he had to share his wealth with inferior colleagues. The stupid rules that they had to live by! What normal man would ban all women from their stronghold? He had started recruiting men to join his band of brothers and ensured they were more loyal to him than the brotherhood.

Alfvine knew that a ring giver was always respected in the world, and he made sure he always had enough wealth to distribute to his followers. He knew the day would come when he would be confronted, he was breaking the rules for some time and the more men he tried to recruit the more likely he would be found out.

Of course that righteous fool Styrbjorn had been suspicious and started having him watched and eventually found his secret horde. The expulsion surprised him as he thought he would be nailed to a tree like the mighty Odin, for his deeds. Alfvine smiled as he remembered his loyal followers choosing expulsion with him and how angry Styrbjorn looked as Alfvine filled a whole longboat with his men. He was also glad that he had hidden some of his wealth in Gotland and Birka, too. Otherwise he would not be able to keep his small band of Vikings so happy.

The expulsion was no great hardship for him as he had already planned to attend Queen Gyda's Althing and try and win her hand. Although now it was more important to him that he did win it. The wealth he had would not last forever and he really did not want to spend a life as a raider.

Everything is in place, he had some wealth, a band of loyal and skilful warriors, and he was a handsome man with a quick mind. He was aware other men had come to attend the queen but he was full of confidence and was sure that he would prevail, after all he usually did. There really was no competition against him and he almost felt sorry for the other fools that had attended.

*

Kari and Brynjolf came in to report to Olaf and Mort, they both looked nervous and Kari spoke up, "Jarl, your best clothes are still a little stained but they stink like an old herring ton."

Olaf looked as if he would explode, "I am going to gut that big red bear, because of that skit all I have is my bad weather clothes."

Mort stood up and spoke, "Jarl Olaf, perhaps you should approach the queen as a humble but powerful man, someone who does not need fine clothes to prove your worth?"

"Mort, it is about the only approach we can make."

Mort watched his lord and saw Olaf start to focus; he looked the same as when a raid was pending. Mort had helped Olaf prepare as best he could, listening to his speech which set him out as the best man here. They had gifts of gold, silver and amber to present to the Queen, plus something very special, but most of all they had Olaf and his heredity. Unless an actual King came here for Queen Gyda, surely Jarl Olaf would be the best match; Mort just hoped that she was a practical woman, not impressed by men dressed in fine clothes.

*

There were many suitors at the Althing, and all their followers made for a crowded event. Jarn Cuaran, as King, watched over events, with his sister, Queen Gyda, sitting on his left.

Olaf Trygvasson looked at the Queen, she was a tall, handsome, woman with long nut brown hair tied back from her face. Her face was very proud and from a distance Olaf could see she had very beautiful blue eyes. While he was studying her she cast her eyes around the room and their eyes met and she gave Olaf the briefest of little smiles. He was so surprised by the time he smiled back her gaze had moved on. What did it mean, was it just a pleasantry? He was not sure but he felt that there was fleeting mischief in her eyes when they met.

Olaf studied his competition; there were wealthy and powerful men from all over Ireland plus a few lesser Norse lords, Alfvine the peacock and one young Prince. The idiot was strutting around in very fine armour with his arrogant horde telling him what a great Jarl he was. Olaf tried to stay calm and concentrate on the task in hand but his instinct was telling him to punch that smug face until he had wiped the smile off it.

The King of Dyflin stood up and the waiting crowd went quite. He spoke in the common language of the kingdom, Norse. "My sister is looking for a husband and as she is a grown women and a widow I have decided to let her choose the one she likes best. Whoever the man is I will have to approve of him obviously, but we are a strong kingdom and we are not looking for any special alliances. Now, all the men that wish to be considered as my future brother-in-law come and stand at the front so Gyda can have a good look at you." Alfvine was first to the front and cheered by his men; he was shorter than Olaf and had very black hair and a finely trimmed black beard.

"I am Jarl Alfvine of the Jomsviking."

"Very nice," said the king, "but where are you from? With such black hair you could be a tartar." The king smiled as all but Alfvine's men laughed at the joke.

Fleetingly Alfvine looked furious but he quickly put on a stony face and replied, "Dear King Cuaran, I was born to the north of Birka, in the land of the Svea and it is not uncommon for my kin to have dark hair."

"Right, who is next?" For all Alfvine's finery the King of Dyflin did not seem impressed.

A young man stepped forward and the King of Dyflin smiled at him.

"My lord I am Murchad Boru, Prince of Munster and son of King Brian."

"Hello lad, how is your father, be sure to give him my regards." The King smiled at young Murchad, but he was so young he could not even grow a beard. Olaf wondered why the King of Munster would send such a young son, but maybe the answer lay in politics.

A few other well-dressed but lesser Irish noblemen came forward, plus a minor Jarl from the Hebrides. Before Olaf had stepped forward the king stood again and addressed the crowd.

"So these are the men who want to marry my sister?"

"Not all Lord King," Olaf stepped forward and joined the line of suitors.

The king stared at Olaf and rubbed his hand on his beard before speaking, "do you not think it wise to dress up a little for a queen, or perhaps my sister does not deserve that kind of respect."

Mort looked on from the crowd and could feel the tension, worried that for all their planning, things were taking a turn for the worse.

Olaf bowed to the King and then the Queen. "My lord King I mean no disrespect toward you or your sister, I am a worthy man with wealth and men. I have sailed here from Frisia and our war gear is wet and needs cleaning, I thought it would be a greater insult to you both if I wore that. Also, lord King I am not comfortable walking around like a peacock."

The king burst out laughing at this and the queen joined him. Queen Gyda then spoke quietly in the King's ear.

"My sister would like to know why she should pick you; you can start by telling us your name?"

"Dear lady, I am Olaf Trygvasson, Prince of Vendland and heir to the Norwegian throne, general to the Holy Roman Emperor Otto III and Viking Jarl to one hundred and eighty men. I bring wealth, soldiers and experience to the Kingdom of Dyflin but to your beautiful Queen Gyda I also bring gifts." At this Olaf turned to his men and Mort brought forward the prepared gifts in a small chest. Mort laid the chest half way between Olaf and Queen Gyda, Olaf then walked forward and opened it for the queen and her brother the king to see.

"I offer you fine amber from the Baltic Sea, silver coins from the Arab lands, gold jewellery from across the world and the most precious of all, a jade statue from the very edge of the world, it is of a woman with many arms."

"Can I see it?" The Queen lent forward in anticipation and Olaf held up the small, pale green statue and presented it to the Queen. When Gyda took the statue, she held both of Olaf's hands for a fleeting second. Her hands were soft, warm, long and elegant, the sensation of her feminine hands on his made his heart skip a beat.

"Jarl Olaf, why have you gone so red in the face," the king said this with a big smile on his face and both Olaf and Gyda smiled back.

"I am not sure if this statue is beautiful but it is unusual and I like it a lot."

Alfvine had had enough of this exchange and feared the game would be over, so he stepped forward and interrupted the exchange. "King Jarn, may I show you the gifts I have brought for the queen and can I present my credentials."

"Jarl Peacock, did I give permission for you to speak?" A wave of anger crossed the face of the King, "the only person I will tolerate interrupting me at this Althing is my sister. Everyone is due a chance to show their worth but I believe patience is something

47

we would be looking for in any suitor. I think maybe you should wait until the end or you can go and prance around somewhere else."

Olaf stayed silent and watched his rival, what would this proud man do to rescue the situation? Was he too proud and important to be insulted by King Jarn? If not he must be a little desperate and gambling on this working for him. His men were grumbling and very unhappy but they had kept reasonably quite so far.

Queen Gyda stood up and spoke, "I am not an old woman but also I am not a young maiden either. I need a husband who I can talk to and understands the needs of a woman and queen in her prime. Therefore, although I am very privileged by the chance to join the family of King Brian Boru, I must thank and decline the offer from Prince Murchad Boru.

I also need to say the only two other suitors that interest me are Jarl Olaf and Jarl Alfvine. So now Jarl Alfvine, your competitor has had his say I think it only fair that you may put your case at this Althing. Oh, and Jarl Olaf, please look after your lady of many arms and keep her safe." As she spoke to Olaf her eyes seemed to convey a message to him. Olaf, being a man, did not understand this gesture but hoped that he would be successful.

He had come to the Althing for the material benefits of marrying the Queen but on meeting her he was smitten. Not only was she a beautiful woman, he felt excited by her manner and intellect. One thing he did not understand was that his stomach tightened every time he had to talk or look at her and when she noticed him he felt like he had sunk a draught of strong Frisian ale.

"I am Jarl Alfvine of the Jomsviking; I bring with me great wealth and military understanding. I have many allies across the northern world including allies in the Holy Roman Empire and the Byzantium Empire." Alfvine turned to his men and waved Ulf over. Ulf approached with a chest twice the size of the one that Olaf had presented.

"I am a simple man and I have not gathered small trinkets from many places but I do offer a large chest of gold coin," at this Ulf opened the chest and revealed a substantial amount of gold.

King Cuaran leaned forward and stared longingly at the contents of the chest. "That is a fair amount of gold, Jarl Peacock."

"Brother, may I speak to Jarl Alfvine?"

"Go ahead, sister."

"Have you a personal gift for me?"

Alfvine looked a little lost for words but recovered and said, "Dear Queen with this gold you may buy yourself anything you want." He smiled, a little to himself; he was so good with words.

The queen, looking a little disappointed, stood still and waited for silence. She was wearing a fairly simple, pale blue dress, with an intricate gold belt enhancing her waist.

"King Jarn Cuaran, Prince Murchad Boru and honourable Jarls, I have made my decision. I choose, as my husband and ally, Jarl Olaf Trygvasson."

"NO! Please Queen Gyda reconsider, this man is a peasant and I am a Jarl of the Jomsviking, a much better man and husband for you!"

The king stood now and he looked impatient, "did you not here my sister you prancing peacock, she has made her choice. This is an Althing so you should know the rules; you only have one other chance, that is if the Queen agrees."

"Very well, Olaf Trygvasson I challenge you to holmgang. You will either face me and my men this afternoon or relinquish your position at this Althing." Alfvine looked smug as his men cheered.

Olaf stepped toward the slightly smaller Jomsviking, "a duel? I thought you would never ask."

Chapter 4

Tristan looked around at his remaining men, they looked exhausted but their spirits rose when they heard the fyrd.

"Men, we must find strength and support our countrymen. When the fyrd attack we must take the fight to the Sais also."

Maban was back at his side and they organised their troops quickly, getting the fittest and strongest into the front line. King Tristan of Kernow could almost taste victory and he dreamed of an alliance with Viking Olaf and a free land for his people.

"Focus, you bastards, I expect you to be able to kill farmers and women easily. We are the Wincanceaster Militia, we kill Danes and Norse so a few country savages will be nothing." Aelle was red in the face, he was angry as to him this was an insult having to fight the fyrd. He would take his anger out on the farmers; he rested his sword in its scabbard and held up his broad axe, watching the horde come upon them.

Drefan had made it back with about half of his men and they were spread about the back row. Earl Godwin kept his horsemen behind the shield wall so he could choose when to use them. The Earl knew that the odds against him were tough but he was confident in his men and he had an excellent captain in Aelle.

As the fyrd of Kernow came within sight of the hated Sais shield wall, Aelle dropped his shield and stepped forward. The shield wall closed behind him as the men cheered their own invincible. He stood with his weight equally balanced and made his axe comfortable in his hands. Aelle was a very fit man and his recovery from the push in the shield wall was quick. Today he felt like he could chop with his axe for hours. He had an old bear skin as a cloak; his arms were bare except for the warrior rings he wore. He had subtle armour protecting him, from a vest of chain mail to iron strips in his leggings. The men thought he was invincible but Aelle knew in a fight, you needed all the help you can get.

The Saxon shield wall was at an angle, partly facing the copse and partly facing the oncoming fyrd. The Kernish guard locked shields and moved forward slowly, the plan was for the fyrd to hit the Sais and then they would engage, too.

Aelle could see the horde running toward him and screaming, holding their weapons high. The ones at the front had some real swords but the most common weapon seemed to be a sichel. What shocked him was he could see women and children in the fyrd and he guessed that almost half of it was women.

He focused his mind on the battle and survival, digging deep to recover his anger. The fyrd attacked the length of the wall and Aelle was in the heart of the battle. He swung hard with his double headed broad axe and cleaved a woman in the side of her head, cutting off any scream. He was aware of the crowd and swung the broad axe back and up, slicing through a boy's jaw. Back again he swung the axe, it was like chopping through a thicket as he cut off the arm of a screaming savage, although the axe wedged itself in between the man's ribs and stuck there. Aelle felt a punch and pain on his arm and in a glance he saw a farmer had hacked at him with his sichel. The fellow was swinging back for another slash so Aelle let go of his axe and hit the man in the jaw with the elbow of his wounded arm. Aelle stepped back and the shield wall closed round him for protection and he took out his sword.

Godwin was waiting, waiting for the whole fyrd to be in the thick of the battle before he sent in his cavalry. Men on foot did not like facing a man on a horse and it was even worse for the untrained farmers. This was his major hope at breaking the Kernish, as they outnumbered his men two to one.

The Saxon shield wall was bowing under the sheer weight of the fyrd and King Tristan had now moved forward and was applying further pressure to the left flank. The whole of the fyrd was not engaged but Godwin could not wait and ordered Edwin, the captain of his horsemen, to attack the back of the fyrd to ease the pressure on the shield wall.

Edwin did not need to be asked twice and he hollered an order to his men and fifty horses were sprung from the Saxon rear. The horse soldiers tried to get their mounts up to some speed so they could hit the fyrd hard and fast. They came round in a curve and saw the undisciplined rabble milling at the back of the horde. Each horseman picked a target and rode hard for it. Edwin was at the front and he picked a screaming man with long hair, the fellow had his back to the approaching horsemen and only turned round as Edwin came upon him. Edwin brought his sword down fast into the enemies face and realised it was a woman just as he cut hard through her. Her head was opened up in the front and revealed a bloody mess. Edwin had moved on but was left with the image of her handsome face just before he ruined it.

He looked up selecting another victim to attack and speared his sword through the chest of a farmer holding a wooden pike up in defence.

The horsemen were hacking their way through the back of the fyrd and causing carnage among the undefended folk. But things changed as about a hundred armed men from the centre of the fyrd came out to face the Saxon cavalry. They were all armed with spears and swords and had rudimentary amour. As a group they rushed at the nearest horseman, spearing him through the neck and lifting him from his mount. Then the spearmen organised into groups of ten, spreading out to defend the fyrd and attack isolated horsemen.

Edwin looked up and saw that he was split from the main cavalry with two of his colleagues. One man was being pulled at by the fyrd, he tried hacking down with his sword but there was a crowd around his horse and he disappeared into the crowd screaming.

Edwin called over to his remaining ally, Frithgist, "Come close to me and we will try and fight a way through to safety."

"Edwin, there must be twenty spearmen between us and the rest of the group," Frithgist had to shout to be heard although he was not far from Edwin.

"Friend, we can stay here and die or we can fight and try to survive."

"Well come on then Edwin, let's get it over with, if I am going to die I mean to kill a few first."

They looked at each other, smiled, turned their horses toward the crowd and kicked back trying to build up some speed over the short distance.

Frithgist realised that they were riding at the farmers in the fyrd and thought they had a chance to break through. As the two horsemen got close to the crowd, the men of the fyrd ran quickly to the side revealing armed spearmen. Half of the spearman had their long spears pushed into the ground with the remainder readying their spears to throw. There was no time to change tactic as they were almost on top of their enemy. Edwin tried to jump the wall of spears but his horses hind legs slammed into the crowd and it fell with Edwin still on it. Frithgist had been thrown too as his horse had been speared in the chest. He hit the ground hard and felt winded but no other obvious pain. Frithgist got up as quick as he could, in time to witness the crowd falling on the half crushed Edwin. There was no scream and Frithgist hoped his friend was already dead before he was ravaged.

The last Saxon this side of the fyrd drew his sword and looked at the crowd and waited to die. A big Kernish man with blood soaking his right arm ran forward and swung his sword at the Saxon neck of Frithgist. He felt the blow knock him to the floor too quickly; as he lay there he saw the rest of his body tumble forward in front of him.

Thirty horsemen retreated back to the safety of the shield wall, having given the men in the shield wall little respite.

King Tristan could feel the Sais moving back slowly, the fyrd was doing a good job on the enemy but he feared that they were suffering heavy casualties. Maban had gone round to direct the spearmen and they seemed to have checked the cavalry attack. The new King of Kernow had used all his resources and he had no more surprises for the Sais, he just hoped this would be enough to win the day.

*

Ealdorman Godwin was worried now, he had lost almost half of his horsemen and his shield wall was shrinking in front of him. The fyrd was taking heavy casualties but the sheer weight of men and women were taking their toll on his ceorls. He guessed he was down to three hundred men including those on horseback and he was facing almost three times that number.

He looked around for a potential retreat and somewhere to regroup, but this was a foreign land to him and he could see nowhere close at hand. A finger of panic touched at his heart and he tried to ignore it. Perhaps he would not get back to his wife after all. He swore that if he survived this battle he would go back to his farm and stay there.

He surveyed the area hoping he would see somewhere they could retreat to, when he saw what looked like horse dust thrown up behind the horde. His heart sunk, it looked as if the young prince had thought of everything and would defeat the Wincanceaster Militia this day with another push from beyond the river.

But through the cloud of dust he saw the shape of the helmet and it was definitely Saxon.

"Please let my eyes be true, is that help for this exhausted troop?"

Thorod doubted himself a little, he had acted on impulse, and having left the small band of savages he was following after hearing Aldred's counsel. He almost did not recognise his man when Rand presented him. Aldred had looked a complete mess; he was dirty, emaciated and shockingly dressed as a monk. The disguise was good, as some of these holy men were filthy and smelled worse than a family of pigs.

However Rand was also worried as Aldred had spoken at length about what he had witnessed around Liddyford, then Aldred had related it all to Thorod.

Aldred had told them that there was a prince of Kernow who believed in training his men and fitting them out with the best weapons. Aldred had seen about one hundred and fifty of these men. This alone should not worry his friend Godwin and the men of Wiltshire but Aldred also spoke of the fyrd being gathered and they ran into thousands. Even the greatest generals struggled when the numbers were so uneven.

Thorod was troubled as he had gone against King Aethelred's express orders and he feared that this would be seen as disloyal by the court, a very bad thing in these dark times. However he loved Godwin like a brother and he trusted Aldred's eyes, from memory the man missed nothing on the battle field.

Aldred had told him how King Cadoc was a fat bloated fool, more interested in securing a long line of young wives. The locals acknowledged him as their king but they loved the young prince. This convinced Thorod to leave the small band he was tracking down and check on Godwin's progress. After all Thorod had twice the men that his southern cousin had.

Thorod broke through the clearing and saw the ford straight ahead; he reigned in his horse and surveyed the scene, while waiting for his men of foot to catch up. What he saw made him glad he had come, and a little scared. The other side of the ford was a raging battle, a disorganised mess of folk waving around anything that could be called a weapon. In small pockets he saw organisation and he caught glimpses of a shield wall defending against the large mass attacking it.

He silently thanked Brother Michael, his old teacher of words, when Thorod struggled with the lessons the holy brother had told him stories of great battles from the past. He learned his Latin words better while reading about the old Roman generals that used to rule over this land when it was Albion. The reason he sent thanks to the holy Brother in heaven was for this alone. He had read how the Roman generals trained their men into

54

peak fitness and would get the foot soldiers to jog long distances to spring surprise attacks on their enemies. Thorod never forgot some of the old Roman tactics and he drilled his men hard also, and today he knew his cavalry would not have to wait long before the bulk of his fighting force caught up.

Thorod had one hundred and fifty horses that only had to wait a few minutes for the first footmen to catch up.

When the first of his ceorls jogged up to the ford Thorod spoke to the most senior.

"Wait here, gather the men together and form a new shield wall the other side of the ford, today we will save our brothers from Wiltshire." He spoke these words to his fittest young captain, Edgar, who immediately started to organise the men into battle formation. Then Thorod gathered his large cavalry and attacked the back of the fyrd, intent on death and mutilation in the eyes of his god.

The Mercian cavalry tore into the back of the fyrd of Kernow, hacking at heads and necks with their long swords. Some of the horsemen preferred the broad-axe and they used it to great effect. The two headed axe came swinging through the air assisted by the speed and weight of a horse.

Although the fyrd looked a little disorganised, Tristan had ensured it was layered with the youngest and strongest fighters at the front, assisted by the trained spearmen. The second layer was mainly young women, old soldiers and boys with the last layer consisting of anyone enthusiastic enough to enter battle.

This last layer of folk was devastated by Ealdorman Thorod's professional cavalry. Arms were hacked to shreds, throats were speared and gouged, and in some cases heads were cleaved clean off. Thorod would remark later it was like shooting pigs in a pen.

Thorod and his horse had been slowed by the sheer weight of people and his arm was starting to ache from all the carnage he had caused. He sat astride his horse hacking first one side and then the other. The spearman of Kernow could only watch the Saxon attack at their rear as they could not move through the crowded fyrd.

Adjacent to Thorod was Godric, one of the nephews of Ealdorman Brihtnoth of Essex. He had been sent along to gain some experience. Thorod thought he was a weak willed, pathetic fellow and nothing like his brave and respected uncle, but hopefully going to war would make a man of him. Godric was now laughing hysterically as he sliced through the poorly defended locals. To Thorod Godric looked like a picture of a devil he had seen in

Brother Michael's bible. The young man was almost wholly covered in blood, his eyes and teeth shone white in his red, glistening face. This did not seem to bother him at all as he continued to hack into his already dead foe. Thorod felt disgust at how the young man looked until he realised he was also covered in the blood of the farmers from Kernow.

The attack from behind had caused a wave of panic to run through the fyrd and they were trying to retreat from the war horses running them down. The panicking people had pushed the spearman away from the rear and onto the shield wall of the Sais. Maban had returned to his brother's side earlier and spoke to him while the men in front pushed at the Sais.

"Brother, get back on your horse and see if you can organise our people, otherwise I fear the battle turning in favour of the scum."

Tristan did not speak; he just nodded at his brother and made his way back to the copse, hoping his horse was still there. Luckily it had been tied up and he mounted his mare and surveyed the scene.

The Sais who had attacked initially were in a shield wall of maybe three hundred men, including all the now unseated horse riders. They were locked tight with his smaller band and the semi-professional fighters in the fyrd. The fyrd were being attacked by a large cavalry force of up to two hundred. Seeing his people hacked down so easily by a ruthless force was not what made him realise the battle was lost. Behind the cavalry, watching and waiting was a huge shield wall, which seemed to be growing all the time. At a guess King Tristan believed there were maybe eight hundred foot soldiers gathered to attack his nation. Somebody grabbed his leg, "brother how bad is it?"

"Maban, we have lost, a massacre will happen this day, this is the end of Prydain as Kernow will almost definitely fall this day."

"Brother, you must escape, take some men and leave this battle; while you live we still have a king to rally around. Go to Dyflin and find the Viking Jarl, a Dane as a master is better than any Sais."

"Maban, together we can try and raise a fighting force to avenge our people."

"No Tristan, you are pure blood and I am nid pur, a bastard, and you inherited your mothers' brains. Do one thing for me brother, make sure I am remembered, I would like songs sung about my bravery."

"Of course brother, I have known none braver than you so I urge you to come with me and protect your king."

At this moment a great shout went up and Tristan looked over at the sound and saw the massive Sais shield wall move forward. The enemy's cavalry had moved to allow the attack and this act panicked the remainder of the fyrd and they started to flee up the incline, run through the brambles and some even ran toward their attackers. Without the fyrd attacking Godwin's men they regrouped and made one last big push on the small Kernish shield wall. It collapsed with some of the younger men breaking rank, trying to escape with the remainder of the fyrd.

Tristan held out his arm to his brother, "get on the horse now, to stay is suicide." Maban clambered up behind his brother the king, and they made good their escape.

*

Aelle was furious, he had cut down and killed every last one of the Kernish shield wall in his fury. He was so close to the two leaders, the prince and his captain were only yards away and he knew if he could have covered those few paces he would have killed them both and so end the fantasy of Kernow. Unfortunately he was held up by the mass of men fighting for their life.

One of his foes was groaning on the ground and Aelle looked down at the dying man. He was asking for something, water probably as most dying men felt a ravenous thirst in their last moments. Aelle threw his bear skin over his shoulder and held his sword up and screamed out loud before bringing the sword down hard and true on the dying man's neck.

"You can drink in the afterlife."

*

Tristan rode hard through the small valleys of his country with his brother holding tight behind him. A valley snaked down toward the rocky coast and to one of Kernow's coastal towns.

The people of Porth Kernow were awaiting news as their young men had joined the fyrd to defend the land. As they saw just one horse, with their new king a top and no other soldiers, they feared the worse. Some people groaned with despair and the rest stood in silence as the horse came down the valley to the small hamlet. King Tristan and his loyal brother Maban climbed off their horse and the last prince of Kernow held his head in his hands and wept.

*

Laughter filled the night to be mixed in with the screams of women. Some men were wrestling their friends and a few others were resurrecting old arguments. Godwin and Thorod had found a quiet place to sit with a sufficient supply of local ale.

"Dear sweet Jesus Thorod, where did you find this sour brew?"

"My old man Aldred brewed it for the locals when he was held captive and you can tell he is no master brewer."

"Although friend, after the first cup I can taste nothing more and feel the effects working. Thorod, I must thank you again, as our shield wall was close to collapse, the fyrd is undisciplined but there was many waves of attack and my boys were just hanging on by the time you turned up."

"Dear Godwin, I would never leave a friend but some credit must go to Aldred as he warned me, repeatedly, that the young prince was no fool in battle and he had been gathering the fyrd. I would ask that you recount this to the king when we next sit in his council as I had to disobey his orders to come here. I do not want to be another Earl subject to the king's suspicion."

"Ealdorman Thorod I believe I have the trust of the king as I defend his capital with my militia. I will, of course, tell him of your great heroics this day."

A chant went up in the nearest group of men as Aelle was representing Wessex in a wrestling match, against a big friendly fellow from the Mercian side. Both men were very drunk and fell over quickly, promising each other lifelong friendship.

Chapter 5

Fain art thou to tell how with Hrungnir I fought,
The haughty giant whose head, of stone was made;
And yet I felled him and stretched him before me.

On a field outside the town of Dyflin, Olaf and Alfvine met. Alfvine's troop in total numbered sixty compared to Olaf's of one hundred and seventy nine. For an equal fight Olaf took the field as one of sixty of his best men. He felt fairly confident as he had a strong disciplined band of men and he had chosen the cream, whereas Alfvine had only sixty and he had to fight with what he had. However, Olaf was not going to approach this fight lightly as he was made aware the men across the field were Jomsviking, renowned as the strongest and best fighters in the northern world.

Both groups stood apart, either side of the field, watching their foe through a fine mist of rain.

Mort spoke first, "Jarl Olaf, can I have the big red bear, I feel I should teach him to respect his fellow man."

"Usually I would want to kick his arse first but the rules of holmgang mean I have to beat his husband first, maybe you can leave a bit of him for me to fight, too."

Alfvine looked over at his men. Ulf was laughing and joking, he was extremely happy as the big man had been bored with all the politics and he could now take out his frustration on the men across the field.

Alfvine was not laughing; he was trying to get totally focused on fighting. He was playing out his opening moves in his mind, while they waited for the King to arrive and adjudicate.

The rules of the holmgang stated no shields and it was not necessarily a fight to the death, although if somebody died during the fight no blood feud could ensue. The no shields rule stopped a long, boring, pushing competition which was common in a real battle but here it gave no entertainment, also a quick outcome was required.

Olaf turned to his men to speak with them before the fight. "Remember what I said, try hard not to kill these men, they are distant cousins of ours but led by a fool and a bully. We are here to show them who are the better fighters, and better men."

Alfvine was ready, he was in his battle mind but something irritated him and he realised he had to speak with Ulf. Ulf was boasting and showing off to Ketil, who was a good fighter but always seemed impressed by the big red head. Berg was over with some of the younger men giving advice and tips on how to engage in the battle.

"Ulf, a quick word," Ulf spun around, a little angry, but calmed himself when he saw it was his ring giver.

"Jarl, what can I do for you so soon before the battle?"

"Just one thing, leave the Jarl Olaf to me, if you chop him up before I get near him, the queen will want to marry you."

"Sounds like a good idea to me," Ulf had a big grin buried in his bushy red beard.

"It might happen if she has lost her sight in the last hour." Alfvine turned to face the foe across the field and focused his mind on the fight ahead.

King Jarn Cuaran and Queen Gyda arrived at the fighting field accompanied by their house guard. The King's brother, Ragnal, had joined them to witness the holmgang. He being a young man of nineteen years and ready for battle of his own, it was said that he always fought beside his father, when he was alive, and would be as strong a leader as his kin.

One of the house guards blew a horn and signalled the beginning of the duel.

Alfvine's Jomsviking, on hearing the horn blow, started to run toward Olaf's men. Alfvine and Ulf weere at the front of the group and Ulf started to scream a battle cry. As ordered Olaf and his men jogged forward a little and then started walking slowly toward the Jomsviking, each one having picked out a target.

Ulf was a big man, but he was not fat and slow, Mort could see the forearms of the big red bear holding his sword out front and focused his mind on his foe. Ulf and Alfvine were a little in front of their men but not isolated. Mort kept walking forward while holding his sword ahead of him with both hands. He expected the big bully to try and batter him with sheer strength and he was ready.

While running across the field, Ulf felt alive, he loved a good fight and it seemed the little skinny one next to their Jarl had picked him out. Very well, he thought, Ulf would abide by the no killing rule, but he would hit every one of them hard and put his weight and strength through each blow. As he came running toward the skinny one with black hair, he lifted his sword above his head meaning to chop down at the fool.

Mort lifted his sword up to take the blow from Ulf, but as the big man came close and chopped forward Mort skipped to the side and swung around, scraping his sword against Ulf's ribs.

Ulf was surprised at the weasels speed and doubly so when he was stung in his side. But Ulf was not such a clumsy fool; he stopped his run and turned, bringing his sword around and just missing Mort's brow.

Mort had leaned back just in time and was now facing a man so big, Mort would have to jump to touch the top of his head.

Ulf started swinging his sword diagonally at Mort and trying to beat him into submission with sheer strength. The first blow was checked by Mort but his wrist felt the whole power of Ulf, and he decided to avoid that tactic. Ulf was encouraged by that blow but as he moved toward Mort, Mort would skip back and sideways, avoiding almost all contact. Then just as Ulf was getting frustrated with the smaller man's slippery ways, Mort would start attacking with small quick jabs at the bigger man. Quite a few of Mort's jabs cut into Ulf, in his forearms, left thigh and he even sustained a slash across a nipple. Ulf could feel the fight slip away, he was getting angry as it did not even feel like a proper fight and he feared losing. He decided to call on his reserves and throw everything at the smaller man.

Just as Mort thought he saw Ulf slow and show signs of tiredness, the big man came at him with even more gusto. This time Ulf caught Mort plum on his sword countless times and Mort's arms were tiring quickly. He was backing away constantly during the onslaught and his heel hit a divot of earth and he went crashing over on his back. Ulf came forward and attempted to hack into him while he was on the ground, but Mort was fast and rolled quickly away and Ulf slammed his big sword into the muddy ground. Mort was up quick and preparing to defend himself when he noticed Ulf struggling to free his sword from the mud. Mort thrust forward and stabbed Ulf in the thigh and the big man fell, leaving his sword sticking out of mother earth. Mort leapt forward and punched the fallen Ulf in the temple and he folded down to the ground. Ulf lay on his side looking peaceful, appearing to lay in a restful sleep.

Mort untied the rope from around his waist and tied the big bear's hands behind his back.

Alfvine had not noticed his big man fall to Mort's attack; he was having fun with the tall Olaf. Alfvine liked to be light when going into battle so that he was capable of moving better. He was using all his favourite moves and the speed he was renowned for. However, Olaf was capable of blocking his opponent's every thrust and swipe and his face gave nothing away.

Usually when Alfvine fought he would dispatch with the enemy quickly, but when he met a better fighter he took joy in wearing them down. He made it a rule to conserve energy in battle. All fighting could be long and drawn out and tiredness could kill almost as much as drunkenness.

Alfvine was fast and Olaf was not sure how long he could defend from this man. He was prepared for a difficult fight, for he knew the reputation of the Jomsviking, but his opponent was very fast and spotted all the openings in Olaf's defence. The one thing that he noted in the fight was that Alfvine did not hit him with one hard strike. So Olaf decided to try and just parry and work out a way to defeat this man.

Alfvine came forward again with an angle swipe at Olaf's sword arm; the heir to the Norwegian throne lent back slightly, lifted his sword and defended the blow. The weapons slid against each other and Alfvine lost his footing slightly, Olaf saw a small opening but their swords were still locked together so the taller man swung his left fist at the Jomsviking and heard a delicious crunch as it connected with Alfvine's nose.

Alfvine was shocked and furious, his beautiful nose! But he tried to recover quickly as he was half blinded by the tears in his eyes and the pain in the middle of his face.

Olaf saw his opportunity and started to hack clumsily at Alfvine, for he was aware of his opponent's disadvantage. Alfvine was disabled from the blow but he was still fast enough to defend himself, but Olaf was relentless. He had had to defend for the whole fight and now he had a small advantage he would push on. Olaf was taller and stronger than the Jomsviking and meant to use this to his advantage now.

Alfvine could hardly see, his nose was definitely broken and his eyes were swimming with tears, what he needed was half a minute to wipe his eyes clear and he would happily continue. He was given no time by the taller man, who was now combining hacking with thrusts, which Alfvine had to try and anticipate. His eyes were finally starting to clear and he thought he saw Olaf stumble in the wet grass. Alfvine made a fast and accurate thrust forward, aiming for neck of his foe.

Olaf had decided on a false stumble to try and draw the injured man in but his plan almost back fired. Although Alfvine was injured and half blind, he was still as fast as he was at the beginning of the fight. Alfvine's sword came at Olaf lightning fast, aimed at his neck, and he had to lean back and jerk his head to the left. Alfvine had put so much into this thrust, as he knew he was disadvantaged, that the thrust carried his sword arm forward, quickly followed by the rest of the Jomsviking. Olaf leant so far backward that he fell to the ground with Alfvine on top of him; they looked like drunken lovers scrambling on the ground. But poor, proud Alfvine did not have the luck of the gods with him, as he threw himself forward his tender broken nose banged into Olaf's shoulder and sent a fresh shock of pain through his head and started his eyes weeping again.

Olaf pushed Alfvine off him and got up quickly, Alfvine took the opportunity to try and wipe his eyes clear. Olaf did not wait and kicked him hard in the side of the head, so hard that he thought he may have cracked a toe. The tactic worked and Alfvine lay still, Olaf slipped off the rope at his waist and tied the unconscious man's hands.

Ketil and Brynjolf had dropped their weapons early on in the fight and were now wrestling each other. If you just wandered across this you could believe it was two old friends practising but this match happened in a field where there sixty individual contests happening.

Brynjolf was getting frustrated, for Ketil was smaller than him and was quite slight, but he seemed to have unending reserves of strength. Ketil was also a tricky fighter, just as the bigger man felt he was getting the upper hand Ketil would trip him and he would have to jump up quickly or lose the advantage.

Ketil would twist and turn and it was like trying to wrestle a pig at the farm. During one of these twists Brynjolf found himself with his arms around Ketil but behind him, it was like holding a woman and he was thankful all his friends were busy fighting or they would taunt him later. Just then, Ketil dropped within his embrace and elbowed him in the gut. He doubled over and the smaller man punched him in the face, catching his cheek hard. Brynjolf heard rather than felt a crunch and waited the second it would take the pain to register itself. It never came, but Ketil squealed and held his hand gingerly.

Brynjolf stood up straight in front of Ketil and punched him square on the jaw. The smaller man was out cold before he hit the floor.

Berg was having a good time, although this was a strange fight. He knew he should not intentionally kill, but slightly wounding someone was hard to achieve also. Berg was thirty seven years old and a very experienced Jomsviking. He had regretted leaving Jomsborg almost immediately and knew it was a big mistake. He had planned to slip away at a convenient time and return to Styrbjorn and beg his forgiveness.

Kjarten, another of Olaf's men, having defeated his own foe, spotted Berg and came toward him, sword high and ready for the fight. Berg braced himself for the fight and easily parried the attack. The man ahead of him was looking for another quick win but Berg would make him regret his over confidence. Berg heard a slight squelch behind him and took a quick look. Another fighter was sneaking up. Berg spun around and thrust at his new opponent, who only just defended in time. Berg tried to back up a little so that he could see both men. As he did he noticed two more men come to face him and started to wonder what had happened to his colleagues close by. He quickly looked around and saw many men on the floor, either trussed up or in the process of being tied. Although they were all Jomsviking, not one of their opponents had been defeated.

The two men nearest him attacked and Berg weighed up their approach, one slightly ahead of the other, and managed to defend both strikes. The man to his left tried another swing, which was slow and over confident and Berg ducked below the weapon, cutting his foes sword arm. He turned to face the other men and found he had five men to his left and another three to his right.

"Brave fighter, lay down your sword, if this was a fight to the death you would be travelling to Valholl this day."

The voice came from behind Berg; at first he was angry with himself for not hearing the approach. He turned around and saw Jarl Olaf standing there with two of his lieutenants. Berg was a practical man and could not see one of the Jomsviking standing. He laid his sword down, surveying the field, and could see almost all his colleagues tied up or unconscious.

"Jarl Olaf, I congratulate you, it looks like you have been successful in this holmgang. I am honoured to have fought against such skilful men."

Olaf stepped forward and placed his arm on Berg's shoulder, "if you ever need a ring giver, you are welcome in Dyflin. I always have space for brave and skilful warriors."

One of the king's young men ran up to join the group, "Jarl Olaf, please excuse my words but they are as the king requested I say them; when are you going to stop showing off and present yourself to the queen?"

Berg watched Alfvine's longship leave the haven of Dyflin, Ketil stood beside him along with some of the older Jomsviking. Ulf had acted like a spoilt child, shouting and screaming at him and Ketil mostly. Berg thought that he may have had to fight the big man until Alfvine stepped in and told Ulf he did not want men that were no longer loyal.

Berg had made a mistake leaving Jomsborg and wished to be back in the famous citadel but he realised that may be too much to wish for. When the opportunity to swear loyalty to Jarl Olaf presented itself he realised he finally had a way out. Here was a Jarl that would be married to the Queen of Dyflin and with a claim to the Norwegian throne.

Berg had followed Alfvine initially as he longed for one more adventure, a chance to settle down and find a wife. Those things were impossible to find in Jomsborg or roaming the seas as a homeless Viking.

What surprised him was Ketil deciding to join them in Dyflin as Berg saw him as a close friend and ally to Ulf. It seemed to bother him more now so he decided to ask.

"Ketil, I was wondering why you decided to stay here with us old Vikings rather than joining Alfvine's adventure."

"I was wondering if anyone would ask, and I am surprised, with all the noise Ulf made, why he did not just ask me, too. It is because of a woman, Berg. I joined the Jomsviking to forget a woman whom I loved and I thought loved me. I was hurt for a long time, but I realised, while I was tied up in that field, that I do not miss her anymore. So I thought I would find another one. Also, I really miss the tupping."

Berg laughed at this, it was not particularly funny, but there had been a lot of tension the last few days and it all came out in that release.

"So we are all men of Olaf now and had better be well behaved as you know the new man is always watched closest."

They all nodded and hoped that life would be more comfortable and less exciting in the Kingdom of Dyflin.

*

65

Gyda lay in the arms of her new husband and decided to ask him.

"Olaf, would you tell me what gods you pray too?"

"That is a strange question, why do you ask?"

"When I was a young girl all I knew were Odin, Thor and the gods of the north. These days, however, many people follow the Christian god and some of the things they say seem to make more sense to me. I feel that the older gods do not care for us and never speak with any of us; it would not matter to them if we gave them tribute or just turned our backs on them."

"I understand what you are saying, when my first wife was sick I prayed to Odin, Thor, Freya, Freyja, Skadi, Njordr and Heimdallr. I used the ancient runes and promised them tribute but all that happened is she got sicker and eventually died. They did not answer my prayers then, and afterward I realised that they had never answered any of my prayers. Then it occurred to me that when I fought for the Holy Roman Emperor we were blessed by Christian priests and all I experienced at that time was success and victory. It seems to me that the Christian god must be very powerful as he alone seems to be bringing about Ragnarok for the army of old gods."

"Husband, I would like to learn more about the Christian god and I wanted to ask you first. If you object, let me know and I will not follow this path."

"You have my blessing."

Olaf pulled her tight and enjoyed being with a woman again, especially one so intelligent and beautiful. Gyda had her eyes closed and seemed to be sleeping and she shocked him slightly when she spoke up.

"Soon, I will show you our lands across the sea. The Fylde is somewhere that needs a strong man and two hundred fighting warriors to help defend it."

Chapter 6

Spring 989

I wake and roll over and see the woman asleep next to me.

Her dark blonde hair has fallen over her face during the night. I can hear her soft, slow breathing while she sleeps and dreams. I move slightly closer to smell her. She always smells good, of fresh flowers and sweet oil. This makes me think of what I must smell of, horse, sheep and sweat. What does she see in me?

I am a big man, skilled with the axe and the sword and with a good understanding of the law. But I am clumsy when talking to women and they always seemed a mystery to me until I met Freyja. I am so happy she has joined me on my farm, Hlidarendi.

She moves a little in her dream state and I notice the sunlight catch the small blonde hairs on her arm, and seeing this I feel my heart grow bigger.

How I enjoy being in love with Freyja.

How things change over the years, the norns weave our web of life and when you look back it is an obvious pathway. I used to be care free and selfish, only looking for my own personal gain. Now so many rely on me, I have a large farm with plenty of land and livestock, two younger brothers to watch out for; I found my sister a husband and myself a beautiful wife. I thank Odin for my fortune and pray that my life can stay steady and boring.

It has been five years since I escaped Gull's kin in Scania, making my way back to Iceland. I had to spend a little time in Orkney in case they searched for me in my home land first, but on returning I heard no news of a man hunt for me.

I miss Gull, Erik and Gustav, we used to have such fun chasing young maids and drinking until we fell over. The laughing we did could go on all night, I remember Erik laughing until he threw up once.

On one occasion we went hunting in the mountains in the far north where the winter deer roam, along with wolves, wolverines and bear. We wanted to have a bear skin each so that we could show what men we were. Erik doubted that we would find any as he claimed they slept all winter. We did capture a winter deer from a great herd of over a thousand djur, but we had only eaten the fillet when fifty mad men of the north attacked us. How we survived that onslaught was a story in itself, but the men of the north were acting as if we had eaten their mother.

We fought, we ran and we killed at least six of them before they fell back, although they then started to stalk us all the way back to our ship. Ten days of being followed across the frozen north, the memory still makes me shiver and not from the cold we all felt at the time. I know what it feels like to be hunted.

I look at my beautiful wife lying next to me and want to feel her warmth. I move into the small of her back and wrap my warrior arms around her, while burying my face into the back of her hair. She groans slightly, and I feel aroused by the curve of her body and softness of her skin. I run my hand down her back and round the curve of her perfect buttocks. I think to myself that husbands are supposed to get bored of their wives, while I find her more and more attractive every day.

"Gunnar?" A voice from the hall, coming from the other side of the curtain.

"Who is it," I shout, already recognising Njal's voice, but stalling so my erection can shrink.

"It is Njal, I am sorry but we need to talk, urgently."

Reluctantly I rise from the warmth of my wife and move out into the hall.

"Hey friend, sorry, I am not properly dressed yet."

Njal interrupts, "There are Danes looking for you, from Scania."

"Where are they?" I feel cornered. "How long have I got?"

Njal sits at a bench. "I believe they are half a day's ride away at least. You better tell me why they are looking for you so I can help, as you look like you know."

I proceed to tell Njal of the events five years earlier in Uppakra Lund.

He never interrupts but patiently listens, making mental notes.

*

Hild 'Yxa' Eiriksdottir, wife of Bjorn Bjornsson, the weak, foolish and wealthy man, stands outside her hall nagging at the servants. She has heard that behind her back that she is called Hild Yxa and is foolishly proud that her servants and enemies are fearful of her. She stupidly misunderstands the moniker 'battle axe'.

Hild burns with a strong desire for power, wealth and respect. She has worked and schemed very hard to get where she is today, the wife of one of the largest landowners in Iceland. Bjorn owns four large farms and employs thirty staff plus eight slaves. He also has two merchant vessels that are constantly ferrying goods across the Scandinavian world. She knows she should be happy but when she looks around, her neighbours are wealthier, happier or more respected than her. Inevitably her thoughts turn to Freyja and she feels her blood boil.

What does that big thug Gunnar see in that skinny, plain dressed tomboy? All through Hild's childhood Freyja has been there, not always winning, but forever winning the battles that matter. The way of things is when Hild scores a success, in the long term Freyja benefits.

A servant girl walks past Hild carrying two heavy buckets of milk and spills a little, it gives Hild the pleasure of shouting at someone; although she usually enjoys bullying the weak this time she is not satisfied.

Returning to her thoughts she thinks about the bloated fool of a husband she has, she concedes he is a fair business man but he never seems to make enough money to look after her. And the bastard constantly complains about her few little indulgences, does he not realise that one of the most important women in Iceland needs a little gold and the best amber jewellery? The fool can make a little money, but he is soft and weak, and in her eyes not a real man at all. In the very back of her mind she hears herself think, 'not like Gunnar'.

As if the Norns are watching she can see, at a distant, a tall man riding hard and fast along the track that borders her land. Even from this distance she can tell it is Gunnar from the way he rides his horse. Instead of riding the mare, he seems to bully it along by sheer will. She watches him at a distance and wonders why he is riding so hard for the quay? He looks as if he is chasing or running from something?

If Hild has one talent above all others, she can smell trouble as if it has been farted right in front of her.

Gunnar obviously has a problem and is working on limiting the damage, if the determination of his ride is anything to go by. Also, she saw Njal going the opposite way earlier. Njal was not riding at that speed but he avoided looking towards her farm or acknowledging her. So Njal was very likely going to see Gunnar and this resulted in the display she has just witnessed. If I am lucky, she thinks, this will turn bad for Freyja.

*

My lungs are bursting and I can taste iron in my mouth with every breath. My arse and balls are aching; my arms, back and legs are straining to stay on the stallion as it gallops on to the quay. I thank Odin my horse is strong enough to tolerate my weight and lack of riding skill. I need to think of an excuse when I reach the quay, and hope somebody has a boat to sell. My brother has a boat but it is far too big for two and it has not tasted the salt of the sea since last summer. I have all my silver in a leather bag hanging round my neck, and the cord cutting into my nape is the least of my problems.

I knew this day would come, I even thought about it on the day I married Freyja. I try and suppress a small choke when I think of my Freyja and spur the big horse onward. I think I mean well but deep down I am a selfish man and can take my wife for granted. I know she is fiercely loyal toward me and will keep forgiving my selfishness. I have been back in Iceland about five years now and I keep kidding myself that I am a farmer and landowner when in my heart I am a Viking. I have retired since killing Gull as I believe that facing the horror of battle so much made me a more malevolent man. If I escape from Harald and his men I will completely change and crush the Viking within me, but for the moment I need him more than ever.

I want a boat with supplies, and I have to escape Iceland and the family of the man I killed. But where should we go, Norway, Shetland, Faeroe or Orkney? Should I go even further, down far south to Byzantium and work for the Emperor? What will be best for Freyja?

I cannot think straight as the sweat stings my eyes and the horse shakes my bones. Oh Freyja, what should I do, all you said is that you would trust my judgement and stay with me.

I can see the quay now within the estuary and there are many people loading and unloading vessels, men caulking beached ships and a few smaller boats bobbing on the water. Ahead I see that rich fool Bjorn Bjornsson directing the unloading of the largest ship at the quay.

I slow the horse a little to give me a few more seconds to think, the story I need has to throw any pursuers off the scent as Bjorn will be cross examined by his bitch of a wife and then the whole country will know where I am heading.

I see the quay master in discussion with some men and head his way.

"Thorgils, hey, can I interrupt, I have a matter of some urgency?" The men talking to Thorgils look at me and my exhausted horse.

"Friend, if you are quick, you may interrupt."

"Thank you," I reply to the Norseman.

"I need a boat, Thorgils, something that can carry Freyja and me back to Scania, as I have urgent family problems that cannot wait."

Before Thorgils can speak one of the Norsemen steps in, "friend, we have a small boat that we were just trying to sell. Although it may need a little caulking it should be enough for a small crew."

I looked at the boat; it is a Faering about thirty hands long, room for two oarsmen, a decent sail but in need of some maintenance. The one big advantage it gave me was that I was buying off complete strangers.

The negotiations went well. For the Norsemen I tried to pay a market rate, but they knew I was desperate and that I had almost no other choice. The only good thing was it did not cost me all my silver.

We all toasted the deal with some quite good Norse ale before I was left to do some quick maintenance while my horse rested. But I had to hurry as Freyja was waiting and no doubt worrying. After buying, borrowing and stealing all I needed to caulk the boat I set to work. In my haste I did not notice Bjorn drift over like skit in a stream.

"Gunnar, I did not know you were a seaman?"

"Bjorn, I see you are hanging around the quay looking for small boys again."

"See you in Hel, Gunnar." Bjorn stormed off towards his merchant vessel.

I am not a natural seaman but I had seen the experts caulking boats before and I continued to stuff as many holes as possible with garn and cover them with hot tar. I tried to work as fast as possible so that I could ride back to Freyja and collect our provisions.

I had finally decided where to go. I had fought alongside Sigurd the Stout, Jarl of Orkney, when I was younger and Orkney seemed the friendly place to be while I worked out what to do. I was sure that Sigurd would welcome me but it meant going back to

71

being a fighting man and what would Freyja think? However I had very little choice, I had already run from Scania back to Iceland and it had crossed my mind to escape to Greenland, but that wasteland is no place to take a wife and raise a family. Hopefully my ruse about going to Scania would buy me some time.

I left the tar to harden, mounted my horse and started back to the farm and my wife.

*

Bjorn hands the reins of his horse to a servant and heads for his hall. He calls to Soren, his farm manager, "bring me some ale and let's talk," and straight away he is thinking of his chair. He is wondering why he always seems to gain weight rather than lose it, considering all the work and rushing around he does. He enters his hall and looks around for his wife; he breathes a sigh of relief when he does not see the twisted hag.

He finds his good chair and lets his ample weight slip into place; immediately he feels relief in his poor aching body. Soren arrives with a jug of ale and two cups; he is used to hearing his master letting off steam and inviting him to join in with the drinking, although, as always, he waits to be invited.

"Sit and join me Soren."

"Thank you, sir."

Soren pours the ale and sits in silence, waiting for his master to unload his problems. Bjorn is naturally a melancholic man, but he is less tense when he has openly chewed through his problems with Soren.

Soren survives in this household by keeping his opinion to himself and only committing thoughts when duly pressed by his lord.

Bjorn sips the sour ale and welcomes the acidic, strong brew. He tries to savour the moment, a small semblance of peace before his wife finds him and harangues him for gossip from the quay and other news across the world.

Bjorn Bjornsson is an unremarkable man, slightly less than average height, slightly too much over average weight and terrible with a weapon. He is very good with numbers and has a way of negotiating a deal that makes the other party feel he has got away with a little bit. His father was an average farmer, but with Bjorn looking after the money of the farm, he ended up quite comfortable. Then Bjorn took a half share in a merchant vessel and his luck really took off. After becoming one of the wealthiest merchant farmers in all Iceland Bjorn almost had the pick of other men's daughters. So how did he end up with Hild!

72

Hild, she was still attractive to look at for a woman already thirty, although she had hair the colour of dried blood and the look of a women that has tasted something sour. He knew what a wicked and twisted hag existed beneath the skin. She never had children, either her womb had dried up or she was preventing them to anger him. Deep down Bjorn feared that Hild was a volvur, a Scandinavian witch, who knew all the secrets of seidhr, the dark worship of the Norse Gods. How else would she have entrapped me and knew that in my future lay wealth and success, that she could leech off and drain me dry.

Bjorn looked up at Soren, but his faithful man stayed silent waiting for his master.

*

Freyja frantically packed clothes and some food into two sacks. She then filled three leather flasks with water and tucked them into a sack. Freyja then sat down and wondered what to do with her small collection of jewellery, should she take it with her or bury it and hope that she would one day return? Always the optimist she went outside the hall and buried all but her special necklace in the sheep pen. That necklace was the first gift she received from Gunnar and meant more to her than all the gold in Iceland. It was a small, many armed green figure hung from a leather strand.

She sat inside the hall waiting for Gunnar to return, she had promised herself she would not stand outside waiting for him, and she would be strong for her man. Anyway, he would be here soon enough.

She picks up a small knife and starts to open some scallops to keep her hands busy.

She hears a horse approach and her heart jumps into her throat, a mix of excitement and fear. In those few seconds she doubts herself and her man. Was he a killer, and was she so love sick and blind that she would follow him while he raped and murdered his way across the north? He is good looking and fair but when really pushed he could be belligerent, and once she remembers seeing the raging fire of anger sweep across his face.

No, she says to herself, Gunnar is no killer, there must be an explanation. He is an easy target because he is bigger and stronger than most men. No man on Iceland can run faster or wield a sword and axe better, although many men and women can ride a horse better.

A shadow fills the doorway.

"Who is this filthy thrall?" the stranger was big but no match for Gunnar, he had an accent slightly different from her husband.

73

She tried to be brave, faced up to the stranger and said, "how dare you insult me in my home," she realised her mistake as soon as it left her lips.

"Gustav, get in here, we have the murderers wife," Harald Sveinsson smirked as he barred exit from the hall.

Freyja could hear more activity outside and she looked around for something to fight with, but all she had was the small shell fish knife in hand. She moved it up her sleeve and prayed to her namesake that she would get through this and see her man again.

Harald is a man of about seventeen and a half hands, with long black hair and a black beard plaited down the centre. He has a scar above, and the length of, his left eyebrow. He is jealous of Gustav's natural ability with a sword and Gull's previous popularity with women. He feels, as the oldest, he should be the best but this is rarely true. Harald suffers from seeing the negative in everything he does and gets his only pleasure from others misfortune.

He looks Freyja up and down and likes what he sees. She is just over sixteen hands tall, slim and fit, but with the added advantage of having a pleasant womanly figure. Her eyes alone could win a man, with beautiful long dark lashes, jade green with a halo of hazel in the middle. He can see that she is frightened but not frightened enough, her breasts rise and fall as she breathes, waking his libido. Her belt is tight around her waist and enhances her figure, she is dark blond and where the sunlight comes in and strikes her hair, it glows golden.

"Harald, is she alone?" Gustav is in the doorway behind Harald, who does not turn around and just nods. "There is no sign of Gunnar," Gustav adds as an afterthought.

Harald turns to his brother and says, "Wait outside; round up the servants and guard the farm, I am going to question her."

"Ok Harald," Gustav looks over his brother's shoulder at Freyja and thinks he knows what will happen, as he can see how beautiful Gunnar's wife is.

"Be careful Harald, we will need her for bargaining."

"Get out Gustav, you worry like a woman."

Harald then pulls the leather door down over the doorway and with his hand on the hilt of his sword he steps toward the wife of Gunnar.

Freyja feels momentarily blinded by the closing of the door but notices the light creeping in through a gap at the side, a line of dust filled light spreads across the hall from the rushes to the beams.

"Now if you are a good hostess and treat me well this will go very well for you." Freyja thinks he is enjoying this.

"And if I do not treat you well?"

"Wife of Gunnar, you will do what I want; there is just an easy way and a hard way. You have to be very nice if you want to live, remember you are married to a dead man and this farm will cover the bludgeld owed to me and my family."

While Harald is talking he edges towards Freyja, but she is not concentrating on what Harald has to say. She needs to think and plan a way out of this mess; she has her small knife and is much stronger than she looks. No man has ever touched her without her permission and she means to keep it that way.

*

Soren is good at waiting; he could remain silent for days if needed. He has a slow way of responding which gives the impression of, at best, average intelligence. But, Soren always thinks before he talks, making sure he says the right thing without appearing to be weighing up all the options. He is a very clever man, born into slavery and having escaped, he values his freedom above everything. He knows that as long as Bjorn Bjornsson is successful, Soren can have a fairly good, free life. Of course Soren also has a little insurance hidden away, just in case.

He sits opposite his master and concentrates on Bjorn's latest whine.

"…he insulted me Soren; I deserve respect from my neighbours."

"Maybe you could work it so that he owes you respect, in some way," Soren only speaks as he thinks it shows he has been listening.

"And how would I do that? Anyway Soren, it is not Gunnar that is the problem, how can my neighbours respect me when my own wife does not?"

"But I do respect you dear," Hild has entered the hall without either man noticing.

"I am here to guide you into becoming a better man, what has Gunnar done to upset you?"

Bjorn then tells Hild of the insult at the quay.

"What was Gunnar doing at the quay?" Hild started to hope that everything may fall into place for her.

"He bought a small boat and spent some time caulking it, although I do not believe it will be ready to sail until tomorrow or the next day."

"Why would Gunnar need a boat I wonder?" Hild appeared to think out loud but really she was teasing her husband, hinting she knew more than he did. She smirked at him and waited to be asked.

"For Odin's sake woman, what are you grinning about? Do you know why Gunnar needs a boat, and one that is only good enough for a crew of two?"

"I would guess he needs to go somewhere and quite fast, perhaps he plans to take his bitch wife with him. I hope so"

"Don't start moaning about Freyja now, what do you know?"

"Nothing husband, apart from seeing Njal ride to Gunnar's farm, then Gunnar riding as fast as he could and stay on the nag toward the quay, and I have just seen him heading back toward his home just as fast, that poor horse…"

Bjorn interrupts Hild. "Soren, get over there and see if you can find out what is going on, there may be some profit from this."

"Yes, sir."

"And Soren, if you don't have to be seen…"

"I understand." Soren leaves the hall to get his sword and horse.

Hild claps her hands together laughing, "oh please let it be bad." Bjorn looks at her and feels the bile rise up. He does not worry about Gunnar having trouble, but he hopes that no harm comes to the lovely Freyja.

If Hild had thought about it she would have noticed that she did not see Njal ride back past her home. Njal was back on his horse but he was not going home.

But deceiving Hild was the last thing on Njal's mind as he rode, as fast as he dared, to Kolskegg's hall.

Kolskegg and Hjort were Gunnar's younger brothers; they were fiercely loyal to their brother and would do anything for him. Kolskegg was a brave and fierce fighter, almost as talented as Gunnar, although a little hot headed. Hjort was less of a fighter but a great thinker, like his oldest brother.

76

Njal hoped they may be able to give him more information regarding Gunnar's trouble in Scania. Already Njal was formulating a plan in his head to protect Gunnar and his belongings at the Althing. Njal was known as the greatest lawyer alive on all of Iceland and he would have to prove it to help his best friend. However, poor Njal had one thing very much in common with Gunnar, he was a terrible horseman, even on the patient and hardy ponies of Iceland. Because his mind was very much on law and less so on riding, the horse had a slight stumble on the rough ground and Njal hit the ground hard, his face taking a great scraping from the gravel. Njal sat up and saw his ride stop and chew on a little tuft of grass. 'I hope it is waiting for me,' thought Njal and said out loud "Njal, you have been called the greatest lawyer alive on Iceland today, but unless you concentrate on riding this horse you will be a dead lawyer." The horse patiently waited for Njal to mount, and for Iceland's greatest lawyer to take a more cautious approach to Kolskegg's hall.

Chapter 7

The hard stony road flashes past and the wind blows into my face, bringing the smell of sulphur. Loki is up to no good, I think.

I am flying with the horse's hooves a blur below me. Yggdrasill has done well, he is a strong and faithful horse and named well. With the practice of the journey down, my ride back seems easier and I am feeling confident. My luck has held and it almost seems too easy, however I still worry for my wife and hope the gods are looking after her in my absence. Njal promised to go straight to my brothers and there is no one else I would want by my side.

If only Yggdrasill had wings I would be home now and holding my beautiful Freyja.

*

Harald was like a man possessed, panting like an animal as he tried to pin Freyja down. He had pushed her against one of the large wooden piles and held one of her arms tight to her side, while trying to feel her with the other. Freyja felt dizzy, in a panic, and the smell of rotten fish from his breath made her feel sick. Over all she was feeling revulsion, disgust and guilt. Had she had time to dress more for a journey maybe he would not have seen her naked legs and arms and become aroused? Although a man like Harald was an opportunist and would take advantage of any situation.

She did not know what to do; the knife she held was in the arm pinned to her side and her other hand was desperately trying to defend her body from his roaming hand.

She detached her mind from her body and gave up on him groping her breasts, it gave her time to think and there was a more important part of her she would defend. His disgusting mouth was slobbering on her neck and he was squeezing her breast so tight she wanted to cry out with the pain. She felt him getting hard against her and a small whimper left her throat. Was she to be raped and die here in her own hall before her beloved Gunnar was murdered?

With his arousal he relaxed his grip slightly and moved his hand down her body towards her groin.

Now, Freyja, she thought, now is your only chance to stop this.

I had flown past Hild and Bjorn's farm and I could now see my own land on the horizon. A raven flew along with me and I felt lifted. Was this Odin telling me he was with me in the hardship to come? I touched the iron hammer at my neck and asked for Thor to help too.

Some of my neighbours say I have the eyes of an eagle, which is stupid, however I can see better than most men over long distances. Thank the mighty Odin for my gift as I could see horses and men standing outside my hall, five men ready for a fight. My throat tightened and tears stung my eyes, Freyja was either facing these men or dead. I had to stay positive; Odin was with me and I was confident the odds were not too much against me, they were standing around looking bored and I was on horseback with my favourite sword at my side.

From a distance I slowed slightly and skirted round the far side of the hall, my eyes always on the men. I counted six horse and five men. From this distance it was hard to tell the individuals but somebody was inside threatening Freyja. It struck me then that someone had thrown his cronies out for privacy, Harald. My wife was in danger and I vowed then that if he dared touch her I would kill the bastard with my bare hands. Tears stung my eyes and I wanted to cry out with the pain of it, my Freyja, my love, my life. The anger was starting to cloud my vision, I wanted to kill them all for this, but I tried to calm down as I neared the hall, plans flicking over in my head as I slid off my horse. Why were the other five all together instead of spread out so they could see me long before I reached my home? With the cover of the hall shielding my movements I dismounted and led my mare up to it. As I was securing her reins to the wattle of the hall I heard some voices, one of which seemed to be approaching.

"…yes I know, I am going to have a piss round there and keep an eye out for the outlaw."

I could now hear footsteps and I slowly pulled my sword from its scabbard, thanking Odin that it was well oiled and silent. I edged close to the corner and waited for my guest.

A burly Dane, dressed in war gear, came briskly around the corner to be welcomed by my sword pommel smashing his nose. aAs he tipped backward I grabbed his shirt and held his weight with my left arm, lowering him to the ground.

I checked that he was out cold and took his sword. His nose was a mess and already purple rings were appearing below his eyes. His sword was lighter and a little shorter than mine but it would be fine for my left hand.

It was then that I heard a high pitched scream coming from inside the hall; it sent me into a mild panic, my heart pinched and tugged as I feared what had been done to Freyja.

Freyja did not know when was best to act, as when Harald released his grip he still had her tight to him, arms pinned down. She almost laughed at his skill in raping a woman; well I suppose it was the only way a woman could be close to Harald. He was panting and slobbering as with his free hand he was trying to feel her up.

But there was one prize he wanted most of all, and to get his hand down to her groin he had to release her even more.

Freyja was not the tallest woman, she did not have weight on her side, she gave the air of one who is quite meek but the truth about Freyja lay in her surprising strength.

She dropped the shellfish knife into her palm and brought it up fast and extremely hard into Harald's groin, piercing his left testicle and sticking the point into his pubic bone.

Harald's scream into her ear was so loud and high pitched it deafened her for some minutes. Harald the rapist completely crumbled to the floor, hands trying to caress and protect his crotch, even though it was too late. He was crying to himself and tentatively holding the knife in place, eventually passing out with the pain.

"Well Harald, you rapist, maybe you should have searched this woman," she whispered at the prone figure.

Although his scream was extremely loud, there was no movement from outside yet, and she scanned the room to defend herself when, inevitably, reinforcements arrived.

Just as she was trying to think what to do, a giant of a man crashed through the wall behind her, carrying a sword in each hand. Gunnar, her husband and only love, had arrived.

*

I had taken a run up at the wall, thinking it may take two or three attempts to break through. I did not count on my size and strength as the old wattle and daub collapsed under my charge. I had held my arms up to protect my face but the rest of me carried a hundred scratches.

I was greeted by the sight of my wife standing over a dead Harald. What had gone on? I came out of my daze and decided we should go before the Dane outside woke up or the group out the front came in to investigate the noise.

"Freyja, come!"

She rushed past me and through the Gunnar-shaped hole in the wall. I turned to follow her as I saw the leather door moving at the opposite end. Outside our friend on the floor had a drunken grip on Freyja's ankle, I knelt down and cracked his head with my pommel for good measure. My wife had the good sense to untie the horse; I mounted and pulled her up with me just as Harald's brother poked his head cautiously out of the hole in the wall.

Gustav Sveinsson spoke, "Gunnar, you cannot run forever."

"Gustav, we both know what your Gris of a brother was up to, maybe you should leave me and my family alone." I said this as I turned the horse and headed for the quay and our boat. As I rode away from my hall and land I heard Gustav shout, "Gull was my brother, too."

I rode hard for the quay, as I was sure Gustav and his men would follow hard on our heels. While riding I tried to concentrate on my beautiful wife's arms griping me tight, but all I could think of was Gull lying dead. For the hundredth time I prayed and begged that Loki had played a trick on me and his death was not by my hand.

*

Bjorn stood in the doorway of his hall looking at his wife's back, "how long are you going to wait there?"

"Until I need to sleep," Hild replied, "I am sure, husband; there will be more activity on the road today."

Although she had to wait longer than she thought, Hild was not disappointed when she saw Gunnar and Freyja, sharing a horse and heading for the river inlet and quay.

"Goodbye, Freyja," she said with a smile, and thought how she would miss Gunnar.

*

As we come thundering toward the quay all looks normal, there are a few men lounging beside their vessels but the majority are working hard readying their boats for a voyage or making repairs. I slow Yggdrasill down so as not to raise suspicion and Freyja speaks for the first time since we left our home. "We have nothing with us, no water."

"I know, but I have a little silver and a horse to sell, it may be enough…"

I said no more as we both knew we had to sail, supplies or none. Although if we could get some supplies we could only sail to one location and hope the gods were on our side, so I planned to go to the sheep islands, the Faeroes.

I see Thorgils up ahead and ride to him.

"Hey Gunnar, Hey Freyja, are you saving your other horses for farm work?"

"She is a good wife and I like to keep her close but we need to sail fast and it would mean leaving two good horses at the coast rather than one."

Thorgils just looks at me, his eyes tell me he knows I have some trouble but he is a good and practical man and asks no more.

"Well Gunnar what will you do for food and water if you mean to sail for Scania today?"

I open my mouth to speak but Thorgils puts up his hand to stop me.

"If you don't mind I will give you what I have, in exchange for your tired old horse," Thorgils smiles at me as we both know that Yggdrasill is a good strong stallion.

"Do you have enough to get to a safe, honest land?" I do not want to put a good man in the position of knowing where I am headed.

"You can have what I have now, I do not have enough water but I have some ale that may be enough if you are not greedy."

At that Thorgils goes into his wooden hut and retrieves some twice baked bread, hard cheese and smoked fish. He also hands over a small barrel of beer and one flask of water.

I have dismounted and I grip his arm, "thank you, I will make sure I repay you this debt."

"But Gunnar you owe me nothing, it is a trade, remember Yggdrasill is now my horse."

Freyja hugs Thorgils and kisses his cheek which brings a big smile to his face.

"A kiss from Freyja is worth the trade alone, good luck."

At this he ties up Yggdrasill to his hut and walks up the quay to speak to one of the workers, he does not look back.

Freyja picks up the water flask and I carry the ale and food to our small boat.

"Thorgils is a good man, but I wish we had more water, a sun stone and a raven to help us on our way."

"Do not worry husband, I trust you will keep us safe, maybe we can rely on your old Viking skills?"

"I will try my love. Did you manage to hide your precious things away before the Sveinsson's arrived?"

"I did but I kept my many armed little lady with me as I think she brings luck with her."

*

No one could call Soren a coward; he was willing and capable of fighting almost any man. But he knew there were many heroes in Valholl and fewer still alive enjoying their reputation. He always thought of the many consequences of any task given him, all the possible outcomes and what was most likely. As he rode the long way round to Gunnar's hall, knowing he did not want to bump into Gunnar, Njal or any of their supporters, he weighed up the reasons for Gunnar's actions in his head.

The trick was to always listen to all information, no matter how small, and weigh up all facts, even the unconnected ones.

Bjorn had mentioned to Soren that there were a group of Danes recently arrived in Iceland. Bjorn was a clever man but he had not connected these two facts. It is known that Gunnar went Viking and spent some time in Scania, so we have a group from the same part of the world landing in Iceland and shortly after Gunnar is running around like a sheep on a hot mountain.

So very likely Gunnar was running from these men; Soren thought it likely that Gunnar was declared outlaw in Scania and had run back to Iceland. This was not unusual as there were many such men here. Soren smiled to himself as he thought this, but it was not the time to dwell on his own past. Although it did make him think of his father; there were two pieces of his advice that had helped him in life.

"Soren, always remember these two things and you shall be safe for many years. Number one; always keep your own counsel, men that talk too much usually end up dead men. Number two, listen to everything and never discount any facts, this will help you see the path you need to take." He thanked his father in his head and wished his spirit well.

So Gunnar is an outlaw and is running; he has a small boat at the quay, so where is he going?

Greenland would be a treacherous voyage in such a small vessel and Scania is out of the question. Even Shetland or Orkney would be a push, in fact if Gunnar's luck held he might make it to the Faeroes.

Soren felt pleased with himself, just some simple thinking and the facts fall down in front of you, although he would keep this to himself for the moment, it may give lovely Freyja a little head start.

While he was contemplating these facts, Soren and his horse were ambling through a small cutting. As he came out of the cutting he could see Gunnar's farm off to the right, at the sight he encouraged his horse to speed up a little for a closer look.

*

Gustav was worried, very worried. At first he thought that Harald was dead but holding the blade of his sword close to Harald's mouth had revealed a little shallow breath.

He cursed Gunnar, and wondered if it was the fate of all the sons of Svein to be slain at Gunnar's hand.

Harald looked like a new born baby, all curled up but laying in a pool of blood covering the floor around his hips. Gustav moved Harald to inspect his wounds, and as he did Harald moaned in obvious pain.

He felt embarrassed as it looked like Harald was maintaining a small erection through his agony, until Gustav realized what he was looking at was the small bone handle of a knife. He winced as he saw it was buried in Harald's groin.

Glum and Helgi were standing behind him and Glum spoke, "we should go now and stop him escaping, he is heading toward the coast."

"No, I want him dead but I want my brother to survive more, one of you go east and one west and see if you can find help for Harald. Tell Hrut and Flosi to let the servants go and stand guard either end of the hall, if Flosi can stand."

At this Glum and Helgi left the hall, mounted their rides and rode for help.

Gustav knew what he had to do, he un-wrapped the woollen scarf around his neck, as he would need this to stem the flow of blood when he pulled the knife out.

*

Soren saw the two men riding away from the hall first, and then the man heading west must have seen him as he turned his horse south. The Dane was in a hurry and reached Soren in a matter of minutes.

84

Soren dropped his hand to his sword, as the Dane was well armed and looked prepared for a fight.

"Well met friend, what brings you here?" A friendly welcome, but the Dane had his hand on his sword also.

"I am Soren, Bjorn Bjornsson's man; I was coming to discuss business with Gunnar."

"I am Glum of Lund, and Gunnar is not here. Is your man Bjorn a friend of Gunnar?"

"I can openly say there is only a business relationship between my master and Gunnar."

At this Glum took his hand off his own sword saying, "do you know anything about healing, my master is very sick and needs help."

"Take me to him and I will see what I can do," this was getting very interesting, thought Soren, and wondered further if he and Bjorn would be able to profit from this turn of events.

Soren prided himself on always being prepared and had with him a packet of healing herbs, he also knew a little about how the body worked and what was good for it; he had learnt a lot during his time in Byzantium.

They arrived at the hall and Glum led Soren inside.

Glum spoke first, "I found this man, Soren, and he says he may be able to help."

Gustav was kneeling by his brother and he looked very afraid. "Well Soren, I am Gustav Sveinsson, if you can save my brother I will reward you in gold."

"Let me see him."

Soren knelt down and looked at the wound in Harald's groin. "Get your men outside to build a fire. We need water boiling, before I remove the blade. Has anyone got any strong liquor?"

"I may have something," Gustav got up and went out to his horse, also to instruct Hrut and Flosi to get the fire started.

Soren looked at Glum, "do you follow the old gods or this Christian god?"

Glum looked surprised, "which is best?"

"I am a man of the old gods, but whoever you pray to pray now because your master is close to death. Anyway, how did this happen?"

Glum gave an embarrassing grin, "I think Harald's charm did not work on the lady of the house."

Soren felt anger build up inside him and wished this Danish fool dead, how dare he touch Freyja in that way? At any opportunity Soren had he would try and talk to Freyja, or at least see her. Strangely he did not feel jealous of Gunnar, as he accepted that Gunnar had got to her first, but if anything should happen to Gunnar then he hoped he would be the man to fill that gap.

Uncharacteristically for Soren, his heart ruled his head for just a moment, as Gustav came back into the hall.

"You do know that raping a woman in Iceland will cost you dearly? You may have a quarrel with Gunnar, but his wife is innocent and has many friends here."

"So you won't help Harald then," Glum started to pull out his sword.

"Glum, enough," Gutsav put his hand on Glum's sword and pushed it back in the scabbard.

"Soren, I think this happened because Gunnar's wife was scared and thought we would do her harm, we only wished to ask questions after her husband."

Soren realised Gustav was talking skit but he also valued his life, thought of his hidden horde and the gold that may come if he saved this vile man on the ground.

"Have you got that liquor?"

Gustav handed Soren a small leather flask, he sniffed at the contents and could smell the foul vapour within.

"You will have to get one of your other men in, Gustav. I need three of you to hold him down while I remove the dagger. Get something to put in his mouth for when he wakes, my job is to stop the bleeding and prevent puss growing in his dick."

Soren had Flosi boil Gustav's scarf for a few minutes before getting on with removing the blade from Harald's groin.

Glum and Hrut sat on a leg each and Gustav held Harald's arms above his head.

Harald was now crying openly and none of the men thought him a coward or weak, they all thanked the gods it was not them in his place. Flosi stood by with the scalding scarf on a stick while Soren took his own knife and cut through Harald's leggings.

The textile was soaked in Harald's blood and hard to cut, but when he had cut through Soren could see the knife was buried to the hilt in Harald's scrotum. He shouted at the others, "Hold him tight now, with all your strength."

He looked around at the others to ensure they were ready, then he took the stopper out of the flask and pulled the hilt of the knife as hard as he could. At first the action pulled Harald slightly across the floor, causing the wounded man to scream and let go of the birch twig he was biting on. Luckily the knife gave and slipped out. Soren threw it to the floor saying, "Now hold him even tighter."

At this point he splashed the alcoholic liquor on the wound, Harald screamed louder and longer. Soren ignored him, stood and walked over to Flosi. He took out a mixture of moss and herbs and wrapped them in the sterilised scarf. The new poultice was then placed gently over Harald's wound, "Gustav, your brother has passed out. Will you hold this in place until we can find something to keep it there."

"Will he live?" Gustav was as white as sheet.

"He now has a chance, the strong drink and the boiled water will keep the worse of the puss away, but he has to stay clean and rest." Soren now felt drained.

"Thank you Soren, you have made a friend today."

"And a little gold?" Soren said this as he left the hall to get some air in his lungs.

*

Njal dismounts at Kolskegg's farm and Hjort is outside to greet him.

"Odin's blood Njal, have you been in a fight?"

"Only with my mare and the ground Hjort, how are you and your brother?"

"Life is good Njal, but you do not normally ride out here, so what is troubling you?"

"Gunnar is in trouble."

At this Hjort called to Kolskegg who came out of their hall.

"What is it, brother?"

"Gunnar is in trouble?"

"Scania?"

Of course, thought Njal, the brothers know.

Inside the hall the brothers sat with Njal while he told them what he knew. Every now and again he had to compliment them on their ale, which was known as the finest in south west Iceland.

When he finished Kolskegg spoke, "thank you Njal, you have always been a good friend to Gunnar and it seems we have our own Ragnarok now. However, I will do everything to make sure it does not end up in destruction for the sons of Hammond."

Njal stood up and now spoke to the brothers of Gunnar, "During my ride here I have thought long and hard about Gunnar's options. He spoke to me of sailing to Orkney but would spread a rumour that he was sailing to Scania. The problem is that he will be sailing alone, apart from his wife. Now Freyja is a clever and resourceful woman to have around, with great stubbornness and surprising strength, but I cannot see how a crew of two will make it as far as Orkney. Therefore his options will be one of two, whether he sails along the coast of Iceland and hides somewhere in land until his pursuers leave our country, or he attempts to sail to the sheep islands."

Kolskegg and Hjort were clever and brave men but they both looked up to their older brother in a state of shock. They both stood and tried to speak at the same time; Kolskegg being older won the small battle.

"Njal, our brother is no coward but he is also not stupid, surely his easiest option is to hide in the hills for a week and try and get word to us?"

Hjort now spoke up, "but brother he has Freyja's welfare to think of, and he is besotted with her and will worry about losing his wife. With this in mind I expect him to sail to Faeroe as I think he has some old Viking friends there."

"I agree with Hjort, Kolskegg, the more I think of it, Faeroe is the obvious option." With Njal's words an understanding fell on the brothers and they discussed how they could help their older brother. They would need somebody to support Gunnar in Iceland, just in case he was hiding in the hills, and Hjort was the obvious choice as Kolskegg had much experience of sailing in his past. Njal suggested his two eldest sons, Skarphedin and Grim, join Kolskegg on his trek as they were great swordsman and were young and needed adventure. Njal promised Kolskegg they were good men and he would be happier to see them go out with a man he trusted. They both knew that young men were always itching for adventure and this would help both Njal and Kolskegg.

Kolskegg had a boat but it needed some maintenance as he had not used it since last year, so they planned to fix up the boat and take twenty men in three days' time. The plans would be known to three of them only, until the boat had left the quay and was sailing across the great northern sea.

Njal would supply ten men from his farm and his kin; the brothers had five men and would go to their brother-in-law, Hroar, for the rest. They felt that Hroar would help as he had some wealth and doted on their sister, Arnguda, who in turn loved her brothers very much.

They decided to gather the hoard of men at Njal's farm on day three and make way for the quay and Kolskegg's longboat.

Chapter 8

And in the south was the Heathen King,
Watching over his domain of hades.
Where the men are abusive
and the women are wanton.

Ivar was drinking, he liked drinking and he was good at it. He liked that it made him feel stronger in battle, that it protected his body from pain and that he was a better lover. Come to think of it he did not just like drinking, he loved it, as much as a maidens arse. Saxon beer, Danish ale, Celtic mead or the burning water from Vendland, give it all to Ivar and he will drink it and his men will cheer.

Yes, thought Ivar, drinking, fighting and tupping, what more can a man want? The answer for a man is nothing, but a king, well a king needs land and wealth, or he is just a man.

He knew he deserved this moment of pleasure, he had secured himself as one of the most important kings in Ireland and he was doing a roaring trade in slaves via Dyflin. Enough for some men but Ivar aimed to be High King of Ireland and he knew that securing Dyflin was the major step in achieving that. He knew that Jarn of Dyflin was young and inexperienced and the Althing called to marry off his sister was so obviously an attempt at securing allies, it made Ivar sure that Jarn Cuaran was getting nervous for his kingdom. The thought of storming through Dyflin wielding axe and sword made Ivar feel excited and horny. He came back from his thoughts to see the slave girl was on all fours in front of him just wearing a vest. Good, Ivar liked that, for some reason a woman looked better wearing a little, when they came in all naked with everything showing, it left nothing to look forward to.

"Hey, girl, where are you from?" he spoke in Norse but she just shivered, so he tried it in Irish. She looked up at him and seemed to understand a little.

"Prydain."

"Ah, she speaks," Ivar continued in Irish so that the girl could understand some of his speech, "you are what the Saxons like to call Welsh, I did not know they had such pretty girls over there in the hills."

She was shaking less now that he was talking to her, and she may be understood every third word. Ivar hated tupping scared women, it felt too much like rape, so he handed her some ale and encouraged her to drink with him. She took the horn and sipped the drink and smiled.

"Woman, you must know why you are here with me, be good to me and you shall eat well and drink well. I like your black hair and pale skin, if your temperament is as fine as your body you shall have an easy time with King Ivar."

She just looked at him; she had very big brown eyes and pale lips. Ivar leaned forward and stroked her hair and she did not pull away.

"You are a clever one; you know that whatever happens, as a slave girl someone is going to enjoy tupping you, so it may as well be the king. And girl, I like tupping even more than drinking."

The girl looked him straight in the eyes for a long time and then leaned forward and took his drink and started to swallow it all.

Ivar was pleased, she seemed to understand her predicament and was going to make the best of it. He started to think he may even give her a little gift, but deep down he knew that he would forget this as soon as he was spent.

"Woman, tell me your name, I like to know the name of the woman I am tupping, even if it is just for the moment."

"Gwenhyvach," she said it and pointed at her chest.

"Thor's hammer that is a horrible name, well for the moment I shall call you Kanin, as your short black hair make me think of rabbit fur."

At this Ivar lent forward and touched his finger on her chest and said, "Kanin, my little Kanin."

"Kanin," Gwenhyvach repeated it, pointed at herself and then laughed.

"Now my little Kanin, let's do what rabbits do best."

But before Ivar had finished talking Gwenhyvach had removed her vest and he realised that he could not wait to ride her.

*

Although it was still before midday the sky was almost black and the heavens had opened. Thor was crashing Mjolnir across the sky and sparks could be seen on the horizon. Freyja held on to the sides of the boat as it was rocking with the movement of her husband, taking down the sail. She watched the man she loved trying to balance and work at the same time. She watched him, wondering if he could kill a man in cold blood. Would he kill a friend and did that mean he could kill anyone? She could not believe it of him, he was so kind and thoughtful and an easy target because of his size. She would trust the Gunnar she knew and not be swayed by these false accusations. While she was thinking she felt a light brushing at her neck and her precious necklace fell into the folds of her clothes.

"Gunnar, can you look after my lady during the storm, I fear losing her."

"Good idea, I have that small pocket you made for me, she will be snug and safe until we make dry land."

The wind was whipping up and the waves were growing around the boat, this would be a bad storm and she hoped and prayed they would come through unscathed.

*

I could hardly see Freyja in front of me in the boat, the rain was like a wall, and she was gripping the sides, jamming her feet into the hull. I was trying to do the same while holding onto the rudder, as the storm lashed me and tried to throw me into the deep.

Concentrating on fighting the storm seemed to clear my head, here I had one thing to fight, one job to do and so far we were still alive. Considering the noise Thor was making in the clouds, the rain slamming into the water and the boat being beaten by waves the size of the hills in Norway, deep in my head I felt calm.

The storm was a bad one; the rain was coming down like a waterfall, which was bad enough. It was the rain and sea water coming up and into our faces that ensured that we were soaked through. The wind was severe and luckily I had managed to take the sail down just before it was torn down. The waves were getting bigger; we would find ourselves at the top of a steep hill of water and then be plunged into a deep dale before repeating this with an even bigger wave. The storm was cruel, powerful and beautiful in its strength; I could feel the power of Thor at work.

I studied my wife, she had her head slightly down and her eyes shut to stop the sea water getting in, or maybe to avoid seeing our cold, watery grave. We had been in the

92

storm for about half an hour and much to my dismay it seemed to be getting worse rather than better. Even if we survived I was worried about what we would eat and drink, as the sea water was doing its best to spoil everything we had.

I prayed to Thor and pleaded with him to stop the storm, I then prayed to Loki and asked that Freyja and I would be spared; I even prayed to Odin but knew that Odin could take pleasure in the misfortune of simple men.

I wondered if I drowned with my sword in my hand, would I be allowed to enter Valholl.

"Dam Loki!" I then shouted at the storm, "WE ARE NOT READY TO DIE."

I looked across at my wife and she was smiling, the kind of smile that is only made with the mouth and mostly a grimace, as all her energy was concentrating on staying in the boat. Oh, how I love her strength, for her alone I was determined to survive this. I hung on to the rudder and roared into the oncoming wave, I hope this storm will go down as one of the greatest foes I have defeated.

Chapter 9

Thor swung his fist
And struck at Hymir's ear
So that he plunged overboard
He sank until you could no longer
See the soles of his feet

Bjarni stood at the centre of the boat, one arm on the mast, and shouted at the man on the rudder, "Litta, do you need a break? As you are only half the size of a real man you only have to do half the work."

"Poke your own arse, you wrinkled bear skin." Litta shouted this with a smile. He had grown up with Bjarni and they were forever insulting each other.

"But, little friend, you did hold the rudder all through the storm and I will give you a rest and some skit Saxon ale," Bjarni patted the ale at his feet while he spoke.

"Skit ale is better than no ale," at this Bjarni made his way to the back of the boat and swapped places with his friend. As Litta made his way toward the mast Bjarni shouted to him again, "oh and can you pass the ale around the boys, as they are all spent after rowing through the storm."

"Bjarni, you are a slimy groda and stink of skit."

Bjarni and Litta were the team that ran Ivar of Waterford's merchant ship; ahead and behind them were two fighting vessels to protect and gather their cargo. Their cargo was stored in the hold at the front and rear of the ship.

The thralls had stopped moaning and crying during the storm; there was so much rain and wash over the side that they concentrated all their energy on staying alive.

Bjarni felt only contempt for them; as soon as they were captured they became a commodity, less than human. Although he did not see them as completely inhuman, especially the young pretty maids. This made him smile, as for Litta they did not have to be that pretty, and when it had been far too long not even maids. He would chide his smaller friend that when Litta was on heat no animal on land or sea was safe.

There were two rules to transporting thralls for Ivar, first do not damage the goods and second save the prettiest girls for the king. Litta was walking proof of rule two; Ivar had cut off his ear lobe and scarred his face when Litta had poked his orm in some young Saxon girl's arse. Not that Ivar cared too much about that, but she bled for days and then died back in Dyflin. Bjarni always regretted not throwing her in the sea days earlier, for he had lost almost all his silver to save being treated the same as Litta.

These thralls were captured from the east coast of Scotland although none of the crew could understand them, so they must be Picts as the language of the Scots was the same as Irish. They were going to head for Orkney but the storm blew up and they were way off course, but at least the night was coming and the stars would be out on this clear day.

As the sun started to set in the west and turn the now calm sea the colour of gold, Bjarni checked the position of the sun on the horizon just to ensure they were heading in the right direction. In this strange light he thought he could see something on the water at a distance, straight ahead. He looked for it again but was not sure if it was a whale swimming on the surface. But Bjarni had good eye sight and could make out a fine line going straight up from the dark shape, it must be a boat.

"Speed up a little, boys, Litta look straight ahead and tell me what you see."

"It looks like a faering, Bjarni, but what is that doing out so far from land?"

Bjarni looks to the longship ahead of him and can see Baldr looking at the horizon too.

"HEY BALDR, WHAT DO YOU SEE?"

Baldr turns and shouts back, "a small boat, follow us."

The three vessels row in the direction of the boat and Baldr's ship is the first to come alongside. Two of his men arm themselves and board the faering.

*

I think I may be waking up soon, but not yet. I am warm, fulfilled and still feel sleepy. I know I have made love with my beautiful Freyja, but I can't remember when. I could sleep some more but I need to drink, I feel so very thirsty.

"GUNNAR!"

Freyja is shouting but why? I open my eyes and I feel blinded by the low sun. Is it morning already?

Before my eyes adjust I am shoved back and my shoulder cracks hard on a plank of wood. I feel the sharp point of a sword on my neck and I look along the blade. At first it looks as if it is a sword made of gold but really it is highly polished and it is stained by the colour of the low sun. At the end of the sword I see a Viking, he looks a little scared, and he only has to move forward by the width of a finger to garrotte me. I move my eyes a little to the left and see another man trying to push a struggling Freyja into a much larger boat.

"Are you ready litta snop?" the Viking addresses me. "You are going to get up slowly and I will take my sword away, but think carefully before you try and fight as we have a dagger at your woman's throat."

I realise the situation we are in, but I cannot risk any harm coming to Freyja. I climb aboard the merchant ship and see the poor pathetic thralls in the hold, my wife is with them.

"Hel's teeth Bjarni, look at the size of him he is a big bastard."

As one man ties my wrists behind my back an ugly man not much taller than a boy addresses the man called Bjarni, who I guess is the captain of this ship.

"I am going to check his bond, I don't want that big bear breaking free," the little Viking comes over and pulls at my rope and somehow makes it tighter, almost cutting off the blood supply.

"Ok big bear, where were you coming from," the guy called Bjarni was talking to me.

"I am from Iceland; I am a wealthy landowner and an ally of Sigurd the Stout - Jarl of Orkney."

"They call him Sigurd the Stout because he is a fat lazy bastard, and he is no friend of Ivar, King of Waterford."

The small man, who must be only thirteen hands tall, comes up to the captain. "Bjarni, can I have the woman, just once?"

I strain in my bonds and roar in the face of these two pirates.

"Ravens skit Litta, I should call you Loki for all the mischief you put me through. Now you have upset our big bear and I am going to have to calm him down."

The captain puts his hands on my shoulders and speaks quietly to me, "now big bear calm down and start to accept your situation. First I will not let my dirty little friend poke your wife, especially as he likes the arse and he has already ruined a few thralls. But do not think you are protected, forget your wife and your life, you are a slave now and behave or you will be broken, or you will die during the process." I looked over his shoulder and saw pirate Litta skulk off looking disappointed.

Not knowing what to do I grunt and look down, trying to look subservient but also thinking long and hard about a plan. I am led along the ship and sat in the hold at the back, I try to keep an eye on Freyja but we are as far apart as the length of boat will allow. I try not to think of all the atrocities that could be bestowed upon my wife, I have to put that out of my mind or I will never think of a way to escape this disaster.

How had we ended up here, after fighting and trying to defeat the storm? Too many times I would look ahead or to the side and see only a wall of water topped with white, like good ale. Each time I thought we would be flipped over or smashed by the storm and end up food for the monsters of the deep. But somehow we survived. At first I thought Thor had taken pity on us but now it seems that Loki had not finished playing. We were both exhausted after the struggle with the storm and when a warm afternoon sun came out we lay down and rested. If only we had not, although I do not think we would have out run the longships.

The captain, Bjarni, and his odious little friend where talking at the back of the boat, while I was stuck with the other poor creatures, bound and with little hope. I feel sure I can escape but I doubt I could save Freyja as well. I pray to every god I can think of, even the seemingly weak Christian god, please, please keep my wife safe.

The slaves around me are a mix of men and women, young and old. It is a naïve captain that puts all the young strong men in one place.

So one thing will be certain, we will be sailing to Dyflin and the kingdom of King Cuaran. Perhaps one will tell me their story.

"Do any of you speak Danish?"

I am answered with a smack on the back of the head with a stick.

"Thrall, no talking, next time I will chop up your pretty face." I wanted to turn around and see who hit me, but that would surely end in another blow. I would spend my time staying alive and looking for any chance of escape. I prayed again for the safety of my wife

*

Freyja was not having a good time at the front of the boat. Being captured as a slave was extremely bad and she thought she would be lucky to live two years, but being a young, healthy woman captured as a thrall meant she could expect rape at any time. She was sure Loki was laughing at her predicament, to escape the clutches of Harald the rapist and then to end up here, heading for the slave market. Already two of the crew had groped her and she saw the small, ugly one leering at her.

She looked around at her fellow slaves; most of them stared off into the distance, already switched off from whatever life they used to have. Some of the women were weeping and a few of the men. Freyja felt like joining them, as she was no longer a person and would be treated like an animal from now on. She had not been searched very well by the men on this boat; they were too keen on feeling her up to do a proper job. She hoped that they would not search Gunnar too well and he could keep her little green lady safe.

She prayed for Gunnar's safety and her own, she also prayed that they would escape these bonds and be together again. While waiting for her prayers to be answered she was going to remain strong and face up to whatever she had to, so that she stayed alive.

*

Litta was holding the rudder again but his mind was not wholly on steering the ship. He could not stop thinking about that new woman they had captured. His mind was filled with how soft her arse must feel and how he longed to touch it. When they pulled her aboard from that small faering she was still wet from the storm and her dress stuck very tightly to her body. Litta closed his eyes and re-lived the moment in his mind. He opened his eyes and tried to concentrate on following the longship ahead, but his orm was rock hard and he did not care what Bjarni or Ivar said, he would at least go down and have a feel of her, when he was free of his duties of course. She would be his little Knulla for the journey and maybe back in Dyflin, too.

"Yes, what a good idea," he spoke out loud to no one in particular. A few slavers looked up at Litta but he did not notice them.

Bjarni would not mind him having a feel of that lovely body, maybe a little taste, as long as he did not damage the goods this time. When he thought about this he unconsciously touched his scarred face.

It was getting dark now and they were heading for a bay in the Hebrides for the night. Yes, he would volunteer to stay on the slave ship on guard duty, and when the time was right, he would have a little play. He wiped the dribble away from his lips and looked forward to the night.

*

Soren prepared a bed in the barn and ordered one of his men to make a screen to protect the injured man. Hrut and Glum carried Harald carefully to the fresh cot that Soren had made up. Harald's brother Gustav fussed around, hindering the progress and helping nobody. Soren thought about intervening but the man could lose his brother and owed Soren a bag of gold if, or when, Harald pulled through.

"Stay with him and I will go and organise refreshment. My master Bjorn Bjornsson will want to speak to you when he is free." Soren went to leave the barn and almost knocked Hild over; she was almost running to find out what was going on.

"Get out of my way you stupid man, and tell me what is happening in my own home?"

Gustav stood up and bowed to Hild-Yxa Eiriksdottir, "my dear lady, my brother, Jarl Harald Sveinsson, is badly wounded and your man here helped save his life. We are most grateful of any assistance you can give and we are willing to pay you for your trouble."

Hild looked closely at Gustav while she gathered her thoughts. He was a very handsome man with shoulder length hair the colour of cut pine. He had a strong nose and jaw, but she was struck by his eyes, they were bright green and beautiful.

"I...I am sorry I seemed harsh, please accept our hospitality, although we cannot offer much as the harvests have been poor and there is a blight affecting the animals."

Soren watched Hild put on her act for the young Dane; he wanted to laugh out loud as he knew how well Bjorn looked after things. They had enough food stored for two winters and the money, which Soren knew of, to help them survive five more.

Hild was speaking again, "and please make your brother comfortable, perhaps your men can stay with him and you can tell me about your troubles over some Frankish wine."

Loki must be playing tricks with Soren's mind, as he had not heard Hild speak pleasantly to anyone before. Even when she wanted something from Bjorn she sounded sarcastic.

"Thank you, dear lady, I would appreciate that. Could we have some ale for my brother and our companions?"

"Of course, now come on Soren, hurry up and fetch the wine and ale, and make sure you bring the good stuff."

Soren understood clearly, bring the good wine and the skit ale. Although he would have felt aggrieved at giving his master's best ale to strangers.

Soren left and Hild guided Gustav into the hall and sat him at one of the tables.

"Now as much as I like being called a dear lady by a brave warrior we should really introduce ourselves. I am Hild Eiriksdottir, the poor, put-upon wife of Bjorn Bjornsson, a man who does not look after his young wife very well. Now you know my name, what is yours?"

"I am Gustav Sveinsson of Lund in Scania, and if you are ready I shall tell you our story.

"Gunnar Hamundsson used to be a great friend of the Sveinsson brothers, particularly my brother Gull and myself. We were all crew on Harald's boat and went Viking to become men like our fathers. Gull introduced Gunnar to us and I thought of him as a good friend. Although my brother Harald was never great friends with Gunnar, after he first lost a swimming race and then at arm wrestling with him.

"About five years ago after a night of celebration in our Hall I was woken by Erik Ericsson, a friend, who told me that Gunnar had murdered our brother Gull in a drunken rage."

"I cannot believe it," Hild loved gossip but she was truly stunned by this news of Gunnar.

"Believe it you must dear lady Hild, because at that time I got up very fast and went with Erik to where Harald was holding Gunnar.

"By the time we got there we found Harald lying in pain next to my poor brother Gull, who was lying in his own blood with his throat cut right open."

Hild gasped. She loved gossip and being the first to know the latest scrap, but she was not prepared for this, especially about Gunnar. She felt excited, she longed for a big strong man and admired Gunnar, but he was not cruel enough for her, she liked a man to put her in her place. This news that Gunnar was a killer excited her so much, she felt a little light headed.

Gustav noticed and held her arm. mistaking her disposition as horror. "I am sorry to be so graphic, it was not the place for a woman, and I wish I had not mentioned it."

"No Gustav, it is fine, I wish to know everything. This man has been our neighbour for some time and if he has a dark past, it is better that we know." She placed her left hand over Gustav's arm and held it there, a few seconds too long.

Gustav noticed, smiled and continued, "Gunnar had killed my younger brother and wounded my older brother in his manhood, and he then escaped toward the quay. He must have secured a boat in the confusion, for at that time we were being raided by three Viking ships. My men and I chased him toward the quay but as we approached there were nearly two hundred men causing havoc. We were less than twenty men so we turned back rather than fight an impossible fight.

My brother needed to recover and we had no idea where Gunnar was. Gull had met him in Tonsberg in Norway, so we searched for him there first. In Tonsberg there were a few men who knew him but they all had different stories, Greenland, Orkney and Gotland. We were stuck so we went home but never stopped wishing him dead. Recently we met a merchant who knew of a Gunnar in Iceland so we followed the trail here, but we have lost him again."

Hild stood and spoke to Gustav now, ready to tell this handsome young Dane what she knew. "I do not think Gunnar and his wife will get far, they have a small boat at the quay a few leagues south west of here, if you had a longship you could out run them."

"Thank you, dear Hild, but I have to look after my brother and ensure he lives first."

"What did Gunnar do to him?"

"It was not Gunnar, it was his wife. Harald was questioning her about her husband when she plunged a knife into his bulle," the real Hild showed herself briefly as she stifled a laugh. She managed to get herself under control but Gustav had seen it.

"I am sorry; I did not mean to disrespect your brother."

But Gustav smiled at her and looked deep into her eyes. "Do not apologise, for it is comical and will be a good story if he lives."

"He does not seem to have much luck down there, but I hope you have better luck with your manhood."

Gustav beamed back at her, "if we were not married…"

"Your wine," Soren stepped into the hall and Hild noticed his face showed nothing as usual. She hated Soren, she was not sure if he was very clever or very stupid. Had he heard her exchange with Gustav, her body tingled all over with the closeness of this beautiful young man and she wanted him inside her. But the nice feeling Gustav had given her faded when the stone headed farm manager came in.

"Your presence will turn the wine sour, Soren."

Soren said nothing as he poured the red vintage for them into two glasses. Gustav's mouth was open as he stared at the glasses, he had only seen the like once before and that was at the court of the Danish King, and from a long way off.

"Lady, where did you get such beautiful cups?"

"They were a gift from my husband, after he had disappointed me for the hundredth time."

"He must be a wealthy man, for these are worth more than gold."

"And we only use them for very special guests."

Soren went outside, as he could no longer stand listening to Hild. What came out of her mouth was worth less than what came out of a sheeps arse.

As he made it into the fresh air he saw his master walking toward him and gesturing Soren to come forward.

"Soren, what has happened, tell me while we are alone before the hag should find out."

"I am afraid it is too late master, she is inside with Gustav Sveinsson, one of the two senior men in the party."

Bjorn looked crestfallen at this news, so Soren took him by the elbow and led him toward the barn to show him Harald and to let Glum tell the story of these Danes.

Soren and Bjorn left the barn and walked a little away from the main hall so that they could discuss the best course of action.

"It seems these men have quite a case against Gunnar, although I am not sure if he can be made outlaw here, as well as in Scania, for the same crime."

"Master, there have been cases like this at the Althing, admittedly cases that happened within Iceland, but the outcome is usually that the suspect is made outlaw and all his possessions confiscated. If that is so it would be a lucky man who got Gunnar's farm land, and if that man moved fast the Danes may be happy with bludgeld, a large sum for them but a small sum to pay for the land."

"Soren, you sometimes surprise me with your fast thinking, I am glad I do not have to negotiate against you every day."

"Thank you, master."

"Let's go and speak to Gustav and I will suggest the benefit of buying the farm."

Both men now walked into Bjorn's hall. It felt like they had walked into the wrong home and they were not welcome. Hild was sitting next to Gustav and moved her hands quickly away from his lap. She actually went red, which was convenient as her colouring now matched Gustav's face. Gustav dropped his hands to his lap to cover his embarrassment.

"What is going on here?" Bjorn spoke quite clearly, and seemed composed.

"What the hell are you accusing me of, husband? This man has lost one brother and his elder brother is at death's door. Can a hostess not show these poor men some sympathy? I was holding his hand while consoling him."

Soren watched and waited for Bjorn to grow some balls and throw the hag out, but as he had done numerous times before Bjorn took the easy route and ignored the indiscretion. As Bjorn faltered and the silence became deafening, Gustav spoke up.

"Dear sir, I am afraid I have shown weakness in front of your wife. I would never have come into your home without following proper custom but my mind is filled with the dire circumstances we find ourselves in."

Soren was surprised at how direct Bjorn was, but it should not be a surprise after what they had almost witnessed.

"Well sir, as you came to my home for some help and assistance why do we not get straight down to some serious business. You and your kin have been grievously affected by my former neighbour and you will wish some recompense for your troubles."

Bjorn had moved into business mode, where no man was his equal, for his mind moved extremely fast in working out benefits and losses. It always came to a very quick conclusion for what was the best outcome for Bjorn. From there he would formulate an effective plan on delivering that outcome. He had approached his hall with a little sympathy for the strangers. However after being humiliated in his own home, Bjorn was about to bite back, with all sympathy gone. This was Bjorn's battle ground and he was the fastest swordsman here. He continued;

"Let me outline the facts as I see them, your brother has been murdered and you were in the process of seeking blood revenge from the individual. Now in that process you now have another brother facing death. So we could see three brothers become one. So should you continue to seek blood revenge against, and I will not exaggerate here, a faster, stronger and perhaps cleverer opponent, or will you choose the other option open to you, accept bludgeld for your dead brother and hope your elder brother survives his wounds. Thus you would be able to return home with something from this sorry saga."

Gustav, who had now composed himself, stood up and turned fully toward Bjorn.

"But where and how will we get bludgeld from a man who has most likely fled the country and to where, we do not know."

"The answer is in your statement Gustav Sveinsson. Gunnar has fled and left his farm unguarded. He has two brothers and a sister so we will have to work fast and legally to ensure you can claim legal right over the farm."

"I have another question Bjorn Bjornsson, what good is a farm in Iceland to men from Scania. We have no relatives here who can manage the farm for us, and we have no plans to settle here in the west."

"It seems simple to me, you ensure that you have legal ownership of the farm land and when that is in place you may then sell the farm and surrounding land, therefore ensuring a sizeable bludgeld. You may then return home knowing your quest was a successful one. But I repeat what I said before, we must act quickly before his family get news of today's events, luckily Gunnar was the brains in the family so we hold the advantage."

"And would you know anyone who would be in position to buy the farm."

Bjorn did not answer; he just smiled a little to himself before nodding.

The performance reminded Hild why she married him, although she would rather ride any other man here than her husband.

Gustav reached forward and held Bjorn's upper arm, looked him in the eye and said, "is there anyone in this country that would stand up for Gunnar?"

*

Njal sat in his favourite chair and worried, had he thought of everything? One thing that he was unsure of was the legal side to these terrible events. Was Gunnar an outlaw in Scania? If so he had already been punished for the crime and he could not be punished again in Iceland? Also there was a chance that Gunnar had not committed the crime, although he was at the scene of the crime, covered in blood and had admitted arguing with the dead man. Perhaps a payment could be paid to the man's family to stop the blood revenge. Njal had plenty of money to lend his friend and Gunnar was not a poor man. He could sell some of his better land to raise enough to pay Njal back.

Njal was sure of one thing, he would have to think long and hard how he would approach the next Althing so he could best defend his friend Gunnar Hamundsson.

Njal's wife, Bergþorar, came over to him and lay her hand on his shoulder, "my dear husband, I am worried. I am worried for my son's travelling on the dangerous seas, I am worried about the problems you have to contend with but most of all I am worried about my dear cousin Freyja. Has love blinded her so much that she will flee with a murderer? What will become of her, if they catch them and she is allied to a killer?"

"Wife, how could you speak so, have you not known Gunnar for most of your life? I believe I am a good judge of character, as is Freyja, and I do not believe for one moment that Gunnar killed the brother of the men that hunt him.

"Yes, Gunnar has killed men in the past, but these were men who would have killed him in turn, without a second thought. Also, you should remember that Gunnar has been punished in Danemark already, and in this country you do not get punished twice for the same crime.

"Rest assured that Freyja is safe as long as she is with the man that loves her."

*

It was night on the slave ship and the thralls were whispering quietly to each other. We had pulled into a bay somewhere to the south; I guess it is Scotland or the Hebrides. The capture was still hurting me but it was so much worse to be separated from Freyja. I had tried to put her safety to the back of my mind but the thought of her predicament haunted me. Later in the evening the boat had stopped and most of the slavers had left to camp on land for the night. A skeleton crew of guards stayed on board to ensure the cargo did not get any ideas. I am a very strong swimmer and feel confident that I could jump off the ship and swim for shore, even with my hands bound behind my back. However, I could never leave Freyja here alone and try as I might, I could not think of a way out of this mess. At least that horrible little slaver did not seem to be on the ship.

*

Litta stayed at the front of the ship, he did not want the big bear seeing him and guessing his reason for being here. He was desperate to get down in the hold to see his little Knulla, and have a feel of that lovely body. Sometimes he had been too swift with other thralls and had either got into trouble, he touched his deformed ear, or his opportunity vanished. Baldr was very loyal to King Ivar and watched Litta like a hawk. No, the best thing to do was watch over the thralls and when everyone was asleep, drop below, gag those pretty lips and have a little play. He was already feeling aroused so he tried to take his mind off it by counting his small collection of coins, although this made him think of the whores in Dyflin and his arousal returned. He looked across the bay at the star lit night and the big shiny moon, telling himself that he would not waste his money on whores, saving some for his old age. But what he loved most of all was his collection, all memories now but good ones.

Litta was actually a Pictish man, born to his mother while she was in slavery, a thrall to Ivar's father. He had grown up thinking all the boys were of equal status, and learning they were not would be hard. Ivar had ensured that he had a status somewhere between a slave and a freeman. But what singled him out most was as they approached puberty, Litta did not grow as much as the other boys. He had been given the name Litta when he was about ten years old, before that they called him Ljot, meaning ugly. Although when anyone called him that they had a fight on their hands. One thing that had always irked him was that Ivar never really released Litta from slavery. Litta knew that if he had not had a good history with Ivar, the king would have killed him when he ruined that young Knulla.

"Dam!" Just as he had stopped thinking about sex, his mind took him full circle back to that incident. Part of Litta thought it was worth the scar and loss of part of his ear. There were remote occasions when he wished that he did not feel like coming all the time. The boat was getting quieter now and it would not be long before Litta could drop below and release his frustration. He could hardly wait.

*

Freyja lay still among the other thralls as they slept, she learned quickly that Gunnar was nearby and strangely relieved to hear him shout out just after she was thrown down here. She thought they may have thrown him into the sea and sailed away, leaving him to drown.

With nothing better to do she had weighed up her options; she suspected they were going to Dyflin as it was the major market for thralls, although she had not written off the possibility of ending up somewhere strange. She had heard that fair and blue eyed slaves were much sought after in the southern hot lands. Being a slave meant, most likely, a short life with little pleasure. Being a woman in slavery meant she could look forward to rape and abuse daily. With her future looking so bleak she contemplated ways to end her life, but she did not believe she would do it. The hope of seeing Gunnar again would sustain for the moment.

There was some movement from above; somebody was climbing down into the hold. She suspected they were checking all the thralls were asleep and tightly bound. It was quite dark so she only half closed her eyes and feigned sleep, as the slave guard checked the prisoners. She could see his outline as he approached. He must have only been a boy, for he was not very tall.

The guard came close to her so she properly closed her eyes and waited for him to move on. He made a small noise in his throat and she felt her head moved by the chin. Freyja pretended she was being woken but the pretence ended as a rag was tied around her mouth. She tried to struggle but the guard sat on her and focused on tightening the gag. It was so tight it felt like it was cutting through the sides of her mouth, but that was almost bearable compared to the disgusting taste and smell of the rag. She felt herself start to gag and she thought any moment she would be sick, when the guard got off her and roughly lifted her dress and under dress up as far as her chest, completely exposing the lower part of her body. She twisted and writhed trying to pull away but he easily held her down. Her arms and hands, being bound behind her back, were screaming with pain as they were pushed against the wooden hull.

"Now be quite my little Knulla, daddy is here to play," the whisper sent a chill up her spine and fear gripped her guts.

The vile guard half lay across her body, pinning her down so that he was free to start running his hand down her body and through her pubic hair. There was no pleasure from his touch; it was an invasion making her skin crawl. She writhed, trying to pull away but she was held tight and now she felt his rough bony fingers feeling for her most intimate place. He was panting with the excitement and she knew it would not be long before the ultimate violation. Tears started to run from her eyes and she screamed inside the rag. Inside her head she prayed for release and for her husband to save her from this horrible rape. But she was bound and gagged and alone with her abuser.

Litta left his hand on her kut and paused, he was so excited he could hardly breathe. There was no rush, he had all night. Earlier he had promised himself he would not penetrate her but he knew now that he would break that promise. He would be gentle and careful and not damage Ivar's goods this time. She is a very beautiful slave and he wished he was a man of wealth so he could purchase her and he would have a Knulla to call his own. He tried to move his fingers into her lips but she started wriggling again, so he sat on her to hold her still and have his fun.

"Litta, what in Hel are you doing down there?"

Litta looked up and saw the outline of Baldr looking down.

"I am just checking everyone is tied up tight."

"You are a lying piece of skit, unless you are tying the thralls by their kut? Or can you explain why that thrall you're sitting on is nearly naked? Now get your disgusting arse back up here, Bjarni was right, you would be up to no good. Ivar will mess you up good when we get back." Baldr did not like Litta and hoped he would be harshly punished by the king.

"Did you not think that Ivar might want that one, could you not wait until he had tupped her until he was bored?"

As the disgusting Litta got off her and climbed out of the hold, Freyja stared long at him so she would not forget him. He looked straight into her eyes and licked the fingers that had been inside her, showing her his enjoyment. He was an ugly man and Freyja felt fear as he looked at her, as he had the cold eyes of a predator. If Ivar did not 'mess him up' she would make sure Gunnar did. The other man climbed down into the hold and approached her. She tried to back away as best she could but he held up a hand.

"Don't worry about me, my wife would beat me severely if she just had a dream that I tupped a thrall, I just came here to pull your clothes down, and it looks like I should take Litta's arse rag out of your mouth too."

When Baldr removed the rag she vomited and it sprayed over her saviour, "brilliant, is that the thanks I get?" Even though he scolded her she felt thankful for this small act of kindness.

Freyja cried for a long time that night, she wanted to swim in a river of cold clean water or sit in a hot bath and clean all the disgusting filth off of her. She felt so violated and ashamed, but she cried for a long time as this was most likely just the first time. That night she felt herself drift into a very dark place and knew that she could not put up with constant violations like tonight. Either they must escape together or die trying, before this horrible lifestyle got any worse. She finally fell asleep whimpering and whispering her husband's name.

Litta sat on the shore in the cold crisp pre-dawn, Bjarni and Baldr's scolding having washed over him. When they tired of repeating themselves they left him alone and he went behind a rock to masturbate. Afterwards he felt free of the constant urge and deep down there was a small, decent part of him that felt disgusted, although this feeling was soon gone.

He stared out across the dark night, the half-moon colouring the bay in a thousand shades of grey. He looked at the slave ship and saw a guard move slightly aboard, perhaps having an early piss.

He thought of the woman, of her breasts, flat firm stomach and soft mound. Yes she will be my little Knulla and I will not let her go. The feeling was back and he welcomed it, he touched himself; hard again he smiled.

Chapter 10

I know that I hung
On the windswept tree
For nine whole nights
Pierced by the spear
And given to Odin
Myself given to myself
On that tree
No one knows.
They gave me not bread
Nor drink from the horn;
Into the depths I peered,
I grasped the runes,
Screaming I grasped them,
And then I fell back.

I had a dream last night, my dear, sweet and beautiful wife, Freyja, came forward into the light of my candle and told me I had to trust him. She was still wet from the cold sea, her soaked woollen vest stuck close to her beautiful body, sea water running down the inside of her thighs and over her calves. The effect of the vest stuck to her breasts, her flat stomach and the line of her groin made me stare, she scolded me for looking at her with lust.

"Gunnar, please my love, there is no time for that you must listen to me and take heed. Trust the King of the North, he will put you on the path to make things right," as she spoke these words she started to fade into the dark again. My heart ached for her to return but I said nothing, I had been struck dumb in this dream. As I started to mope and long for my wife I heard the approach of another. I looked up and Njal stood before me, my friend and adviser for these last years, he looked tired and strained as if a great pressure lay upon his shoulders.

"Gunnar, listen and listen good, only trust the prince of Vendland, the scourge of Jarl Gilli and the King of all Norsemen. He will turn his back on the old gods but will lead you to your heart's desire."

And then, as Freyja did before him, Njal faded into the dark.

I closed my eyes to the light of the candle and when I opened them Hild-Yxa Eiriksdottir was standing in all her fine jewellery and a purple silk vest that must have cost a king's ransom. The silk clung close to her body and she watched my reaction, but nothing stirred as it had for Freyja, I only felt revulsion.

"Gunnar you should know that I have won at last, I have beaten you and it feels good, so good. I never dreamt that revenge, over Freyja, would be so sweet."

Hild approached me and I realised that my hands are bound, she leaned forward and whispered in my ear, "I will rejoice in your deaths" and then she laughed. The laughter carried on as I awoke and I realised I was now listening to the hysterical laughter of a mad fool in the hold.

As I sat there I wondered who my allies meant, was it Jarl Haakon of the Norse and how I would gain his support?

I wish Njal was here to interpret the dream but I am a fool to wish, all I can do is wait on this boat, and see what the Norns have in store for me.

*

Kolskegg, Skarphedin and Grim joined their men as they dragged the longship up the beach. There were a few other ships grounded here and a collection of men milling around and acting out repairs.

Kolskegg went to the nearest man to gain information, "Well met friend, we are trying to catch up with my brother and his wife. They have sailed here from Iceland in the last few days, have you seen them?"

"I have not, we have been here for a week and no other boat has come to this side of the island since we arrived."

"Thank you," Kolskegg moved back down the shale to his party. "There has been no sign of Gunnar and Freyja in the last week, but we will need to check before deciding what to do, I suggest we go to Tinganese and see if the market is on."

"Will there be fighting Kolskegg?"

"Not now Skarphedin, this is a friendly visit and hopefully we will find my brother and his bride here."

They ensured the ship was pulled high up the beach, beyond the tide mark, before collecting their packs and heading for the central peninsular of Tinganese in Faeroe.

*

Out at sea, half a day from Dyflin, sailed a merchant ship, escorted by two longships, a new cargo was on its way to the slave market.

Bjarni lent on the rudder and made some small adjustments to stay on course behind Baldr's longship. He was thankful that Litta had not tried to tup anymore of the thralls, although it did not stop his hands feeling the women every chance he could get. Bjarni was not a reasonable man; he did not look out for the thrall's welfare. He did not care if Litta stabbed his disgusting orm into all the thrall's holes, but he did care for his own welfare. Litta had ruined it for all the men who ran the slave ship. One of the perks of the job was to tup the pretty slaves, and the captain would get first choice. Now that Litta had literally plowed a slave to death, Ivar was extremely concerned that his cargo was safe.

Bjarni hoped that after a few more trips without any problems, Ivar would relax his grip on the slave ship.

Baldr was glad to be on his own ship, far away from that horrible little man. He was going to work hard at staying clear of him. Litta had no shame, after pawing the thralls he would walk around with his erection visible beneath his jerkin. Baldr thought that if he saw that again he would teach him a lesson by kicking Litta hard in his cock.

Litta was unaware that his two allies were thinking about him, he was still obsessed with that Knulla. It was a warm day and he was checking the thralls, making sure none of them had any obvious illness or disease. It was a job he enjoyed a lot; he could feel all the women without anyone looking at him suspiciously. It was also a good cargo, as there were a lot of young women, at marrying age. Litta laughed, nobody would be marrying these women now.

He moved onto another pretty Pict woman, he checked her teeth, and then felt her ample breasts for a good time, then checked her below before finding a new one to grope. The male slaves were getting very agitated and he supposed they still thought they owned these women. One bearded fellow was speaking to him, but Litta had no idea what he was saying. The man was angry about something and looking at the woman with big breasts.

He decided to try an experiment and squeezed one of her breasts again and the fellow went red with rage. Litta smiled, the man was an idiot, and he was trussed up on a slave ship, with no rights and no help.

"Do you want me to stop, hairy face?"

Litta was answered by more incoherent noise and he was getting sick of this. He slapped the weak fool round the face and saw hatred cross the man's eyes.

"What are you going to do? You are nothing, get used to it, aersling."

Litta moved on as there were many women to check.

*

I knew that we were near land; I had been able to smell it for some time now. I guessed we were sailing south and it seemed I was right about their destination. My treatment had not been as bad as expected, although they had only given me a little bread every few days with not much more water. It was true with most of the men, I suppose they wanted the strongest to feel weakened and have no energy to rebel.

The thirst was the hardest thing to deal with, if you did not count the shrunken pervert in the crew. I saw him feeling up the women but was more surprised when witnessing him feeling up some of the younger men, too.

I felt compelled to defend the women near me but there was nothing I could do but wait and hope. This inevitably led me to conclude the obvious, that this little skit had groped my wife, too.

I had a plan, it was a skit plan, but it was all I had. I tried acting very subservient toward all the crew so that they would not worry too much about me. From what I observed I was by far the biggest man on the ship and felt confident in my fighting skills. I needed the crew to think that I was something of a gentle giant, but I kept watching all the time hoping to pick something up. I learned all the names of the crew, watching all their little habits and preferences. An opportunity may present itself and I had to be ready to spot that opportunity and take advantage. The only member of the crew that did not fit was Baldr, the leader of one of the longships. I suspected he was forced into this skitty job against his will, but who was I to try and understand the secrets of men's hearts?

*

Baldr steered his longship south through the Irish Sea on a slightly warm and calm day.

"Not long now lads," he was feeling happier, they had passed west of Manu and he knew that soon he would be eating his wife's food and hopefully enjoying her in bed.

Baldr did not fit in this crew and he did not fit easily in King Ivar's guard, for he was one of the few Christians among the senior men. He had started to feel the conflict between this life style and the teachings of the priests. Father Niall had tried to justify the lifestyle in Dyflin to him, saying there were necessary evils in the world. The slaves brought in were the enemies of Dyflin and pagans, who worshipped the devil and other demons, and their import was a great source of income for that kingdom, something King Ivar coveted from afar. Baldr was not sure as he had heard other crews boasting of capturing Christians and laughing at their weakness. Also Jesus taught that you should love your neighbour and this was so far from His teachings. The sooner Dyflin had a Christian ruler, the better.

However, if Ivar's plans came to fruition the kingdom would be far from having a fair and Christian ruler. Baldr thought for the hundredth time about a better way forward for him and his wife. They both wanted to farm and raise children, and they were almost the only two people they knew who were pure Norse.

He had heard of a land beyond Greenland where grapes grew, and wild wheat that continued to the end of the earth. Although he liked to think of it he suspected it was a silly dream; perhaps he should try and take his wife to Iceland as there was still a little land to be had there. Whatever he decided he must get her and himself away from this odious lifestyle.

*

Freyja looked up at the sky and saw three pure white gulls flying around the boats; they screeched with something like excitement and sometimes flew fast down toward the water. They looked beautiful against the bright blue sky and the beauty of the scene brought on another dark attack of melancholy. She fought it off because she did not want to give up, like some of the other thralls aboard. If you gave up, and do not keep a spark of life inside, you are already dead.

She forced herself to believe that she would be free with Gunnar again, and unmolested. She hated herself for tolerating the hands of that horrible little man, even thinking about him she could almost feel his dry, rough fingers against her soft skin. For a while now she had been able to smell grass and wet soil, so knew that they were not far from land. Although the smells would come and go, depending on what way the wind was blowing. She looked forward to setting foot on dry land and she constantly dreamed of drinking cupful's of cool water. Her tongue felt too big in her mouth and she longed for something to eat. She almost laughed at her wish list, while hoping for food and drink maybe she should wish for a bath, scented oil and all the gold in the northern world.

She tried not to think of what would happen when they set foot on land and she prayed to her namesake that she would not be too far from her love. Her faith in Gunnar was still strong; she still believed he would save her from this nightmare and make her heart happy again.

*

Not only was there no market at Tinganese, there was also no sign of their brother, Gunnar. They had stayed the night on the sheep islands but there was no reason to stay longer, as they had plenty of supplies, although they did top up on fresh water.

Kolskegg was now sailing for the western islands off Scotland, his logic went against the knowledge that a drifting boat would head toward the kingdom of Norway. He knew his brother was resourceful and he did not believe that he was in great danger. Therefore, Gunnar must have had a plan that nobody would be able to follow. Kolskegg had thought long about the very last place his brother would head for. He decided that it would make sense to head for Faeroes, Shetland or Orkney, so he discounted the other two earldoms. The only places Gunnar's small boat may have a chance of sailing to, if his luck held, were the mainland of Scotland or perhaps the western earldom of Hebrides.

They would start with the Hebrides, as it was a smaller place and he remembered Gunnar talking fondly of it once.

Skarphedin and Grim were a little bored, they had expected adventure and all they had to amuse them was the vast vista of the grey northern sea.

"Boys, you did know this was not a chance to go Viking," Kolskegg smiled at their disappointment.

"Not wishing anything foul to have befallen your brother, but I hoped he had been captured and we could spring him and defeat a great enemy." Grim was the younger of the two and still thought about the world too much like a boy.

"Brother, you should not say things like that, Loki could be listening and intend mischief on Gunnar or us. And you are forgetting that Kolskegg will be worried about his brother, as I would if it were you."

"It is no problem, Skarphedin, it is just the youthfulness of Grim, and I have taken no offence."

"So Kolskegg, what will be the plan when we arrive in the Hebrides?"

"We will sail to the island of Coll and pay tribute to Jarl Gilli, hoping we find out some information. If there has been notice of Gunnar this will be the best place to start."

*

"We will be leaving in the morning as my brother is fit enough to sail. I wish to thank you and your husband, dearest lady." Gustav managed to stutter the words out, for he felt awkward and uncomfortable around Hild and Bjorn. She had come on quite strong to Gustav and it was something he was not used to, also it had been a long time since he had seen his wife and been touched like that.

Hild stood before him, smirking; she was weighing him up and seemed to be getting some enjoyment out of his obvious discomfort.

"My husband is away for the night."

If there had been more light, Hild would have seen Gustav blush, she loved these games and it heightened her excitement flirting with this handsome man. Gustav stayed silent so Hild reached out and pulled at his hand until he came into the hall. She brushed past him and lowered the leather door ensuring she brushed against him again.

"What shall we do now, my handsome Viking?"

Gustav looked straight into her eyes but stayed silent; she sensed he was trembling a little. He started to speak and she placed her hand on his lips to stop him from breaking the moment. Her hand moved down, brushing his beard before settling on his chest. She felt his heart beating under the tense muscles of his breast, she stared into his eyes and he held her gaze. Hild was not sure if she was still breathing but she was enjoying this and her most intimate place tingled with what she hoped would happen. She moved her hand lower, brushing his stomach until she found the top of his trouser, pulling it down and forward, expertly exposing his arousal. She liked what she saw and went down on her knees to pleasure this beautiful man.

*

Soren stood in the dark, outside the hall, listening, spying. He liked to gather information, digest it, and then decide on a course of action. He had never spoken to Bjorn directly about his wife but this latest act made him want to remove the whore Bjorn was married to. He moved silently away from the hall, not wanting to hear the adultery.

*

Erik Eriksson sat on an old stump, watching the harbour and eating freshly baked bread, while sipping weak ale. The warm bread was a pleasant breakfast that he enjoyed, knowing that he would be at sea again soon, living off salted herring and flat bread. He had been in the kingdom of Dyflin for a month now and he had noticed his anger finally subsiding. He had left Harald and Gustav's side two years back and made a little money trading skins from north of the Svea lands out of his small stall in Dyflin.

Three ships had come into the Longport of Dyflin, two longships and a fatter merchant vessel built only for the sea. More slaves for the market, Dyflin ate up people from all over the world and spat out lifeless men and women who left without a name.

Erik watched the thralls disembark while finishing his breakfast. They took the thralls off in small groups, men and women tied together at the end of a sword. A man, much shorter than average, was slapping the women on their behinds and laughing, he was getting the same pleasure from the first until the last.

Erik was watching, while eating, but not really registering. He had been here long enough to see scores of thralls come to the market and be sold onward. He was just finishing off his bread and washing it down with the last dregs of ale when he saw a big man leave the ship. He was tied to three women and had his head down, but Erik knew the gait and shape of him. He nearly choked on his last morsel, it was Gunnar and he was a thrall, a slave.

Erik stood up and watched the group and followed them to the slave enclosure, trying to appear inconspicuous.

*

I saw him while I was disembarking, my hair hung over my face but I would recognise my old friend Erik anywhere. He had hair like straw and it always had a mind of its own. I loved Erik but I now feared him, he was obviously here on behalf of Harald to scout for me. Now I was enslaved I was very vulnerable, Erik was fiercely loyal to Gustav and

117

Harald and he had loved Gull above all other friends. He would surely kill me at his first opportunity.

I tried to keep an eye on him as we were led away and he must have spotted me as he started to follow us to the market. At no other time in my life have I felt this low, I was cornered, without rights and with no one to speak up and defend me. But the worst of it was my beautiful Freyja would not have me to protect her, and the full horror of her future lay out before me. The tears started to roll down my face and I did not care, I would soon be dead and my wife would be raped repeatedly until she was no longer of any use.

*

Erik followed the group until they were led to the holding area for the thralls, which was very close to the market. After the men and women had been separated and the entire furore had died down, Erik approached the man on the main gate.

"Well met friend," Erik tried a friendly approach.

"What do you want," the guard looked as if he did not want to be disturbed.

"I just wondered who these new thralls belong to."

"Have you silver?" The guard must be used to earning a little on the side, thought Erik.

"I have a little; do you know the answer to my question?"

"I might but it will cost you to find out if I do or if I don't."

Erik fished out a small silver coin and held it in front of the guard.

"Friend, this coin is for information and not for smart arse remarks. If you know the answer to my question I will leave you with this, but if you offend me, I will get very angry."

The guard took a good look at Erik, before him he did not see a tall man but he gauged that Erik was a hard man. His eyes noticed that Erik wore many arm rings, not fancy but the more simple the arm rings normally meant a more accomplished fighter.

"I know the answer to your question but it will cost two silver coins."

Erik fished out another coin and handed them over.

"The new thralls are the property of King Ivar of Waterford, a good friend but a terrible enemy."

Erik walked away meaning to find out when the next market was and hoping he could find a way to succour Gunnar.

"Harald, this is ridiculous, we have the blood money, and if we continue this we will be outlawed."

"I am your older brother and you will obey me, I am the head of our household."

Gustav stared at the belligerent fool of an older brother and shook his head.

"I would like to see Gunnar dead as well, but I do not want to spend my whole life chasing him across the world, I have a family and a farm to keep, it is different for you," Gustav stopped, realising he had gone too far.

"Go on brother, have you some comment to make about my wife and land?"

"No Harald, but I want to go home to my wife and I do not think you feel the same."

"Gustav, do not become my enemy, you must be under some strain to say such hurtful things to me. Do you not think this is difficult for me, I am not fully healed and sailing is painful in my current state? Anyway brother we will not chase after Gunnar immediately; I want to try and find Erik Ericsson and ask him to return to our side. He should be pleased we have found revenge for his good friend and our brother."

"So we are sailing to Dyflin then? I wish you would tell me your plans and then we would not have had harsh words."

"I am telling you now, thanks to our new ally Soren Guldhuvud, we can estimate the outlaw is heading for the sheep islands. Once we have searched there we will go and find Erik and I promise we will discuss the way forward together."

"Well brother take note, unless you change your mind and come with me, I will be returning home from the kingdom of Dyflin."

119

Chapter 11

Mother bore a son and clothed him in silk.
She sprinkled him with water and called him Jarl.
He was fair of hair, bright of cheeks,
and his eyes pierced like an adder's.

Sweyn Forkbeard king of Denmark, son of King Harald Bluetooth, had overthrown his father three years ago and seized the throne. He thought about his father now, just two years in the grave, and felt some pity toward the old man. For himself, he had craved power and could not wait for the old man to die so he had speeded up his ascent to the throne. The one thing he did for his father was make sure he died with a sword in his hand, you never know. Although his father had changed allegiance and followed the new Christian god, as did Sweyn, it paid not to upset the old gods. Anyway, he suspected his father was not worthy enough to be let into heaven so gave him the insurance of entering Valholl.

King Sweyn sat with his two most loyal Jarl's, Justin and Guthmund, raised his glass of fine Danish ale, made a quick toast and sunk a healthy draft.

"Well met friends, I can say the advantage of being King is you rarely have to drink skit ale."

The two men laughed, not a nervous laugh in front of their King, for they had been loyal friends since their younger days.

Sweyn was a stocky man, seventeen hands high, as his name suggests he had a forked beard, his hair the healthy brown of a bear's coat. His eyes were a bright blue, like the ice in a cold winter, and they were always watching and calculating the thoughts of others. But at this moment he was relaxed with two men he trusted.

His two friends were an odd couple; Guthmund looked taller than he was, as he carried no fat. Guthmund was not exactly skinny but he looked as if he had missed a few meals. He was not a weak man; his composition fooled you as he was strong and sinewy.

Justin was not small but he was shorter than the average man, and next to Guthmund he looked smaller still. He had white pale skin, jet black hair and narrow eyes betraying ancestry from the icy wastelands in the north.

"Well boys, what are we going to do about Angle Land? My father never got round to it but I mean to claim my birth right. The Danes ruled the north of that land for many years and it is about time it returned to Danish rule."

"It is a big job, Lord. We should line up our allies among the Saxon Jarls." Justin paused and looked to Guthmund to continue.

"And dear King, the Kingdom of Dyflin has land in the North West of Angle Land. An alliance with Jarn Cuaran and his new brother in law, Olaf, we think is wise. In fact I have already sent word to Jarl Olaf; he would appreciate our friendship as he has enmity with King Haakon of Norway and is looking for allies himself."

"It is a start, but promise him nothing as I intend to extend my empire over all the northern lands and am not ready to give any of it away."

Justin stood up and waited for the chance to speak, and the King granted it. "We should organise large fleets, make them appear as Vikings initially and then on a signal bring them together to annex a large chunk of eastern Angle land, we all know it has worked before. We can raid the eastern coast and retreat repeatedly, demoralising the Saxon and make their militia march up and down trying to find where we will strike next."

"I like it Justin, let us make contact with all potential allies and you can meet up with them at Shetland, as I do not think Sigurd the stout would mind, and who cares if he does."

Guthmund now stood and the King allowed him to speak, "King Sweyn, I also have two contacts among the Saxons. Their King had his brother killed and one feels loyalty to a dead King, the other is of Danish blood and can bring in others like him."

"Good, they can now show loyalty to a very much alive King who will reward them with gold. But dear Guthmund, do not spend my money freely, save some of it for yourself and Justin the Black."

With that the men took another draft of the good ale and had the beginnings of a plan.

*

King Aethelred sat alone in his compound at Wincanceaster, drinking weak beer. He fretted over the problems in his Kingdom although his southern and eastern coasts had been quiet for some time. Importantly he had finally removed the annoying tick of Kernow. Perhaps he should let Thorod make plans to clear Mercia of the threat from the kingdom of Dyflin.

Danes were not his biggest problem at the moment, as he still had the problem of his own Earls loyalty. He believed that some of these men would even prefer a foreign king if it meant they gained a fraction more power.

It had been ten years since his half brother, Edward, King of England, had been murdered at Corfe Gate, and the tremors of that act continued to be felt across the nation. He knew his mother, Aelthryth, was heavily implicated in the murder, but what did they expect, that he put his own mother on trial and jeopardise his right to be king?

Some of the Earls blamed him for the act, although he was only ten years old at the time. Others looked to their paymasters among the pagan nations of the north, which left the weak and sycophantic.

His man Godwin was strong and loyal so he kept him close in Wiltshire, also he knew he could rely on Ealdorman Brihtnoth but they were the only ones he could be sure of. Thorod was a friend of Godwin, but that meant he could only be half trusted. If he was going to half trust some of his earls he could include Aethelbald of Devon, having just secured his border and Edgar of Kent. It was almost as simple as counting the earls based on their location going back to the Danelaw, although the worst being Ealdorman Alfric of Hampshire. Those to the north of Watling Street seemed to be discovering their old Danish roots, whereas most men to the south of that ancient highway had Saxon blood and Saxon loyalties.

He supposed that at least the Earls gave some clues to their loyalty but the Bishops were worse. They would smile, send blessings and impart advice while plotting behind his back to depose him. The worst of these, and the man the king suspected of being the ring leader of his opponents, was the Bishop of Rochester, Aelfstan. The man was driven by power and wealth, looking jealously on the King, coveting all he had. Aelfstan seemed to have even more sway than the new Archbishop of Canterbury Aethelgar. Aethelgar seemed to be just a front for Rochester and greatly favoured his sponsor. In amongst this was Sigeric, who was no great supporter of the King but despised the Bishop of Rochester. The King thought that he should support Sigeric a little more and ensure that he is the next Archbishop, therefore blunt the threat from Aelfstan. It would be hard to bring Sigeric round as he was a great supporter of the deceased King Edward. But Aethelred could easily praise his dead brother and complain about the evil Earls who conspired against his family.

"Yes, that is a good idea," Aethelred spoke to himself and smiled, rewarding his cunning with another draught of beer and saying a small prayer to the Holy Mother that she would help protect his Kingship.

Chapter 12

Now within the streams of elf circle conceal
Great counsels of mighty men.
In the body of the mother of the foe of giants,
Jord.

He was under the earth but not afraid. He lay on his back, his eyes still closed, and he could smell the damp soil pressed against his face. The earth was wrapped all around him and the roots of a tree snaked down, over and around his body. He knew the tree was Yggdrasil and he welcomed its warm embrace. While in the bosom of the tree of life he knew then that Gunnar and Freyja had made the safety of land. This was the reason he had been brought here, deep underground, into the heart of mother earth. Jord wanted him to stay but he knew he could not stay for long or he would be held here until Ragnarok. Jord, the Goddess of the earth, spoke to him now and her voice entered him through every pore of his skin.

'Njal, servant of the Gods for so long, in man years, stay with your mother earth and worship her for eternity.'

"Dear sweet Jord, favoured among the Gods, I have come to you on behalf of my two friends, and for them I ask for your protection."

'Give me tribute Njal, venerate me above all other Gods and I will watch over the mighty warrior, but Grimnir is not as fair as his wife. The price for the safety of the warrior will be harsh if He chooses so.'

"I will venerate mother earth and pay you tribute as soon as I return to the realm of men. But can you protect us from the roving eye of Odin the Great?"

"I will distract him but be warned, he has only one eye, a spear wound in his side and long did he hang, crucified on the tree, but he always sees and cares little for men."

With this statement Njal felt a change in the environment and realised that Jord had left him and he was awakening. The warmth of the soil and the roots of the tree of life left him like morning mist in the wind.

He awoke recalling the dream he had just had; now certain of what he had to do. Having much on his mind Njal had decided to spend time in the sanctuary of his small shrine. He felt glad that he had decided to rest a while here, as it was his most holy place, and where he felt close to the gods. He can see his hall from here but it is well known that if he is here, he should not be disturbed. There was much to think about, nearly all of it concerned Gunnar and his possessions. His mind had been full of all his problems, it needed order and he needed a clear head to ensure his friend's safety. When his mind was cluttered he felt the only way to clear it was to talk with the gods, which would result in him writing his message in ancient runes on a birch stick and disposing of it in many ways. (Taking the sacred stick to the top of a mountain, throw it into the sea or place it under ground, all depending on which of the Gods he wished to communicate with.) This rune writing would be dedicated to Jord, the wife of Odin the mighty, and buried in the ground. Njal would ask for her help in guiding Gunnar and Freyja safely across her sacred ground.

Iceland is a land where Asgard meets the human realm and is therefore a venerated place. The process of cutting the runes into the stick concentrated Njal's mind, giving it something to focus on and clearing the clutter. While working he thought about the ancient Norse Gods and pondered the usurper, Christ. He wondered if this new God was all powerful and if he alone could bring about Ragnarok, and what this would mean to the realm of men.

His mind drifted back to his friends. Soon enough, he thought, tongues would wag and the news would spread that Gunnar and Freyja had left the country. He did not doubt that Gunnar's crimes would increase as the gossip progressed across Iceland, he would use this to his advantage when he presented his case at the Althing. The plan was to defend Gunnar initially against the charge, and if he failed he would insist that no man should be punished twice for the same crime, assuming Gunnar had been outlawed in Danemark. Furthermore, if he lost both arguments, something that had never happened to Njal yet, he would offer bludgeld for the crime. He made a mental note to visit Hjort and see if there had been any developments that he had not heard of yet.

Just as he was finishing off his holy runes, Njal heard the sound of a horse and looked up to see Thorstein approaching his refuge. Njal put down the finished stick and stepped outside to meet his farm manager.

"Well met Thorstein, I believe you have news for me or you would not have ridden here to disturb my work."

"Please excuse me, but the news I have is of great importance."

"Ok, come down from your nag so we can talk face to face and I will pour us some ale."

Njal waited for his man to join him and they sat down. As soon as Thorstein was seated, he spoke.

"Bjorn has possession of Gunnar's farm; the Danes claimed the farm and all the land as bludgeld for their dead brother. Apparently it was witnessed and agreed, as soon as they had a hold on it Bjorn paid them half its worth and they left. The belief at the quay is that they still intend on killing Gunnar."

"You did well coming to me so quickly, we will have to lodge a complaint at the Althing and prize Gunnar's possessions from Bjorn's fat, greedy hands. This act of stupidity may be enough to give me an advantage; nobody likes to think that anything he owns will be taken from him before he has had a fair trial."

*

Hild was furious. She thought about shouting at her servants again, but they were already running around Gunnar's farm liked panicked hens. They had searched everywhere and then repeated the search; however they found no money or jewellery. It was common to bury valuables and they had searched the obvious places; the whole floor had been dug up inside the hall and any piece of earth that looked as if it had been recently disturbed. The trouble for Hild and her helpers was there had been a great storm just after Gunnar and Freyja had left, and she knew that this could cover up a fresh dig. They had even dug up around some of the out buildings but to no avail.

*

Soren and Bjorn were riding around the perimeter of Gunnar's land on a surveying trip.

"This is good land, I think we will do well out of this, but I will miss seeing Freyja."
Bjorn looked a little melancholy for a moment as he pondered his neighbour's fate.

"Lord, we will have to be careful and ensure we have allies, as I have heard that Njal is working hard on clearing Gunnar's name. I suggest that we find someone who is willing to say that Gunnar wished his possessions to be left to you to administer."

"Soren, have you been drinking? It is well known there is enmity between our families. I mean Gunnar and myself, we keep the most basic pleasantries, but Hild has never hidden the fact that she despises Freyja."

"But people know what women are like and surely this is a business between men only. But what I was thinking is there may be an acquaintance of Gunnar that is struggling, perhaps somebody that has suffered blight to their animals, drinks all their savings or is in heavy debt. If we find someone like this then we only have to find out their price for a small betrayal. This will give us an insurance against Njal, and the longer Gunnar is gone, the tighter is your grip on this land."

"Actually Soren, I believe some of Gunnar's cousins are in debt to me already, we should check our ledger and you can start by visiting the one with the biggest debt."

Soren said nothing in reply. Sometimes he wondered how Bjorn had done so well, but he remembered that he only came good when scheming within business negotiations; when he tried it in any other walk of life his heart was not in it. Soren had already formulated a plan but felt it best to let Bjorn think he came up with the idea. This was Soren's little insurance as he had not forgotten how resourceful Gunnar was, and expected him to return and clear his name, therefore reclaiming back all his possessions. Soren did not want to be on the wrong side of that man's vengeance.

They started to ride back to the hall and could still see the servants busy scouring the place to find the smallest trinket. If they did not find anything Hild would see it as another defeat to Freyja, and Bjorn would be nagged and harangued for at least a week. Soren looked at his master and could almost see the strength sapped from him as he approached his wife. He decided that if they got through this episode unscathed he would formulate a plan to get rid of the hag.

*

She had thrown everyone out of the hall and closed the leather door. The only light came in through the hole in the opposite wall. The only thing of any value that had been found was a polished metal mirror which she held in her hands as she sat on a bench. She faced the light and held the mirror up to her face and looked at every detail. They were still there, little cracks, like tributaries from a river; they broke away from the edge of her mouth and her eyes. She had tried everything to stop their progress and when asking around she was told to visit Njal, but her pride kicked in and she would not give the scrawny lawyer the pleasure of knowing age was creeping up on her. Although behind her back people would say they are the marks of bitterness and greed on an unloving face.

It wasn't fair, the last time she saw that bitch, Freyja, she still looked as if she was not yet twenty and Hild knew she was only a year older than her nemesis. She wondered if Gunnar had been in love with her instead of Freyja, would he still love her as she aged?

Hild sat and stared out the hole in the wall and thought of her future. She did not like it. She gathered wealth and possessions close to her sagging bosom like a bloated magpie, but she always craved more, and the possessions did not love her back.

*

Ragnal walked with his brother in law and decided he would be direct when talking to the older man, for one day he could be King of Dyflin and kings were always direct. Although he did show the other man respect when addressing him. "Jarl Olaf, will you defend my lands across the sea for me if I am your King."

"Prince Ragnal, your brother is very healthy and full of life, we should not think of his demise just yet. But I speak true when I say I am sworn to defend your family and ensure safety to my dear wife."

Ragnal did not like the answer, it was too ambiguous, he wanted a direct yes but he loved his sister and would trust her judgement. After all, Jarl Olaf had impressed him greatly during the Althing, when Olaf and all his men had defeated the famous Jomsviking. It was an act the young prince had not heard of before. However, Prince Ragnal of Dyflin was a little surprised by Olaf's next question.

"What are your hopes for the future?"

Ragnal gave the same answer he always gave to any question like this, "I intend to be High King of Ireland and gain a reputation like my father, for without reputation a man is nothing."

"That is an ambitious goal. Dyflin is a wealthy kingdom and the only true Norse one on this land, but the other kingdoms of Ireland are large and can call on many fighting men."

"That is true Jarl Olaf, but we are perhaps the richest kingdom of Ireland and this will help buy allies when the time is right."

"But dear Prince, an ally that is a friend is worth two allies that are pure mercenary. Although this is just my belief, but if I was looking to expand my kingdom I would gather friends close, perhaps Jarl Sigurd of Orkney."

"But Sigurd is a fat fool; he sits in comfort getting fatter every day. I am a warrior like my father; I have no time to appease the feelings of old men whose best days are behind them."

"Prince Ragnal, I am not just your friend, I am also your family and I invite you to listen to my counsel. Make friends with powerful men then keep them close and watch them like Odin watches all of us. Do them some small favours and if you cannot stand them, loan them gold and silver so that they owe you a favour in return. Work hard at building up alliances while training your men well. And one last piece of advice that I was told by the Holy Roman Emperor, be lucky."

Olaf's loyal lieutenant's, Mort, Brynjolf and Kjarten, where sent with the majority of his men to Kirkham, the fortress guarding Dyflin's territory of the Fylde. The remaining men, some of his closest warriors, plus the men who defected from Alfvine, stayed in Dyflin to help police the kingdom and the lucrative slave market. He was not happy with the location of Dyflin's split kingdom, one half surrounded by the Irish and the half across the sea surrounded by the Saxon. Dyflin generated huge sums of money from the market and was eyed enviously by the surrounding kingdoms. The Fylde had large areas of fertile lands but was viewed by the Saxons as rightfully theirs. He paused from his thoughts to acknowledge two of his guards as he and Ragnal walked by.

*

Berg and Ketil saluted their commander as he passed alongside the Prince of Dyflin, both men thinking how easy and comfortable their life had become.

*

King Ivar was pacing up and down, mulling the problem over in his head. Kanin sat in the corner hoping her master would not get any angrier as he could be rough with her if the mood took him. His captain, Tyr, waited for his king to come to a decision.

"What the Hel is wrong with my people, Tyr, we are getting ready to expand our kingdom and the peasent idiots are fighting about which god is the best. I am not a man of patience and it seems to me that the arse loving Christians are causing trouble. I do not argue that Thor is greater than Grimnir or that Freya is stronger than Loki, so why does Jesus have to be the best over all the gods?"

"Lord King, there are not many Christians that are for this, but they cause more trouble than the rest of the kingdom."

129

"Well Tyr, I have had enough of their whining, so if they cannot live in harmony in my kingdom they can join Jesus in his."

"Sir?"

"On Sunday I want you to go to both Christian temples and kill all inside; I will end this skitty religion in my realm."

Chapter 13

With her death dealing hand,
And the hounds she loosed,
The thralls she awakened
And a firebrand threw
In the door of the hall;
So vengeance she had.

Her head burst through the surface of the ice cold water, gulping the crisp clean air into her lungs. Through watery eyes she could see land not far off and started to swim in its direction. Her strength sapping now, she dug deep, confident in her ability and stamina. She reached the stony shore and pulled herself up the beach. There was a small incline, topped by a grassy knoll. She climbed up the knoll and hung onto the grass, resting for a moment, but not too long. He was here, she was sure of it, they had been together until the great storm and he was the strongest swimmer in all of the north, why should she worry, you do not worry about a seal when it is in the sea?

As she lay on the grass she could hear talking far off, far enough so you could not make out the words or the language but it was definitely a human sound. Surveying by the light of the full moon she looked across a large plain toward a hill on the far side. On top of the hill was a dead tree, killed by a bolt from the wrath of Thor. Her eyes were good and she could see something in the tree, perhaps a man?

Freyja stood up to get a better look and saw by the size and shape of the man it could well be Gunnar. Her heart was squeezed with pain and for a second she let herself think her man was dead. But she shook off the dark thoughts, intent on rescuing him. She was an accomplished runner and she gauged that the tree was only a roman mile away, a distance she could run easily in six minutes. She ran down the knoll and started to get up to her running pace as she entered the plain.

'Do not worry my love, I am here to rescue you, soon we will be together.' She focused on the run but her heart betrayed her a little and small tears pricked at her eyes.

She tried to focus on each footfall, as the ground was uneven and she feared pot holes, but Freyja wanted to maintain a steady pace so that she could cross the plain and help her man. It was going well and she was half way across when she heard a shout to her left. She glanced toward the sound and saw a crowd of over a hundred warriors running toward her. A glance to the right and she saw a similar number, although at the front of the crowd on her right was the disgusting Litta. Both groups were some way off but they were slightly ahead and running fast to cut her off. She needed time when she reached Gunnar to cut him down and treat him. She moved up a level and ran flat out, knowing from experience she could maintain this for almost half a mile. Eventually the change in speed paid off and she was slightly ahead of her pursuers.

Freyja managed to put a little distance between her and the horde following; they had joined up now and Litta was still maintaining a pace at the front. The incline ahead was approaching fast and she could see it was Gunnar on the tree. He had been pinned to the branches with big iron nails and he was in obvious pain, but he was alive. She focused on the man she loved and who loved her. He was saying something. Freyja strained to hear the words but the wind was snatching the sound from her ears, although eventually she understood.

"Leave me Freyja, run for your life."

He cannot have said that, she would never leave him to die; she loved him so much her heart ached if she imagined life without him. She pushed on up the incline but it was wet and muddy and she slipped and slid down. She slid a few feet to the bottom of the small slope and tried to scramble back up.

Hands grabbed her from behind, many hands; they pulled her down and held all her limbs. She was pinned to the muddy floor and many faceless men held her arms and her legs tightly. She could not move or even struggle to any effect. She looked between her legs and saw him standing there, Litta. She could see he was aroused and he was smiling.

'No, not now, not when Gunnar and I are so close.'

Litta pulled a short sword from its scabbard and knelt between her legs. He lifted it above his head and brought it down repeatedly into her torso. She looked down at her body and saw her stomach and chest shredded and bloody. She felt her life force draining away and knew now that she would never hold Gunnar again. The last thing she remembered was Litta laughing loud with gratification.

Then she woke up.

*

Aldred was now very used to freedom; he had made it as far as Wincanceaster and had even delighted at the hard bed of the countryside. In fact, he had been bunking down next to Rand who found his happy bearing slightly annoying. He had travelled with Thorod's Mercian's as far as the capital of England, as Thorod was to report to the King, with Godwin and the other high born Saxons.

Aldred was enjoying himself in Wincanceaster; he was now sitting with Rand and drinking some good Saxon beer while they waited for their lords to finish their audience with their prince. Together they had been enjoying their time in the capital and had had some fun with the local ladies who were happy for a good night as long as they left with some silver. Rand was a pragmatic man, a Christian, but in a relaxed way. Although it had been over a year some of Aldred's old colleagues were offended when they found out he had been living as a monk among the savages of Kernow. They were very devout men and had made some noises about a sufficient penance to atone for his sins. Aldred was not too sure what would come of it but he hoped the penance would not be too boring, as most things Christian are.

*

Aethelred sat quietly listening to Godwin recounting the battle at Liddyford, only interrupting if he needed more detail. When Godwin finished the King held his hand up for silence.

"So it seems we were lucky to have a spy in the camp of old Cadoc, and lucky too that Ealdorman Thorod listened to him. So please tell me what happened to the young pretender, Tristan?"

Thorod stood and spoke, "I had some men follow him, lord King but it seems he left in a boat with his captain. We threatened some of the locals and found out he headed for Ireland."

"Ah, another place of savages, he should be happy there. Ealdorman Thorod, what of this Aldred, is it true he lived as a monk for two years trying to convert the savages to Christ's teaching?"

"Well, my lord, it is true he was dressed as a monk but there is little detail about him being pious, although he was a prisoner all this time. But I do remember him having good eyes and a good memory, so when he informed me of the forces within Kernow I took note."

"I am not very happy about him dressing as a holy man, but he seems to have paid us back for his sin."

"That is true lord King, but I have many unhappy men who are not so forgiving. In fact I was hoping one of my peers may be able to use a good soldier?"

"I need observant men," Ealdorman Brihtnoth had spoken, and "that is if he does not mind fighting the devil's horde regularly."

"Thank you Brihtnoth, who shall I tell him to report to?"

"Send him over to the camp of Essex and get him to report to Wulfgar."

*

Aldred was being shaken and somebody was shouting at him, "Get up you old drunk."

He tried opening his eyes but they felt sticky and his tongue had grown to twice the size. Rand shoved him again, "hurry and wake, friend, I have been told you are going to join the Essex militia."

Aldred thought that maybe he was dreaming, but there is no way he could dream through this pounding headache. He managed to mumble to Rand, "What?"

"Come on, hurry, the Essex militia will be leaving soon and they are expecting you, you have to report to Wulfgar in their camp."

Aldred panicked a little but calmed down when he found his bag of silver still around his neck. Thorod and Godwin had been thankful to him and rewarded him with too much coin, although he did not complain as he had nothing to his name. Luckily the money helped him buy some good, hard-wearing clothes and a new sword. He collected his few possessions, said his goodbyes to Rand and left through the town gate to join his new command.

*

"You don't look much like a fighter, though I have learned to never judge by looks alone," Wulfgar handed a spare shield to Aldred while he spoke, "if you want to get on in the Essex militia fight hard and drink well, is that a new sword?" Aldred handed over his sword for inspection, "yes, just had it made in the capital."

"Not bad considering they have no Essex blacksmiths here, won't be long before it sees work. I have been told you are a senior soldier, so I will put you in charge of a small troop. Oh and Aldred, don't balls up under me."

*

Berg was almost enjoying his time in Dyflin; he had found a widow who he now shared a home with. Helga had lost her man to an infliction of the heart and was glad of the company of a man, a father for her son and the silver Berg earned. She was a practical woman, good with the home and able to serve up delicious fare at the end of the day. But what made Berg very happy was that she had an appetite for sex that he sometimes thought he could not keep up with. He smiled to himself while thinking of the nights with Helga. If he was to complain, and it was not generally in his nature to do so, he would gripe about Ketil.

Ketil had decided that Berg was his friend and Berg felt a little responsible for the younger man. However, he did not want to see so much of him and Helga said that he gave her the creeps. Berg could not really say what it was that he did not like about Ketil, perhaps it was that Ketil had said he needed to find a woman but showed no interest in even the prettiest girls. Or maybe it was his ability to be coarse and vulgar in front of Helga, something that Berg never did. But what seemed to grate on Berg the most was that occasionally Ketil would talk fondly of Alfvine and Ulf while criticising Jarl Olaf, a man that Berg very much respected.

Ketil was returning to his side after going for a piss. "Berg old friend, we should tour the sheep pens and make sure all the thralls are safely tucked up inside." The two men walked around the cells and spoke with the men on the gates, picking up gossip and exchanging stories. Half way round they came across a man sitting in the dirt openly crying, wracked with emotion and not caring who saw him. Berg bent down to talk to the stranger.

"Friend, is there anything we can do for you?"

The stranger looked up at Berg, his eyes red and his nose running into his beard.

"There is nothing anyone can do, I have lost my wife and I have nothing to live for, all I want is to join her at the side of Jesus our saviour."

"What is your name, friend?"

"I am Baldr, until recently I was a captain under King Ivar, but I wish only God's wrath on that evil man."

"What has he done to you?"

"He has killed my wife and all the good Christians in Waterford; I have nothing to live for, no wife to love and no ring giver."

"Have you anywhere to stay?"

"I have lost everything."

"We can use a good soldier here in Dyflin, if you can hold a sword and show loyalty to your Jarl."

An idea struck Baldr then, deep in the dark recesses of his mind. He could exact revenge on Ivar and all the plans of Waterford.

"Could I speak with your Jarl, I have some important news for him."

At this Berg helped the man up and started to take him back to the soldier's quarters.

"Ketil, you will have to tour without me, I will take Baldr back and get him something to eat and hopefully soothe his soul."

*

Ketil had made a few acquaintances with the men who guarded the cells of the thralls. The many structures were built and owned by the kingdom of Dyflin and then rented out by the slavers who needed somewhere to store their goods before the weekly market. The huts were well built with strong wooden posts, driven deep into the ground, and a new wattle & daub wall finished with a wooden shingle roof, held in with heavy iron nails, unlike the straw roofs of the houses in town. He approached the two men standing outside the nearest barracks.

"Well met Bjarni, Litta."

"Ah, it is our friendly guard of Dyflin. How are you, Ketil?"

"A little tired and tense, I was wondering if I could have a chat to Litta?"

"Ok, but don't be long as it is his job to stand guard, not mine."

"Come on Ketil, let's go inside." Litta did not question Ketil as he had been doing business with the guard for a few days now and knew what he wanted.

"So Ketil, you filthy bastard, what do you want today and have you brought enough silver for your little friend?"

"The same one as yesterday, he is just what I need."

"I am sorry I cannot do that. Bjarni thinks you are paying just to feel up the thralls, if he knew you were poking them I would be in trouble and we would both lose. At the moment I give him half of what he thinks you give me. I am only telling you because I know you are a dirty aersling and you cannot stay away. If you want to stick your orm in the same one it will have to be another as that poor bastard will have a ruined arsehole if you had your way."

Ketil did not like Litta and was no fan of his straight talking. He did not like to be spoken of in that way, although it seemed Litta did not care either way what his sexual preferences were. He guessed Litta's were a lot worse.

"So tell me what you fancy Ketil, and I will choose you the best hole you will have today, how about a young boy?"

"Litta you are a disgusting man, what do you think I am? I do not want children, just let me choose one and I will be on my way."

"Well make the most of it, arse lover, as the market is nearly upon us and they will be all gone soon."

"Litta, this is Dyflin, there will always be thralls."

*

Everything happens for a reason and Olaf smiled to himself at how obvious things looked. He had not yet been able to settle the problem about which god to worship and yet another thing was nudging him toward following Jesus. He had been brought one of the slavers from Waterford and the man was completely broken. He told Olaf about the plans of King Ivar to spring a surprise invasion on Dyflin. Jarl Olaf would get prepared for the attack and would ensure a solid defence was in place. Initially he was thinking of killing the informer, Baldr, but the man pleaded with him to fight and die defending Dyflin. Jarl Olaf promised him he could fight with Dyflin if he could explain Christian worship to him.

*

Njal was tired of riding. He did not like to do it too much as he was sure his body was not built to sit on the tough ponies of Iceland. He was returning home again after a day of negotiating with his neighbours. Most of them were allies and friends of Gunnar so he knew he could count on their support at the Althing. He was pleased to find that even the men who did not know Gunnar well were appalled at the quick and devious job done by Bjorn Bjornsson, and no doubt his evil wife Hild Yxa.

Iceland was a special place; it was ruled by the law of the people and paid no homage to any king, not Norse or Dane. Every year they held the Althing and discussed the law of the land, hopefully resolving any disputes among neighbours and enemies. The Althing relied on a collection of wise and learned lawyers to remember the law and advise in all logged disputes.

Njal was said to be the greatest of all the lawyers of Iceland and did not just rely on his reputation, but had a fine memory and an appetite for hard work.

However, riding ponies long distances were not his idea of enjoyable work, his bones seemed to rattle as the pony walked across the stony ground. He promised himself a bath in one of the hot springs to soothe his aching body. He would stop visiting allies for a few days and spend time relaxing and thinking about his case. He was nearly home now and looked forward to sitting in his chair and drinking good ale.

*

Erik was a simple and loyal man, somebody that put his friends and family above everything. He was a capable fighter and skilled in hunting. However, he was not the greatest thinker and would never be a leader of men, he was a good second in command. If he suspected foul play, or that one of his friends did not show the same loyalty back to him, he would drop them and never call them a friend again.

He had needed the time away to think and be sure of his conclusion, for he wanted to give Harald the benefit of the doubt. About five years ago he had heard Greta, Harald's wife, crying in the woods. He had gone to comfort her and, at the time, he had come away confused. Again he tried to remember her words;

"Dear Erik, you should not be angry with Gunnar, for Gunnar loved Gull and he would only defend him, never causing him harm."

"But Greta how can you defend the man who killed your brother in law, we caught him kneeling next to the body, soaked in Gull's blood?"

"Erik, I spent a lot of time speaking with Gull and he trusted Gunnar as much as he trusted you. And dear, loyal Erik, I believe I knew Gull best of all."

When she had mentioned Gull's name she had sobbed, and the emotion had wracked her body. If this had been an isolated instance then maybe he would have let it lie but six months after that, he had visited Harald's hall in the late evening and had heard shouting as he approached. He still felt a little guilty to this day, for instead of entering the hall or turning and leaving he waited outside and listened for a moment. He heard Greta crying some more and also heard Harald ranting at his wife.

"My own brother, you filthy whore; how many times, you gris? I know of the time I caught you but I want every detail."

Erik had felt ashamed and had stolen away hoping he was not heard. At the time he had thought Harald was talking about Gustav, but the next day he came upon Harald with Gustav and the older brother had his arm around Gutsav's shoulders telling him how good a brother he was.

Both instances were six months apart and Erik did not put them together until over two years later, when Harald told him that he was glad that Gull was dead as he could even betray his own brother. Erik had been angry with Harald and had told him what he thought of his remarks, before storming off. Then the penny dropped.

Gull was very popular with the ladies. He was good looking and a fit young man with plenty of charm. All the women liked him and Gull liked the ladies; Erik would fail to keep up with which one he was tupping. Gull was Erik's closest friend so he had eventually got used to Gull's need for chasing women and escaping their husbands. Although he remembered telling Gull that he did not approve when Erik found out he had been tupping the wife of a local Jarl. After that Gull would not confide in him and he had preferred it that way.

The night he died he had been arguing with Gunnar, and Erik recalled they were discussing a woman. Erik assumed it was somebody that Gunnar knew and felt, at the time, it was up to Gull, the woman and her husband to resolve.

So Erik linked all these together and strongly suspected that Gull had been tupping Greta and Harald had found out, and in a rage Harald had killed his brother. Perhaps luck had shone on Harald as he had had a drunken Gunnar stumble in to take the blame. Over the last two years Erik was sure that this was closer to events than the version that presented itself on that terrible day five years ago. Now he had all this information laid out in front of him, it sat more comfortably with his gut feeling, that Gunnar would not kill a friend.

He decided to go out on his own, trading skins and travelling, hoping to find Gunnar's trail and tell him what he now knew.

Erik was frustrated, he was honour bound to rescue Gunnar but it was an impossible job. The huts they held the thralls in were very secure and guarded day and night by the slave ship owners. The kingdom of Dyflin made a healthy profit from the slave market and they would not look kindly on anyone trying to disrupt their core business. So he was left with one option, to buy Gunnar at the market. It should not be too difficult for Erik as he had a large collection of coin with a further horde buried in his secret place.

The slaves were generally sold collectively at the market but a wealthy man could get in early and have first pick, although this meant paying a higher price. Erik knew he had to do this as he had failed Gunnar in the past, even though he was used by the devious Harald. Erik approached the small guard at the place Gunnar was held.

"Well met friend."

"I am not even your friend in Hel, arsehole."

"That is not the way to make yourself some extra silver." Erik was trying to remain calm but he instinctively wanted to punch the smaller man in the face. He was ugly and rude, and that was putting aside his job was selling thralls.

"How much, and what do you want? Most come here to poke young boys or girls but you look like you would like to do a man in the arse."

"You disgusting little ugly orm, respect the warrior in front of you or I will run you through and be gone. No one will know who killed the ugly aersling standing here and no doubt many would rejoice in your death."

Litta could see he had gone too far and the stocky warrior with crazy hair had taken out his sword so fast Litta was not sure it was ever in the scabbard. Then he noticed the man had arms full of war rings and would look better suited on the battle field. But it was not in Litta's nature to be conciliatory and he stared the man in the eye and grunted to acknowledge he was at a disadvantage. Erik spoke some more.

"Now little ljot, you may be thinking of pulling out your baby sword but I warn you, your guts will be opened up before your hand touches your pommel."

"I am not going to reach for my sword, now if you want to spend your silver, do it or leave."

Erik was not sure if the little man was brave, stupid or just stubborn but it surprised him that he had not humbled him. He decided this was not helping his old friend Gunnar and decided to free his friend.

"You are a piece of skit, little man, but let us do business so I can be on my way. I want to buy a thrall now and I know he is in here, so I will point him out and we will then discuss the price."

"I can't do that, and do not look so angry. I am on this guard duty as I am still being punished by Ivar's captain and only he can sell a slave before the official market. Come back here before breakfast and speak with Bjarni and you will get your choice of thrall. But if you want to tup one of the women I can be paid to look the other way for ten minutes."

"Tempting though that is, I do not want to be anywhere your disgusting orm has been. I will be back here after sunrise and make sure you are not pissing on me as I have a long memory."

Chapter 14

Once were the gods together met,
And the goddesses came and council held
And the far famed ones the truth would find
Why baleful dreams to Baldr had come
Then Grimnir rose, the enchanter old
And the saddle he laid on Sleipnir's back

Ivar pulled out of Kanin and rolled over on his back, spent. She moved over next to him and held him tight, like lovers do. Sometimes he would forget that she was a slave, he had had many pretty thralls and none of them were anything like Kanin. She knew how to keep a man interested and wanted to try different things in his bed, and she liked to drink too. For a fleeting moment Ivar wondered if he was in love and then laughed out loud at his weakness.

"We need not love, eh Kanin, we tup, we drink and we tup some more. But you are like a drug to me woman, I want you again but it will have to wait as Tyr is expecting my orders."

Kanin looked him in the eye and he knew she was disappointed there would be no more loving this hour.

"Woman, do not look at me like that, your kut is hungry for orm, but we have a kingdom to conquer and soon, my little Kanin, you will be the lover of the High King of Ireland. Tyr, come in here."

King Ivar of Waterford was a strong and confident man, bullish and without any shame. He stood naked waiting for his captain, too excited about his plans to get dressed.

"My lord King, the troops are ready and waiting your orders."

"Good man, I cannot wait until the early morning. I am looking forward to crushing Dyflin quickly and kicking that fool, Jarn into the Irish Sea."

"We are ready to start riding toward Dyflin; all we need is our King."

"Do not scold me Tyr, I was with my woman and the men understand how important that is. In fact I will be bringing her with me to battle as I wish to have her as King of Dyflin, too. Now Tyr we will have a drink together as I know you cannot turn down good Danish ale."

Tyr laughed as his King was a very likeable man and a generous ring giver. His men would say that Ivar hated gold so much, as he gave it away so often. Also Ivar loved fighting and killing, he was a formidable foe to be against and the men loved having him on their side and leading them into battle. His loyal friends would say that Ivar had created Valholl in the realm of men. They never went too long without a fight, a drink, or a woman, and word spread so that disenchanted men would flock to his side just for the chance to experience Valholl on earth.

Ivar felt so confident he was going to take his son Sihtric with him. He had a large force ready to smash the defences of Dyflin, and he had a small band of men in the town guarding the few slaves they had returned but ready to attack the local guards and make his job easier. Yes, thought Ivar, he could rely on Baldr to get the men together and cause havoc in the town.

*

Baldr was still in a dark place but now he had a purpose, a chance to gain revenge for his wife and all the innocent Christians in Waterford. He sat in an empty hut, surrounded by stacked spears and spare shields. Ivar may think he is clever but Baldr had informed Jarl Olaf of the plot against Dyflin by their larger neighbour. He thought about his lost loyalty to Ivar and his friendship with Tyr. He thought how he would kill them both and then he hoped he would be killed too, for it was his own fault that Astrid had died.

She had pleaded with him to leave Waterford and find a better life for nearly a year. But he, the foolish Baldr, had insisted they needed more money to set up somewhere new. Why did he not listen to the woman he loved, for now he will never see her beautiful pale blue eyes again, and never feel her soft skin against his. The pain was almost too much to bear, but he had stopped crying now, his eyes were raw and dry. He could not stop the pain in his chest, he supposed his heart was broken and it would kill him eventually. He spoke out now, not sure if it was to his god or his broken heart he addressed his statement, "Let me live long enough to kill the tyrant then you can let me be with my wife for eternity."

143

Erik crossed to the huts holding the thralls, including Gunnar. A few men were milling around tolerating the boring job of guarding their cargo. He noticed one man seemed to be directing things and approached him.

"Well met, are you Bjarni, leader of these men?"

"I am, Litta told me to expect an early shopper; did he explain there is a premium price to buying early and avoiding the competition of the auction?"

"How much is the price, for I cannot magic up silver?"

"First you need to tell me the thrall you want to buy and then we will decide on the price, in gold."

Erik wanted to punch the fat bastard in his smug face, but he knew that he owed a debt to Gunnar and this would be a way to repay his old friend.

"Let's get it over with, I am a busy man."

"Patience friend, let me see your bag of coin first, so I know that you can afford to pay and will not be wasting my time."

Erik was fuming. This fat groda was insulting him and he would try and get revenge on the arsehole in front of him. But before he could unhook his money bag he heard a commotion behind him. A troop of the Dyflin guard was marching their way, at the head of them was Jarl Olaf, husband of Queen Gyda. The soldiers stopped in front of Bjarni the bastard and Jarl Olaf spoke,

"Are you King Ivar of Waterford's men and is this his cargo of thralls?"

Bjarni forgot Erik for the moment, wondering why Olaf had brought such a strong show of force.

"I am Bjarni, the captain of King Ivar's slave ship," before he could say any more Olaf spoke to the man next to him.

"Berg, arrest all these men and confiscate the cargo they have brought here."

There were almost fifty men in the Dyflin troop and Bjarni had about ten men at his disposal. He tried protesting. "Jarl Olaf we are allies, you cannot arrest me it will cause great anger to the King of Waterford."

"Shut up you disgusting fat pig, either you think I am stupid or Ivar thinks you have a loose tongue. I believe you know what is going on and so do your soldiers. Let me ask you a question and do not lie to me. Why have you two fully armed longships, one hundred and twenty men to round up thirty thralls?"

"Jarl Olaf, we had bad luck and did not find enough, we were hoping for more...."

Olaf hacked his sword across Bjarni's fat stomach, causing the slave captains jaw to hang open in shock. Bjarni's belly opened up like a cutting a whale on the beach, the skin was holding back a lot of fat and guts which slowly oozed out, before spilling out in a waterfall of gore. He fell to his knees and proceeded to try and scoop his innards up from the dusty ground.

Olaf looked away from the dying man, as there was a problem with one of the men they were arresting.

"Berg, do I have to come over and shut him up too."

"Jarl Olaf, I am not one of these men, I have no allegiance to Ivar or Waterford." Erik was trying to remain cool but he knew that if he could not talk his way out he would die with the rest of Ivar's men.

"Where are you from, and please note how I do not like to be lied to." Olaf had a hard look on his face, the look of a man prepared to kill.

"I am a Dane, from Scania, I sell skins here at the market and my friend has been held as a slave by these arseholes. If you speak to him he can vouch that I am no slaver."

"What is your name?"

"Erik Ericsson of Lund."

"Well Erik, Berg will get the first thrall he finds and they can say whether you are with Waterford or Dyflin."

Berg looked after his sword well; it was freshly sharpened and made quick work of the thick rope holding the large hut closed. He entered the place crowded with over a dozen male slaves. The nearest was a black bearded man who he hauled to his feet.

"You will do friend," Berg turned the confused man toward the doorway when a voice from the back of the hut spoke up.

"You will not get much out of him; I think these people are Picts as nobody can understand a word they say."

Berg peered into the dim recess of the cell but was not sure who spoke, "So I suppose I have to take the only man who speaks Norse from here? Do not try anything, thrall, for I am a Jomsviking and very skilled with my sword or without."

145

"I am trussed up like a pig ready for the fire, I have not eaten for four days and had little water, I would be thankful for a few moments outside this dark cell."

Berg pushed the Pict-man back down to the ground and moved to the back of the cell. Among the rest of the thralls was a great bear of a man sitting on the floor with his arms bound behind his back. Berg grabbed the big blonde Dane under the arm and helped him get to his feet. He got behind him and held onto his binding, pushing him toward the doorway. As he did something hit the floor and the slave groaned.

"Hold on thrall, what have you been hiding?"

Berg saw something strange on the floor in the gloom. He picked up a small green lady with six arms, her legs crossed over. Somebody had added a loop of metal and tied a crude leather lace on to it, creating a necklace.

"Give that back, it is all I have left."

"You are a thrall, you can own nothing."

*

I had been in the cell for days; it had become our bed and toilet, how glad I felt to be leaving this small part of Loki's realm. I wanted to get outside but I felt cautious as I was not sure what was going on, but I had heard the filthy slavers being arrested by the guard of Dyflin.

The sunlight blinded me after days in the dark, like the Icelandic sun in midwinter, so I had to wait a few moments for my eyes to adjust. Although having lost Freyja's necklace I did not care if the sun blinded me or I was struck down, all hope was lost. As the scene before me became more clear I recognised the scruffy hair of an old friend and recent foe.

"Jarl Olaf, the thrall was hiding this on him."

Berg handed over the small figure and Olaf looked shocked.

"Slave, look at me, I am Jarl Olaf, husband of Queen Gyda and guardian of Dyflin. Where did you get this figure? Speak true slave, it may help you."

"I bought it in the market of Byzantium, although the journey there is a long story to tell."

"A man of the north at the heart of the empire, you should not be a thrall, now tell me who these men are that I am holding."

I had not worried about the other men as I could not stop looking at Erik, he was being held with a sword at his throat along with some of the slavers, although I could not see Baldr or Litta, Bjarni lay still on the floor bathing in his own blood.

"Jarl Olaf, may I ask one of the men here a question before I answer your question?"

"Be quick as we have little time. Berg cut his bonds and return his necklace."

"Erik, do you mean me harm?"

"No Gunnar, I know you are innocent, but you need to reveal to Jarl Olaf the slavers here."

I turned to the leader of the troops and addressed him directly, "Erik with the bad hair is not a slaver, and he is in fact here to release me. I am a merchant from Iceland and I was caught by these pirates while trying to sail to Faeroe, and my wife is among their female thralls."

Olaf spoke to Berg now, "Berg release this poor merchant and his friend Erik, leave a guard here to protect the new cargo of Dyflin, and kill these pirates."

My arms were cut free and Erik came over and gave me a big bear hug, repeating how sorry he was he doubted me back in Scania. I had a tear in my eye as I loved Erik like a brother and had missed him terribly. I pulled out of his embrace and spoke to him as a friend again, "Erik, we will have to catch up later, my dear wife is held among the female thralls, she needs to be released and taste freedom again."

*

He had been sitting in the shade eating some smoked fish and fresh bread whilst watching the work being done by his colleagues. At first he felt pleased with himself that Bjarni was doing all the work now that Baldr had disappeared. He thought he would finish his breakfast, drink his ale and then reluctantly go and help Bjarni get the slaves ready for the market. Then, what seemed like the whole Dyflin guard turned up and Bjarni was on the ground lying next to his guts, dying. Shortly afterward they released the big bear and killed the rest of his colleagues. Litta was sitting among some sacks in the shade and was afraid to move in case they saw him and cut his throat too. He knew they would be moving on to the rest of the slavers now, which meant he should get to the quay and hope there were still enough men left to get one of the longships out to sea and down the coast to Waterford and warn Ivar. He took a circular route to the quay, being an expert on the layout of the city. Litta realised with Bjarni dead and Baldr gone that he would now be

147

captain of the slave ship. Immediately he knew what a great advantage this would be for him. He would be able to acquire greater wealth and have his pick of the slaves, with no one to tell him what to do. He did not mourn for his old friend or worry about the danger; he could only see the advantage to be gained. Today was going to be a good day for Litta.

*

Olaf had killed the rest of Ivar's men and recovered the thralls for King Jarn. He had made free the Icelandic man's wife and was now escorting them both back to the king's residence, along with Erik of Scania. He thought the look on Berg's face showed that he did not approve of releasing any slaves, but Olaf knew what it was like to be a free man subjected to slavery and he saw some of himself in Gunnar. The man's wife was quite distressed and he could only guess at what trauma she had had to deal with. He had witnessed his own mother being abused and it haunted him still. His dear mother must have been around the same age as this woman when they were enslaved. Olaf stopped the march across to the town and addressed the husband and wife from Iceland.

"You must have suffered among those terrible men; I will do my best to return you home."

Gunnar gave the small jade figure to Freyja and she kissed her husband again. Olaf saw the exchange and spoke up.

"This strange statue, I did not think there was another one in the north."

"Have you seen another one, and if so can I see it?"

"My wife will show you, but you must tell me more of your adventures, Gunnar, when we have more time."

It was a long story how I ended up with the many armed creature and I promised to tell Olaf the story when we had time and some ale.

We followed Jarl Olaf in a dream state; I could not believe that Freyja and I had managed to escape slavery, and part of me felt for the poor Picts still encased in the cells near the market. Jarl Olaf came across as quite a stern man but he had explained the kingdom was under threat and he needed good fighting men to help the cause. He did not ask out right but it was an obvious hint so Erik and I offered our services to Dyflin, as one favour deserves repayment. I had not told Freyja yet as she was still very shaken by the ordeal on the slave ship. I thought about Litta and I was sure he was still alive as I had not seen his disgusting corpse litter the streets. If he had touched Freyja the way he abused the other women I would have to kill him. It makes my blood boil to think of him coming near my wife and I intended to exact my revenge as soon as I can find him.

We entered the kings' compound and Olaf stopped us to explain his thoughts.

"Dear Freyja I wish to take you to my wife so that she can help you clean up and get you something to wear. Gunnar and Erik, wait for me here, as you will need to be supplied with armour and weapons."

"Jarl Olaf, what do you mean, why will my husband need a weapon?"

"I am sorry Freyja, wife of Gunnar, but Dyflin is going to be attacked by Waterford and we need every able man to defend the kingdom. I helped Erik and Gunnar this morning, and this will be a chance to repay me."

"I am sorry my love, I was so happy to see you free I forgot we had promised to support Jarl Olaf in his time of need."

Freyja looked at me and conveyed everything in a look, the way only a wife can communicate with her husband. Her face said that she did not like my decision and that she was annoyed that I had not told her what was happening, it also told me to stay alive and be there for her after the battle.

"I will apologise again, but I need to get you to my wife, Queen Gyda, who will ensure that you are fed, well dressed and safe."

My beautiful wife left then and we were left with Berg and another man, called Ketil, to get fitted with our war gear.

Ketil came over to me and spoke. "Do you trust our Jarl to keep his hands off your wife big man?"

I grabbed the fool by the throat and roared in his face, "Do not talk about my wife like that, worm skit."

Berg put his hand on my forearm, "Gunnar, please put him down, Ketil is a dumb idiot with no control over his stupid mouth." I released the fool and tried to calm myself, I felt a little light headed from the strain and lack of sustenance. "Berg, is there any food or drink around here?"

Erik fumbled in his bag and produced some bread and a small flask of ale, "I am sorry Gunnar, I should have produced this earlier, please eat." As I started to eat Erik finally had a chance to talk.

"Gunnar, when we are alone I will tell you of what has happened but I know that you are innocent of the charge laid upon you in Scania. I am so glad I have found you and I believe that Gustav will be happy when I tell him of what I know."

I swallowed the last of the bread and washed it down with the warm ale, "but what about Harald, will he be pleased to see me?"

"Do not worry about him Gunnar, I will deal with Harald."

*

Freyja stood outside the Queen's hall waiting to be called in; her head was spinning with all that she had gone through and she felt weak from her lack of food. She was going to be presented to a Queen and she was still wearing the clothes she had left Iceland in over a week ago. She was desperate for a drink followed quickly by some bread and meat. There was a guard standing at the door of the hall who she now spoke to, "please, I have not eaten for days and I am desperate for a drink, can you help?" She felt herself swaying as she spoke and her thighs seemed to empty of strength. Blackness filled her vision and she was out cold before she hit the ground.

Freyja woke lying on a bed made comfortable with deer skin, there was a woman speaking to her in a strange language.

"I don't understand, please can you speak Norse?"

"I am sorry Freyja, I am Helga and you are in the Queen of Dyflin's hall, I am sorry but you passed out."

"Can I have something to drink, and then maybe some food?"

"Of course, I have some fresh water here."

Behind Helga were a couple who looked good together, both of them tall and handsome. She recognised Jarl Olaf who addressed her, "Freyja, I am sorry for what you have been through, rest here until you have strength enough and then my wife Queen Gyda will make sure you have fresh clothes, and as soon as our little trouble is over you will be reunited with your husband."

Freyja tried to take a draft of water but it hurt her mouth, so she proceeded to sip the water while Helga prepared some food for her. It was a feast for somebody so hungry, there was pork, herring, hard cheese, bread and earth berries.

*

150

Wood quay was busy and there were many men milling around, helping ships unload or getting them ready to leave. Litta had rounded up eight of Ivar's men and decided that they would be enough to man one of the longships. Lacking a leader they all looked to Litta to get them away safely. He could only assume the rest were executed or arrested. He took the rudder as the eight oarsmen worked the longship away from the quay and turned south in the direction of Waterford. Litta hoped the men of the little kingdom were too busy on defence to notice a poorly manned ship sailing toward their enemy, for they must now know Ivar's plan. He kept looking back at the quay worrying that a fast ship would be sent to cut them down, but none came. When the coast of Dyflin was out of sight he began to relax and think of the fallen. They were all fools and he was glad to know that Baldr was dead, the self-righteous bastard. None of them were as resourceful as Litta; he was a survivor and could not be touched.

*

Sitting in the small hall I felt shocked and angry at what Erik had told me, but it made sense. Killing Gull was as bad as me killing my own brothers. The anger came as I realised that Harald had set me up. I was not sure how much Gustav had known but he most likely just believed the facts in front of him, a dead brother and the man he was fighting with the night before covered in his blood. I realised I would have to make sure Erik stayed alive so that he could help clear my name.

"Gunnar, we have company," Erik pointed at the approaching men, Olaf and one of the slavers.

"So Gunnar, have you eaten enough yet?"

"Yes, thank you Jarl Olaf, but before you tell me how my wife is, why have you let this slaver of Waterford live?"

"This is Baldr, a Christian man, who revealed the plot hatched by Ivar of Waterford."

I looked at Baldr and he looked a broken man, you would have thought he was a thrall rather than the slaver that caught them. I felt no sympathy for him, just hatred toward his lifestyle.

"Jarl Olaf, I am happy to repay you but I do not want to fight alongside this aersling." But before Olaf could reply to me I heard a familiar voice from the doorway.

"Gunnar, my love, this is the man that saved me from rape by the ugly pirate, Litta."

151

"What?" I was shocked as some of my worst fears were being suggested by Freyja, as she entered the hall with Helga.

"It is true Big Bear, and I wish I had killed that revolting skit when I had the chance, but at least he is dead now, as I will be soon."

Olaf stepped forward and addressed Erik and I, "Baldr has requested to be at the front of the fighting. Ivar murdered all the Christians in his kingdom, including Baldr's wife, and now he wants revenge against the devil king before joining his wife in heaven."

I was a little stunned as I did not want to fight alongside this man, but he had stopped my wife being abused by that horrible little man.

"Jarl Olaf, do you need my husband to fight? He is weak from the treatment we suffered and I do not want to lose him so soon after our new freedom."

"Wife, I will fight for Jarl Olaf, as Dyflin will need all the men they can muster to repel the enemy. I will no longer owe a debt to anyone and we can return home and claim back our land. Do not worry, my love, I will not be cut down as I have much experience in battle."

Dear Freyja looked angry and upset with me, she knew I could be stubborn and to back down in front of Erik and Olaf would have made me look like only half a man.

"My dear wife, do not despair, I have to stay close to Erik so that he does not get himself killed and can clear my name."

"Gunnar, you are an arsehole, I do not need anyone's helps to stay alive in a fight."

I slapped my old friend on the back and insisted we had a little practise outside to see how slow he was.

Helga turned to Freyja, "Men are insensitive beasts that do not know how hard it is to wait around hoping they do not get killed."

Before Freyja could reply Olaf spoke, "But your husband speaks truth, we need every man to fight or we could all be staring at death soon."

Chapter 15

Here for Baldr the mead is brewed,
The shining drink and a shield lie over it;
But their hope is gone from the mighty gods.
Unwilling I spake, and now would be still.
Who shall vengeance win?
For the evil work, or bring to the flames
The slayer of Baldr

Kolskegg was pleased he had some news at last; he celebrated with Skarphedin, Grim and the men. They had heard that a slave ship had anchored a night in the same bay that Kolskegg had landed at, although he was told that an escort of two longships had beached in that very bay too. The helpful local said he remembered the slave ship as it had a faering tied to it, a strange vessel for a large boat. This sounded like Gunnar and Freyja had come across some very bad luck and it meant that they were most likely at or on the way to Dyflin. It was evening and they had all been at sea for too long, even though Kolskegg was keen to chase down his brother and release him from the slavers, they decided to leave at first light after a good meal and a decent sleep.

Skarphedin and Grim were very excited, as there definitely would be a confrontation and nobody cared much if you killed a slaver or two.

"Ok boys, I know you are ready to fight, but I mean to return you to Njal alive. You must promise me not to be too rash and let me take the lead in saving my brother and his wife."

The young men agreed, although in their current state Kolskegg believed they would agree to anything. He was very worried as he did not know how Gunnar would react as a slave, and he did not want to think what Freyja would have to tolerate. He held the iron hammer at his throat and sent a small prayer to Thor, to protect his brother and sister in law.

*

King Ivar of Waterford sat astride his horse in front of his house troops, mercenaries and the Waterford fyrd. With him was Kanin, his favourite slave and lover. He held out his horn of ale and drunk it down in one before his men. The men cheered and raised their weapons high, shouting praise for Waterford and their king.

Ivar addressed his men in Irish rather than his native Norse, "Brave men of Waterford, brothers, we are an hours march to the border of Dyflin, a kingdom that is rightfully part of Waterford. Let us deliver the kingdom from foreigners and restore it as an Irish kingdom." A great cheer went up among the crowd, a crowd ignoring or ignorant of Ivar's ancestry.

"Fight for Waterford and your king, but mostly fight for the prizes on offer, Dyflin gold, Danish ale and plenty of women to ride," another big cheer, men loved a ring giver and there was none greater than Ivar.

"We will attack from the south, around the black pool, and drive our enemy into the Liffey. Do not show mercy to these outlander, kill the men, rape the women and capture the slaves. Now drink ale with your king and ride to glory." At this Ivar took another horn of ale and joined his army in a toast to victory. When the toast was done they turned toward Dyflin intent on bringing bloody slaughter to the Viking kingdom.

*

Dyflin was built across the Poddle River, a tributary of the Liffey River. The Poddle flowed south from the Liffey into a lake named the Black Pool; the lake giving its name to Dyflin. The kingdom straddled the tributary with the main town being on the west side, with the slave enclosure and Thing field on the east.

Olaf was expecting an attack from the south; it was the direct route toward Waterford and as Ivar thought he had the element of surprise on his side, he would assume he could just march straight into the town. As Olaf was the most experienced warrior he organised the defence of the kingdom. The King would defend the main town with his house guards while Olaf and his men would defend the slave enclosure, leaving the kings younger brother, Ragnal, to defend the middle ground between the two. All able men were called to arms to defend the city. Dyflin did not have a fyrd as such, but everyone wanted to defend their livelihood and women folk.

154

Olaf was ready and waiting, sure that he had thought of everything. He just wished he had Mort and his trusted men with him, but they were guarding the lands over the sea from Saxon threats.

*

Odin says "Don't leave your weapons lying about behind your back in a field; you never know when you may need your spear." I missed my atgeir, my very best spear, but I had been well equipped by King Jarn's armoury. I had a shield, a spear, a bow with arrows and luckily for me, a sword. Erik had kindly given me a knife and some chain mail, which was a little short and tight but better than nothing.

I was not happy to be fighting with Baldr, but I did not remember him being cruel to the thralls, as Bjarni and Litta had been. Baldr was standing alone, a little in front of the other warriors; he was obviously impatient for the battle to start.

"Friend, it is good to be fighting with you again."

"I am glad Erik. It still hurts that Gull is no longer with us, but I am glad to have his death lifted off my back. When this is all over perhaps we can go hunting with Gustav?"

"If he can leave his wife alone for just a moment," Erik looked disgusted that a man would rather spend time with his wife than with his friends, but I understood Gustav better than many men.

Erik started talking to the man on his left and I already knew the man on my right. We would be in a shield wall together and we had had little practise together. But I had come to like Berg; he was a straight talking man, much like Erik but somebody of deeper thought. I was glad that he had been a Jomsviking as they were known to be accomplished fighters.

"Big man, when was the last time you were in a shield wall?"

"Well Berg, I think it has been at least six years but I will never forget the experience, and I am not looking forward to it."

"Nobody does Gunnar, but do not forget to watch out for me, as Erik will watch out for you."

"Rest easy Berg, I will kill anyone that even thinks about coming close to you."

Berg slapped me on the back and we both felt a little better.

People call me a great warrior back in Iceland, but that is fighting one man or at most maybe two. A shield wall is completely different, you are fighting as a team and if the wall

155

breaks you could all die that day. You have to fight hard and look out for each other, defend yourself and your colleagues with your shield, and watch for small jabs under and over your defence. Although the most important thing to do in the shield wall is to push and push as hard as you can for as long as you can. The best walls are those that have good warriors that practise a lot, as Erik and I were new we were in the second row. The job of the second row was to protect the man in front with your shield and to stab over their head if you saw an opportunity. But ultimately the shield wall is a wall of death and destruction, a wall of cutting and maiming, of much sorrow and little joy. I reached inside my vest and held onto my hammer amulet, praying to Thor and Odin that I would survive this day and hold my wife again.

*

Ivar rode along the Poddle Valley feeling exhilarated; he loved war but most of all he loved victory and everything was in place. The people of Dyflin would be hit by a double hammer blow, he would come along the west side of the valley and Tyr would bring the mercenaries along the east side. Tyr should easily annexe the slave enclosure and the Althing field. He knew there would be some resistance at the town but he saw his house guards attacking the troops of Jarn, Tyr crossing the tributary to assist and Baldr terrorising the rear of Dyflin's troops. He had thought of everything, and soon he would set up his court in Dyflin and rule a large chunk of Ireland. Kanin held on tight to him and he enjoyed the feeling of her warm body being so close, although he knew it would restrict him in battle but he would not really be needed to fight, as it would all be over soon. He contemplated the future and decided to leave his nagging wife back in Waterford and rule Dyflin with his slave Queen. At least the old queen had given him Sihtric, a fine young man.

"How do you feel son, facing your first battle?" Sihtric rode alongside his father.

"I am excited; I cannot wait to kill my first man."

"Well do not get too excited as you will be at the back, you are too precious to be thrown in at the beginning of the battle. When the fight has turned in our favour, you may join in alongside your father."

The prince looked unhappy but knew better than to argue against his King.

*

King Jarn had garrisoned the town well with his house guard, they all knew their job and were almost equally spread across the south west of the city to face an attack from land. He had sunk two old longships beside Wood Quay, to halt an invasion from the sea, and had placed his reserves at the Longport. It did not surprise him that Ivar was trying this, the man could not keep still and when things were calm you could rely on the King of Waterford to stir things up. He had sent word to King Brian Boru, the High King of Ireland and requested some support but he expected the High King to sit back and let them both weaken each other so there would be less of a threat to his realm. Still, Jarl Olaf had done well and he was a seasoned warrior that drilled the troops of Dyflin regularly, ensuring a fit and professional army. King Jarn hoped he would get the chance to face Ivar himself, and cut down the loud mouth bastard.

*

Jarl Olaf was thinking of all the possible outcomes of the day. He had thought of mostly everything, and thought he had done well to position Prince Ragnal in the middle ground, just in front of the Christian church of Dyflin, Saint Michael of the Black Pool. It would give the prince a chance to lead a troop of men while not exposing him to the main push from Waterford. He expected Ivar to attack the town first, and the well trained house guard were there. The east side of the river was the overflow of the town and the outlying districts such as the slave enclosure and the field. If Ivar was as experienced as he thought, he would send warriors this side, too. Prince Ragnal was a good fighter but young and a little inexperienced, so Jarl Olaf had given him the Jomsviking Ketil. This was a little worry as Olaf knew, deep in his heart, that he wanted to get Ketil out of his sight. The man was irritating and Olaf always felt the urge to slap him around the face. However he was a good warrior and that is what we needed today. It was early and dawn had already broken, with the morning mists starting to lift from the valley floor. Olaf could now see his men positioned further south to give warning of an approaching invasion force. The man with a claim on the Norse throne set his battle face and readied himself for war.

*

King Ivar and Tyr marched their men either side of the River Poddle, with the horsemen trotting alongside at the easy pace of an army on foot. His small cavalry to the front were ready with their bows in case of an unexpected force. One of the cavalry men ahead of Tyr had spotted something and rode forward a few lengths and stopped before unleashing an arrow along the valley. Tyr looked ahead and shouted over to his king, "Lord, we have taken down a look out, we must be close."

Ivar acknowledged Tyr and raised his arm and waved on his troops; this was the signal for the men on foot to start jogging so they could surprise King Jarn and butcher the inhabitants of the town.

*

Jarl Olaf had good vision and was looking at his watchmen down the valley when he heard a voice from behind, "Jarl Olaf, one of you watchmen is down." He was about to answer when he also noticed there was only one man and he was waving back at the defenders.

"Ready yourself, trust your comrades and concentrate. If any of you are drunk I will throw you out the front so that Ivar can practise on your corpses." He then turned toward Gunnar, "you have good eyesight, you saw before me, that is a rare thing, now be ready to defend your woman."

Southward, down the valley, they could see horsemen and foot warriors jogging into view, all carrying the long spear and a round shield. The front row of Olaf's men loosely locked shields together, ready for the dreaded battle.

"Where is my runner?" At this request a horseman rode over to Jarl Olaf and received his orders.

"Inform Prince Ragnal the men of Waterford are here and then ride and warn the king." The runner turned his horse and galloped back to warn their allies.

*

King Ivar kept to his side of the river and concentrated on entering the town while Tyr and his mercenaries made straight for the slave enclosures to the south of the town. Tyr was a little stunned to see a shield wall defending the thrall town, with a further shield wall to the left in front of the Christian church. He slowed his horse down and gestured for his troops to stop in sight of the towns defenders.

"Men, we are expected at this party after all, but we cannot let our king down. We will still win the day. First we will kill these fools and then we will go and help our king plunder." There was a slightly muted cheer, the mercenaries had expected to hit a town that did not expect them, and they expected to run through the area causing havoc.

However now they would be in a shield wall facing hardened warriors and they knew that some of them would die this day.

Ivar could see the shield walls across the river but decided to ride on knowing he had more men than King Jarn, supremely confident he could win even though he had lost the element of surprise. Ahead of him, instead of a docile town, was waiting a third shield wall. It was made up of Dyflin's best troops, the king's house guard. King Ivar halted his men and wondered for a moment how that pompous fool Jarn had guessed his intentions.

The house guards of Dyflin stood in a locked shield wall with spears pointing toward King Ivar and his men. The invaders would need to think fast if they wanted an easy victory today.

Ivar wanted to curse out loud at the betrayal of his surprise but he knew this would further demoralise his men. He suspected the ugly fool Litta had ballsed up somehow, he would find out later. Now he must rouse his army, he turned his horse toward his now growing shield wall.

"It looks as if our surprise has been ruined, but remember this, we have Valholl on earth and Waterford is a kingdom full of warriors, ahead of you are few of the king's troops bloated with the soft bodies of merchants. The men of Dyflin will sing no songs of today, they will tell no sagas as dead men have short memories. My brother warriors, remember your training and think of the prizes on offer. Kill these men and you will have plenty of gold and silver to share, your heads and dicks will be sore for days."

The Irish had now formed into a sturdy shield wall that was two hundred paces from the Norse wall of Dyflin. Ivar positioned himself behind the wall with his small cavalry and they moved forward to engage King Jarn's defences. Sihtric stayed close to his father, watching and hoping for a chance to become a man.

*

We stood in semi silence looking at the Irish advance, the only noise was that of nervous men coughing and farting. I felt more confident now even within this terrible moment before battle, when men's hearts could fail. I had been in shield walls before and there were many signs of fear before battle, men vomiting and pissing themselves with fear, even cases of men's bowels opening as they faced death. But I believed I was standing with professional soldiers, hardened warriors, as there were no outward signs of dread. The silence was killing me but I knew I could rely on my fighting skills and I was between my old friend, Erik, and the Jomsviking, Berg. Then the silence was broken by our new ally, Baldr was shouting at the Irish.

"Tyr, come to me now and fight like a man, aersling. Let me warm up on your corpse before I kill that gris of a king!"

Baldr started walking away from us into the empty space between the two armies. He removed his helmet and chain mail standing with his shield slack, axe in his left hand, before lifting his sword in the direction of our enemy.

"Come on, you coward, I wear no armour or helmet. You killed my wife you cunt, and now I am going to kill you."

A spear flew out of the ranks of the Irish but fell well short of Baldr, who threw his shield down so that he could wield his broad axe better. To me he had lost his mind with grief and cared nothing for his own life, I imagine he would be a difficult foe to fight in his current state.

A man on a horse rode round to the front of the Irish wall and stopped, the rider just looked at Baldr, possibly weighing up how to deal with this maverick. It must have been Tyr, as Baldr became more animated.

"Come on then, try on your horse first, would you like the first strike, as you are such a skit fighter but a good coward? Be a man for once Tyr; do not hide behind your women anymore."

The rider, Tyr, snapped then and did the most unprofessional thing, he rode toward Baldr and it looked as if we would see our first action of the day. Tyr pulled the horse up a few lengths from his foe. He seemed to be trying to reason with Baldr but we could not hear his words, only the shouting reply of Baldr.

"No, you are a skit and a liar, I know how things work. The aersling king gave you an order and you carried it out. He is an idiot and only thinks about tupping and drinking but you knew my wife was a Christian, you knew you were killing your friend's family."

I could see Tyr's face and he looked very sad, he was obviously an old friend of Baldr and he was pained in having to fight his kin. I realised then that Tyr would not strike out against Baldr, no matter how much the broken man wanted it. Then Tyr gave up talking to Baldr and turned his horse back toward the Irish troops. As he neared them he gave an order and the Irish shield wall started to move forward. All this time Baldr was shouting abuse at his old allies, willing them to fight him one by one. Soon he would be joining his wife in the Christian heaven. I held onto my hammer amulet and thought of Freyja, my reason to survive this day.

The shield wall moved forward, slower than walking pace, as even the bravest wished to put off the inevitable carnage. Tyr joined his cavalry behind the army and felt sick. Baldr had turned against Ivar, obviously because of the extermination of the Christians in Waterford. Now he knew how King Jarn had been warned of their coming. He felt responsible for the death of Astrid although he had tried to help her escape, but she wanted only to stay with the Christians although it meant certain death. It seemed that their heaven must be as great a place as Valholl; well Baldr would be joining her soon.

"Kill Baldr quickly, make sure you get it over with." He shouted this at the front row of his warriors. He had thought about killing Baldr himself but he remembered that he always lost when they practised together, and his troops morale did not need to be dented further.

As the Irish wall came closer to the shield wall of Dyflin, the Norse warriors launched their spears over Baldr and above the heads of the front row of the Irish. Men put up shields, but not quick enough, and many of the men in the middle were wounded, some mortally. A cheer went up among Jarl Olaf's men as they could see they had struck the first blow. Confusion reigned in the Irish ranks as the back rows stumbled over the fallen comrades, exposing the front two rows for a few seconds. Baldr ran into the Irish shield wall like a man possessed, he swung with his axe and chopped down with his sword, a one man army halting the Irish advance. Jarl Olaf saw his opportunity and ordered his shield wall forward quickly. The Norse warriors ran forward and slammed their shields into the Irish wall, knocking them backward over their injured. The Irish wall collapsed, Baldr falling on the shields in front of him, and some of the men of Waterford were scattered. Tyr and his cavalry ran around trying to get order back into the mercenaries. The killing had finally started.

*

At the order from Olaf we ran forward and pushed hard against the Irish. A shield wall usually consists of hours of exhausted pushing but our spears had been very effective and the Irish dead and wounded were tripping up their companions. Instead of finding myself in a pushing match and trying to defend with my shield, I found a little space as our shield wall demolished the Irish wall. I looked around me and saw an Irish sword lying at my feet; I quickly picked it up looking around for any attack. I prefer to fight one on one and I am blessed with ability in both arms, knowing this I held the enemy sword in my left hand and drew my own sword from the scabbard. Our shield wall needed no help from us, so I gathered Berg and Erik and we went to the side to mop up the stragglers and defend the wing of our warriors.

A big black bearded Irishman came straight at me, holding a broad axe. He had no chain mail on, just a leather jerkin to protect his chest and a big heavy shield kept high up his left arm. He was swinging the big, two handed axe, hoping to chop into me. Although I am a big man I am quite fast and it was easy to dodge my opponent, especially as he had broadcast his intentions with his weapon. I stepped back and he swung harmlessly past me fast, I tried to stab at him but also missed. He gathered his balance and then held the axe in one hand while letting his shield drop back along his left arm. He attacked again and this time I defended the blow with the sword in my left hand. I met the full weight of his blow and my arm shuddered as sword cut into the thick wooden handle. I quickly thrust with my own sword and he managed to bring his shield up just in time. We were fighting in a crowd of men which was descending into many bouts, although out of the corner of my eye I could see Berg had two foes to contend with. My ability to use my left hand almost as well as my right proved useful to surprise my enemy. The Irishman was weighing me up readying, for another attack when I launched at him. I swung quickly with left then right, although surprised at my speed the Hibernian giant parried my first blow with his axe and blocked my second swipe with his shield. But as he lifted his shield to block the attack from my right he left a little area exposed that I chopped at with my left. It was not a heavy blow but I cut into his ribs where his jerkin did not protect him. He roared at me in frustration and hopefully pain. He brought up the broad axe hoping to cut into my groin but again I could see it coming, stepped back and thankfully he missed. I thrust forward and stabbed into his armpit and the axe fell to the ground. I started swinging both swords at him, first left than right, pushing him back while he tried desperately to see off each strike with his shield. He fell backward over a dead Irishman and I swung wildly at his legs as they flew up, hacking deep into his left calf. I stepped forward and buried the left hand sword into his exposed guts. He would be dead by noon.

I turned to my right to support Berg but he had finished with his two adversaries and was moving through the Irish, killing and maiming at will. In that moment I realised why he was a Jomsviking, a man born to fight. I turned to my left and could see Erik defending against three men, he was keeping them at bay but I knew he had been out of practise and could do with some help. One of his opponents was slightly turned away from me so I chopped at his neck, cutting deep into his spine. I knew from experience that although relatively small, the neck held most of the blood in the body, and I was rewarded with a great spray of red gore.

"Hello Gunnar, have you come over to spoil my fun," Erik had to shout his little joke as there was the noise of battle all around. I knew he was having fun but it is better to step in and kill the enemy rather than have sport with them.

Erik's opponents had seen their friend fall and realised they had two Vikings to deal with. Erik took on the stocky one with hair that behaved like Erik's, although his was jet black. My fellow was a wiry man with red hair. His hair would have sat well on top of one of the Svea, but his pale skin was covered in a rash of brown spots, something that was common amongst the Irish. He looked a little nervous, he had been one of three fighting a single Norseman and now he faced a well-equipped man of the north, and I was confident I was the better fighter. I waited for him to attack, but he was doing the same so I decided to act. I thrust forward with my right and with a flick of his hand I had lost my sword. I was a little shocked at the move and the fellow gave me a thin lipped grin. He must have used this move many times. I chopped hard with the left and he was forced to defend the hard blow. But before he could recover I was chopping repeatedly with my sword in the left hand. He stumbled a little but it bought him a few paces and I was too far back to capitalise before he gained his balance. I swapped hands and attacked again, but he came forward to meet the attack and as our swords locked he grabbed me round the neck with his left hand. We were in a tight embrace when he butted me with his head; I reacted in time for his blow to hit me on the cheek rather than my nose. The pain was intense but it did not disable me as a broken nose would. His plan foiled, he now could not let me go and release my sword, but I had my left hand free and I punched him hard into his side just under the ribs. I knew I had winded him and quickly pulled out my belt knife, my seax, and stabbed him hard where I had landed my previous blow. He released his grip and folded down. I kicked him hard in the face and looked about for the next adversary. But the Irish had pulled back and were running and riding back down the

Poddle valley. We did not chase them as we had taken many casualties. I saw Jarl Olaf walking over toward me holding a sword soaked in blood.

*

Baldr had found himself splayed across two Irishmen, stuck under their shields. He did not recognise them or any of the warriors with Tyr, suspecting they must be mercenaries. He got up quickly and the two below him moved fast as they knew they were vulnerable to attack and death lying prone on the floor. The ugly weasel to Baldr's left was fastest to his feet but his neck was met by the blade of Baldr's broad axe and his body was devastated by the blow. Baldr left the axe in the Irishman as if it were placed into wood awaiting further use. The other Irishman was thrusting hard at Baldr with a short sword, the man had gambled and it nearly paid off but Baldr managed to block the blow with his own longer sword.

In a shield wall it is good to carry a short sword for stabbing at close quarters while keeping your long sword ready for open fighting. The short, stocky Irishman, who looked like a dwarf from legends, had hoped to cut Baldr quickly but he was facing a man with a longer reach and a proper sword. Baldr did not want to waste time with this idiot; he had to kill Tyr before finding Ivar and cutting him down. He hacked hard at the shorter man, cutting into his side on the third blow. The dwarf man fell and Baldr looked around for the man he must kill. There were many individual battles going on around him, Jarl Olaf's men stood out as they were all well-equipped and Tyr's mercenaries all carried a collection of their own combat gear.

He felt a sharp pain across his hamstring and tumbled to the floor. The last thing Baldr heard, before joining his wife in paradise, was a whispering in his ear as he had his throat cut. "Never under estimate a little Irishman you Viking skit."

*

Jarl Olaf had been in many battles and knew that when you gained an advantage you had to push on and use it. He had acted fast and his troops had devastated the Irish mercenaries under Tyr. He had lost a few men and some would never fight again but that was to be expected. He had sent a rider over to Ragnal to tell him to go and support his brother against King Ivar, and he had also organised a few men to carry the injured back to the slave enclosure, where some women were waiting to tend their wounds. The dead

164

could wait until the invasion had been dealt with. He was on his way to talk with Berg when he saw Gunnar and Erik with his man.

"Gunnar, you fight well for a slave and a merchant."

"I have had some practise but it went well, thanks to your quick thinking, and I am better at one to one combat than shoving in a shield wall."

Jarl Olaf patted Gunnar and Erik on the shoulder, turning to speak with his man. "Berg, if I were the enemy I would be trying to cross the Poddle to join my colleagues attacking the town; we should follow him so that between us and Ragnal we can finish off the Irish."

Berg did not say anything; he just nodded and started to gather the fit men together. Jarl Olaf and his troop of warriors jogged after the attackers, confident they would win the day.

*

Tyr and his cavalry hung to the back to defend his retreating troops. He was furious; if he had had longer to work with these mercenaries they would not have made the most basic of errors. Perhaps they should have ensured that all men were supplied with shields, but they had been so confident in their plan; Ivar and Waterford were acting as an ally of Dyflin so the element of surprise should have worked. Dam Baldr, and dam his stupid wife, only a Christian would die for his god. A shout went up ahead as they found a ford to cross the river.

*

Kanin hung on tightly to her king; she buried her head into his back and shut her eyes tight. She had opened her eyes briefly and saw terrible sights of death and gore. As she shut her eyes again the image of dismembered bodies stayed imprinted in her mind. She felt sick and scared, hoping her king would keep her safe from the fate that had befallen the men she had seen from the back of his horse. She had seen a few horrible things when she had been snatched from the green valleys of her home. The Dal Riata had come to her village looking for young slaves, and she had hidden and escaped, but later that month King Ivar's men had arrived and swept her away. She was lucky that the King liked her and he kept her close, not treating her too badly if she kept him happy.

The most frightening part was when they broke through the town's defences. She had hoped, as king, Ivar would not be at the front of his men but he could not wait to engage the enemy of Dyflin, and she had clung on tight to him while he hacked and killed the enemy soldiers. She could hear him whooping and laughing as he fought, he was very brave.

Kanin was not too sure how old she was, her mother had thought she was at least sixteen summers old, which meant she was probably older. Her father had been killed in a raid, by pirates, perhaps ten years ago and now she could not remember what his face looked like. She had wanted to leave the village as soon as she came into womanhood. The men of her age, she knew, were all idiots and she had dreamed of a better life. She had been frightened when she was captured by the slavers, and had hated the attention of the small, ugly slaver. His hands were always groping for her most private places, and she had been happy when she was presented to the king. It seemed to her that all men wanted her for was to plow and when they had finished their grunting and grinding they would move on till they needed another poke. King Ivar did not know it but he was the first man to treat Gwenhyvach well, and for the first time in her life she felt like a respected woman.

*

Ivar hacked down from his horse and his hard iron weapon cut through the defenders helmet as if it were a mere turnip. The man crumbled to the floor and Ivar swung to his left, trying to garrotte another Dyflin warrior who moved but lost part of his ear.

"Come on boys, there is gold to be had and women to be tupped." King Ivar held his sword aloft and surveyed the battle. Kanin was holding him tight around his waist and he was already in the mood to have her, but it would have to wait.

He had hit the defenders shield wall hard with his cavalry; all carrying a long spear to batter and pierce his enemies' shields. The men on horse disposed of their spears and drew their swords to attack the ranks of men trying to repel them. On King Ivar's signal the cavalry rode to one side to let a volley of spears rain down on King Jarn's house guard. As soon as Ivar's warriors had loosed their spears they ran forward and engaged the cities defenders. Now there were around two thousand men fighting a hand to hand battle for the richest kingdom in all of Ireland.

Ivar sat calmly upon his horse and planned his next move. He looked south west, along the valley of the Poddle and saw Tyr and his mercenaries approaching. It was annoying as he had told Tyr that he should find a ford across the Poddle and attack the city from the east side. Perhaps Tyr's troops did not like getting too wet and had found an easier place to cross? He looked back toward the town and saw reinforcements coming for King Jarn. With King Ivar's mercenary troops the numbers would even up, perhaps it would be good to form his men back into a shield wall again. To help him think better Ivar decided to ride through the battle and cut open a few Norsemen. Strangely he found a kind of calmness within the chaos of battle; it was as if the act of fighting calmed King Ivar's excited spirit. As he killed and maimed, with his long sword, Kanin held tight and prayed that she would survive this terrible and exciting ordeal.

*

As Tyr approached his King's men, he saw the warriors of Waterford fall back in some order to form a new shield wall. He knew what was expected of him and took his troops to one wing of the shield wall. Tyr knew that King Ivar would be angry with his failure to fight through to the river, so he set his troops on the difficult north end of the shield wall.

Eventually King Ivar called him over and he rode to the centre of the attacker's wall.

"Tyr, you are not a coward in battle, tell me what stopped you attacking Jarn on his eastern side?"

"My Lord King I came face to face with a very professional army and at its centre I saw Baldr."

"Why in Hel is Baldr betraying me to that pompous fool Jarn?"

"Baldr is a Christian, King Ivar; his wife was killed in the cull of Christians. I sent word to her to come to me so I could protect her for Baldr's sake, but the word is she walked of her own accord into the burning church of her fellows."

"She sounds like a bloody idiot; did you kill her traitorous man?"

"Baldr is dead; Beag cut his throat but is carrying a wound of his own."

"If Beag lives, we will give him some gold, now Tyr, go and defend my left flank and kill me some Norse."

Chapter 16

On the host his spear did Odin hurl,
Then in the world did war first come;
The wall that girdled the gods was broken,
And the field by the warlike Wanes was trodden.

"I hate this, do men know the pain we suffer? Will they ever understand the pain of child birth or the pain of awaiting the fate of your husband at war?" Queen Gyda was not really talking to Freyja and Helga; she was cursing the gods for putting her husband's life at risk.

"My dear Queen, all men are blessed with thick heads and small hearts, for them to understand a woman you may as well ask them to understand a skraeling." Helga looked as if she was used to speaking in front of her Queen this way.

Queen Gyda posed a question to Freyja then, "And Freyja, I am sorry that my husband needed your man and his friend but please tell me there is one man who thinks of his wife before he goes hunting or Viking?"

"Well, I love my husband but he is not free from making mistakes, but I know he loves me most and will often prove it."

"And I know Olaf cares for me greatly, it is other men that cause us to be apart. Also, my husband has a strong claim to be King of Norway and I must support him in this. Perhaps it is easier to be a farmer in Iceland, I could be happy with Olaf near me all day."

"Queen, may I ask a question?" Gyda nodded to encourage Freyja to continue.

"Are we safe here? I can hear the fighting and I am spending all my time distressing about my husband, not knowing if he is alive or dead. But what if the worst happens and the army of Dyflin is over run?"

"My house guard have a ship by the Wood Quay and we will leave for The Fylde, but Freyja, my Olaf is a remarkable warrior and has led men to many victories. I am sure we will be eating with our men before the sun sets."

*

Jarl Olaf had crossed the Poddle with his men and told them to rest for a while. He wanted the Irish bandits he was following to think they had a clear passage back to their King. He was not worried for King Jarn's welfare as he knew that the King had the support of his younger brother's troops. He had the men drink a little weak ale and check their weapons.

"Berg, how are the men?"

"They are in good spirits Jarl; they are frustrated they did not finish them off in the field."

"We will finish them Berg, they are joining a battle they cannot win and we will hit them hard in the rear while they are busy engaging King Jarn and Prince Ragnal."

"Jarl Olaf, I must admit I am enjoying this, it has been a little while but I love a good fight."

"There will be more Berg, it was a good day when you came to me, and you fit in well here."

Jarl Olaf moved on and Berg had a big grin on his face. Olaf could be quite a stern character but you knew where you stood with him and he rarely gave out compliments, perhaps there would be a little extra silver for Berg soon.

*

Gustav was miserable, he missed his wife, he missed his farm and he was beginning to hate his brother. He had never got on that well with Harald but they had been brought together by the death of Gull. Gull had been only a year younger than Gustav and they were not only brothers they were friends. While pulling on the oar through the cold, salty sea, he thought of the happy times in the past with his brother. Most of his best memories were tainted as they involved Gunnar. How could Gunnar have done that to Gull, they were so close, in fact some people used to think that Gunnar was their kin.

Gustav hated Gunnar for killing the only brother he truly loved, but he also mourned for the old Gunnar, his friend the hunter, fighter and drinker. They all thought that they would spend eternity in Valholl together, fighting old foe and drinking until they were sick. But Gunnar had denied that to Gull, murdering him in cold blood and sending his spirit to Loki's realm.

These thoughts were making him feel melancholy so he tried thinking of his wife. He closed his eyes briefly so he could picture Thorgerd naked in their hut, washing herself.

He thought of the sunlight coming in and playing across her full breasts and pale nipples. His mind drifted down to her small waist and wide hips. How he wanted to feel that beautiful soft skin against his, instead he was rowing this Karve into the Irish Sea.

When he got to Dyflin he hoped Erik would still be there and he could spend some time with his old friend and away from his arsehole brother. At least there would be some peace in Dyflin; by all accounts it was a calm kingdom much like Iceland.

*

Ragnal was excited. He had been in to battle with his father and brother before, but this time he was leading his own troops and they tasted only success. He must be a great commander. He had arrived in the town just in time, the Irish had over run the defences of his brother the King and he had seen Jarn in one to one combat with a common soldier. He knew how good a warrior his brother was and it was confirmed when Jarn cut through his foes defences, chopping off the Irishman's arm.

The Poddle was quite deep near the town but Ragnal had lived here all his life and he knew a good point to cross, although they all had to hold their weapons above their heads to keep them dry. When they were all on the bank they jogged into the town and straight into battle. It was a shock to the men of Waterford, as they must have thought if they broke Jarn's men they would take the town. Prince Ragnal himself killed two men easily, as they were focused on fighting and did not see him jog up. The invaders made a small retreat into a shield wall, but one man turned and faced Ragnal to gain his friends some time. The man was the same size as Ragnal, about sixteen hands high, but he seemed to be made only of muscle and he had a sword almost as big as himself. He lifted it two handed above his head and brought it down on Ragnal, meaning to open his head up. The young prince lifted his own sword to defend the blow and the heavy long sword hit it hard and the blade snapped. The long sword followed through and hit the earth; although his opponent was muscular he must have been tiring as he left the sword a fraction too long on the ground. Ragnal jumped at him using only his shield and aimed the boss at his face. The fellow moved his head away from the blow but they both tumbled over with the Irishman dropping his great weapon. Ragnal had managed to pin his enemy to the ground under the shield but it was like trying to hold a boar in the forest and he had soon wriggled free. The Norse Prince punched him hard in the jaw and it did nothing apart from bruising Ragnal's knuckles. The Irishman was up on his feet fast and Ragnal scrambled up, leaving his broken sword and shield on the floor. He tried to pull his seax from his belt and his foe looked longingly at his dropped weapon, before deciding to run back to his troops.

"I suppose you will need a weapon, lord Prince?" His captain, Kent, was standing by and Ragnal suspected he had been watching closely in case Ragnal slipped up and got himself killed. He hated Kent for this as it made him feel like a child and not the man he claimed to be. He grunted in reply to Kent and his captain threw him a sword made from pig iron.

"Lord Prince, I suppose you will be asking me to tell the men to join your brother in the shield wall?"

"Of course Kent, I was just going to suggest it." It was amazing how Kent made him feel small and useless.

Kent turned away and Ragnal just saw the smirk on his face as he brought order to Ragnal's troops. Even his brother did not treat him like this, but in the back of his mind he knew that Kent was almost forty years old and had sons older than him. Also, Kent had been in the Varangian guard and fought at the Battle of Tara, he had been a warrior longer than Ragnal had lived and was still alive to fight again. His troops were now lining up alongside his brothers in the shield wall and he realised he did not know where to stand.

"Lord Prince, your brother is in the centre, perhaps you could help protect him." Ragnal's face was red with anger as he marched over to his brother's side and Kent had to stifle a laugh, but he would protect the young prince with his own life, no matter how much it hurt Ragnal's pride.

*

Tyr had come over to King Ivar and told him there was another troop of Dyflin warriors roaming somewhere. He did not recognise any of the men in the shield wall of the defenders, and was worried about the men he had engaged on the land behind the slave enclosure. This made up Ivar's mind to act quickly to try and turn the battle in the favour of Waterford. Tyr was getting irritated with his king, as he felt the woman he carried was now a hindrance to his ability.

"Lord King, would it not be better to fight without the slave behind you?"

Ivar looked annoyed at Tyr nagging him again, but he knew that carrying Kanin with him had been a hindrance when attacking the shield wall of King Jarn. He peeled her arms from around his waist and spoke to her in Irish, "My little rabbit, you must dismount and wait behind the soldiers, Sihtric will protect you. You can come up again when I have finished with the men of Dyflin."

He lifted her by one arm and encouraged her to dismount; she dropped to the ground and looked pathetic and small. Ivar already missed the feel of her kut in the small of his back but he dismissed this thought, knowing he would have his share of that later.

Kanin was very afraid, she knew she held a privileged place when close to the king but in reality she was nothing but a slave, and who cares about another dead slave? She huddled behind the now dismounted prince on the bank of the Poddle before shouting up at her King in a mix of Irish and her native tongue, "Don't forget me King Ivar, I miss your orm!"

Most of the men laughed at this, underlining their opinion of Ivar as a King to be proud of.

"Don't you worry, my little Kanin, I have not finished ploughing your furrow this day. Me and the boys just need to kill the King of Dyflin and have an ale together first."

*

Further south west, along the Poddle valley, the grass was growing long in the fertile floor of the dale. The bird song was limited as the fighting men had scared away most of the fauna. Fat bumble bees, weighed down with pollen and nectar, fluttered between the local flora. In a large patch of long grass, adjacent to the small island in the Poddle, there was movement.

Jarl Olaf had his men crawl on their stomachs for two hundred paces until they were in sight of King Ivar's shield wall. He kept them all down low and told them to wait while he and Berg crawled nearer by another twenty paces. He was intent on destroying the threat from Waterford and meant to end it this day.

"So Berg, I am thinking we should wait for the shield wall to engage and then get as close as possible to time our attack just right. We should not let Dyflin suffer too long, but if they are doing well against Ivar and his pirates we should let them wear down our enemy a little before we cut them down."

"True, Jarl Olaf, but we will have to time it right, if we wait too long we throw the advantage to the invaders. Attacking Ivar from two sides with these men should see us win the day."

Olaf clapped Berg on the shoulder and indicated the men behind, "Bring the troop up to join me and I will make the right call."

The two shield walls stood apart facing each other, the abuse had started immediately but had died down now and neither side moved. King Ivar sat astride his grey horse and gave a signal to Tyr, his captain started banging his pommel on his shield and the men joined in. This was no battle of Tara but there were substantial men facing each other, up to three thousand on the battle field, although Tyr had been right earlier about the amount of men Dyflin could call on. King Jarn's house guard were proper warriors and the majority of men fighting for Olaf too, but Ragnal had the older troops, and the enthusiastic. Jarn was no fool and placed his best men in the centre and the Dyflin fyrd in the rear. He knew Olaf was out there somewhere planning some surprise attack; he had better not leave it too late.

The Waterford warriors stopped banging their shields and launched themselves across the gap. Each man determined to break through the Dyflin shield wall.

Jarn sent out a signal and the Norsemen locked their shields tight and braced themselves for the strike.

The Waterford militia hit the Dyflin shield wall hard and it stumbled back slightly but the rear rows dug in and held their peers in place. Men were grunting and sweating as they pushed hard against each other. Both second rows were trying to pull down shields with broad axe so their friends could stab with short swords. Usually in a shield wall weapons would be thrown to disturb the enemy, the Saxon liked to use a small throwing axe and the Viking preferred a spear but all the spears had been thrown earlier. In the front row men were being crushed behind shield waiting for an opportunity to stab with a short sword or seax.

King Ivar's men were feeling confident; they had already broken Jarn's shield wall once and they meant to do it again, although now the numbers were more even. The shield wall can consist of hard men pushing for hours at a time and after this ordeal you were expected to fight and kill. Only the fittest and best fighters would survive, the weaker and lame would be found wanting.

King Jarn stood next to his younger half-brother at the back of his troops watching and waiting for one side to break.

"Brother King, I wish I could be at the front of the shield wall, not stuck back here unable to fight."

"Ragnal, you are a prince and expected to lead, it would break the men's heart, in battle, if they should see you fall."

"Why does everyone think I cannot fight, when I was only nine summers old didn't our father take me into battle? I am more of a veteran than a young warrior."

"Ragnal, there will be fighting enough soon, be prepared and show me the great warrior then, until then stop the childish whining."

The prince shut up then but was even more determined to be the greatest warrior on the field today, he would show his brother and he would show Kent, and then they would give him the respect he deserved.

*

"What do you see, Berg?" Berg put his hands over his eyes to cut out the sun and tried to concentrate on the shield wall. From his standpoint he could see the back of the Waterford militia, their cavalry milling around at the back away from the core of the conflict. In the land between them and the enemy there were some ravens nonchalantly standing about, but he knew they were here to pick over carrion. He focused again on the shield walls and gave his summary.

"Not much movement jarl, but I think I can see the men of Waterford getting excited, which means they think they have the momentum."

"I thought so; we will wait a few moments more before springing our surprise."

*

Kent had joined the fighting in the core and three rows back. He had experienced this many times before and was well prepared. On his back was his shield and his sword slept in its scabbard. He had his short sword tucked into his belt and held on to his pole spear, ready to use it if the wall should be breached. He was struggling to concentrate, as the morning was warm and they had been here for some time now, pushing, shoving and grunting at each other, but each army was equally matched. Ahead a broad axe came over for the umpteenth time but this time it caught the shield plum and pulled it down. A sword came out of the Irish ranks and stabbed into the gap and all Kent saw was the man crumble. The Irish pushed hard before a replacement could come through from the second row, as the fallen man became an obstacle.

The Irish poured through the gap and panic rippled through the Norse, as if a stone had been dropped in the lake of Hel. With the Norse pushing back Kent was squeezed tight and he could not move to wield his pole. All he could do was watch as the Irish chopped and hacked their way through with broad axe and sword. It was a carnage that was all too familiar and Kent knew that when this happened it was always best to be on the attacking side.

*

We were up and running on Olaf's command and we had covered over twenty paces before the Waterford horsemen saw the danger behind them. We had collected our spears from the previous battle and Olaf had made sure we were prepared for this attack. The men at the front, including Erik and me, had chain mail, shields, sword and spear. The scabbard banged repeatedly on my leg as I ignored my own trepidation and covered that small space. I am a fast runner and can sustain it over some distance but although Berg is an older man he kept pace easily. We both were a little ahead of our warrior friends as the enemy on horseback turned and moved to engage us. Each of the men had a spear in hand and was protected by their own shield. I had never seen King Ivar before but one of the men was upon a large grey horse and seemed to be leading the other men. Quicker than I expected the Waterford horses were up to speed and almost on us. Our orders from Jarl Olaf were to defend ourselves and lame the horses.

A brown sturdy mare, bigger than our Icelandic ponies, came at me with a bushy eyed Irishman astride her. He looked supremely confident in his approach and I briefly thought of Freyja and how I must live through this for her. He lowered his spear at the last moment hoping to run me through; I met the tip with the boss of my shield and managed to scrape the horse's ribs with my spear. The horse screamed and bucked, desperate to get away from the attack. Bushy eyes on her back struggled for a moment to hang on before he was thrown, his arms were out and he landed on both hands. I ran over to him and could see he had broken both his arms below the elbow. He watched me with those dark eyes and knew that his death was near. I saw him struggle to hold his sword in preparation for his death, for only a man that dies in battle with sword in hand can enter Valholl. I slowed my approach a little to give him the chance to rest his broken and painful hand on the pommel. I looked in his eyes and wished him well in the next world, as I jammed my spear into his throat.

"See you in Valholl, Jarv."

I surveyed the scene around me and the Waterford horsemen were having varied success against Jarl Olaf's troops; a few of them had been unseated and dealt with but King Ivar and his surrounding troops had carved a furrow through our men on foot. I looked to the battle on the edge of town and the rear of Ivar's force had formed a shield wall against us. We needed to deal with the horsemen and attack them as soon as possible to relieve King Jarn.

*

With the gap opened ahead of him the pressure around Kent eased and he let go of his pole and pulled out his well-maintained sword. He was facing the back of the man in front of him and as he watched a sword came toward Kent from the centre of the man's back. His ally fell and Kent was prepared, with his sword held ready to attack. An Irish warrior was pulling his sword from the belly of the dying man and Kent hacked at his neck without a pause. The well sharpened sword sliced easily into the exposed neck, opening it like a yawn. It was amazing how much blood was stored in the neck, whereas a leg seemed to hold little blood. Gore gushed from his foes throat and the fellow looked shocked at his sudden death. Kent lifted a boot and kicked the man over, looking for more invaders to kill. Two men approached him as all around the disciplined shield wall became hand to hand combat. They shared a quick glance and a smirk knowing they had the advantage.

"Old man, looks like you could do with a warriors help." It was Ragnal; he had seen his captain's predicament and come to his aid. Kent nodded at the young Prince and showed him the briefest of smiles; the battle field was not the place for too many niceties. Kent took the man on their right and Ragnal the man to the left. He attacked the man in front using his favourite move of slashing left and right across the body. He wanted his foe to defend and it would help Kent feel for weakness.

Ragnal had less time to work out his attack, as his enemy had already attacked him with a thrust to the body, hoping to gut the Prince of Dyflin. The younger man was quick and easily dodged the sword; as it passed his side he grabbed the sword arm of his foe and brought up his knee to break the enemie's nose. Now he was holding a disoriented but dangerous man by the arm and he quickly brought his sword down on the fellow's exposed back. He let him go and turned toward Kent, who was still finding his way to defeat the enemy. Ragnal felt a stinging blow strike his ear, the blow seemed to echo through his head and then the pain exploded on the side of his face. He feared he had lost his ear and turned to his assailant. There was a scrawny Irishman with a shock of red hair, the colour of an unmaintained sword, and he was swinging a thick wooden branch that had been worked into a club. It looked as if the invader was going to try and crack open his crown so Ragnal tried to block the cudgel with his sword. The Prince of Dyflin was feeling dizzy, and as the shillelagh came down it broke his wrist and he dropped his weapon.

Kent heard the scream to his left but his opponent was an awkward bastard that refused to die. Kent had cut both his arms and stabbed him in the belly but he did not seem to weaken. The Prince was in trouble and it was his duty to protect him. He threw caution to the wind and launched a frenzied attack on the Irish pirate, blow after blow he landed, all but the last were defended. He managed to chop into the man's sword arm and he dropped his weapon. Kent ran him through and turned to defend his Jarl.

He saw young Prince Ragnal, a year younger than his own son, lying still on the ground. Standing over him was a scrawny red head eyeing the prince's fine armour. Kent was only a few paces away and crossed the distance quickly, plunging his sword in-between the man's ribs, cutting up through his kidney and up into both lungs. He checked for any more invaders to fight and saw that the men of Waterford seemed to be retreating; he supposed Jarl Olaf had finally decided to make an entrance. Kent knelt down next to the Prince and rolled him onto his back. The boy's forehead had a dent in it, as if you had put your fist into freshly risen dough. His eyes were closed and his body was limp, Kent checked and saw that he was not holding his sword when he died and hoped the boy was a Christian, as there would be no place at the table for him in the hall of Valholl.

*

Litta hated riding a horse, but he hated marching more, so he tolerated the fact he looked ridiculous and feared falling at every step. He had been lucky with the wind and sea, having got to Waterford as quick as it was possible. Most of the best warriors where away with King Ivar but he had managed to collect fifty men together and they were trying to cover the hard march to Dyflin as quick as they could. In his dark heart he rejoiced at his luck; Bjarni and Baldr dead plus quite a few of King Ivar's men would die on the battle field. Litta was showing loyalty and support for his childhood friend and could become a close ally of his king again. Not that he cared much for anybody else, but his actions would benefit Litta and maybe lead to silver and some gold coming his way. He imagined Ivar having to retreat and Litta coming to his rescue, followed quickly by a nice reward.

If only they had all been on horseback they would have covered the distance in half the time, but they were constantly waiting for the men on foot to catch up.

*

The horsemen, including King Ivar, retreated to the bank of the Poddle and I saw the King sweep up a young woman, she clung onto Ivar like she was holding on for her life. A young man also mounted a horse and readied his sword. The Waterford warriors were still numerous and they formed a circular shield wall to protect against King Jarn and our troops. We had moved a little away from the river's edge and we could see our allies defending the town. Jarl Olaf had us form a formidable shield wall using as many spears as we could recover to deter the horsemen. The two parts of the Dyflin militia did not have enough strength to punish the invaders but if we joined we would be superior. We tried to edge our shield wall closer to the town and its defenders. As we did this the enemy shuffled a little down river, giving us more freedom to move. Just as we were getting close to King Jarn's troops King Ivar and his horsemen burst out of their defences and attacked the Dyflin shield wall. We stood still and watched until Olaf shouted for action.

"Attack the horses with your spears on my order, Now!"

We unlocked shields and ran at the side of the horsemen and resumed our earlier battle. Ivar had decided on attacking Jarn's wall as they had very few spears and he held the advantage, but with our attack their cavalry scattered but whirled around and feigned attack against us but did not engage. Jarl Olaf spotted the problem and passed on the news.

"They are retreating; the army of Ivar is running from Dyflin."

Behind the horsemen's attacks their house guards and other infantry were jogging away from the battle ground. The horsemen were bravely facing a large shield wall to keep us occupied, so their men would have a chance to escape. King Jarn had sent a runner over to Olaf and asked him to stay and defend rather than pursuing the retreating horde. We were told to hold position but it looked as if Dyflin would be left in peace for the time being. I kissed my hammer amulet and looked around for Erik hoping he still lived.

I saw him chatting with Berg and they looked like they could have been friends for years. The bond you build with the men you fight with is strong, especially after victory and nobody would have known that so recently Berg had been close to killing Erik.

Chapter 17

The son of a King,
Shall be silent and wise,
Bold in battle as well;
Bravely and gladly
A man shall go,
Till the day of his death is come.

After sailing the northern sea for weeks Kolskegg now had a trail to follow. It was not a definite, iron clad trail, but it was better than none. Now he felt, at last, he was getting closer to his brother. He had prepared the men for a fight, something Skarphedin and Grim did not need as all they spoke of was engaging an enemy.

The Irish Sea was frustrating as it generally had high winds and rain to accompany a vessel, but now there was sunshine and no wind. So if they wanted to get anywhere they would have to row through the still, stagnant water.

"Boys, keep a steady rhythm as we may need warriors in Dyflin. I would rather we got there a little later and you all had something left to fight with."

He tried to stay positive but his hand went to the iron hammer around his neck as he prayed for his brother's safety.

*

The smoke twirled around itself as it rose from the pyre. In the dusk the great fire danced and shed flickering light on the crowd standing around the burial. A great trench had been dug into the ground and a longship had been placed in the hole. The light from the great fire cast dancing shadows within the boat, revealing in all his warrior gear Prince Ragnal. He looked as if he was sleeping but he was of course, very dead.

A helmet had been place on his head to cover up his broken crown and a shield lay across his chest with the boss placed over his heart. His sword was now held in his hands and his favourite spear had been tucked at his side.

I was surprised at the burial as I had heard that Ragnal was a Christian, but the burial was set out as we always had under the Norse Gods. The only difference was that after the initial ceremony was over the wailing Christians joined in and ruined a good funeral. After what seemed like hours of crying and screaming to the roman god, we all used our shields to fill in the grave with fresh earth. Olaf came over to me with that stern look on his face that I was now getting used to.

"Did we do the young prince justice, Gunnar?"

Not wanting to offend this powerful man, I kept my reservations to myself.

"It was fitting that a prince should have such a funeral," Olaf smiled and I suspected that he had arranged the ceremony, as his wife and her older brother were distraught after losing their youngest sibling. I could not work out if Olaf was a Christian or he followed the old gods, as he seemed to appease both camps while upsetting no one.

"Gunnar, did I ever tell you that I was once captured as a slave? Something in you reminded me of my own plight in the past. When I saw Freyja's necklace I knew that we were somehow connected and I believe that our fate follows the same path. Life was very hard for me and my mother when we were enslaved; she endured terrible abuses but always managed to protect me. Unfortunately I did not have a Jarl Olaf to emancipate me; we spent many years as slaves until eventually my skill as a warrior was rewarded with my freedom. I tell you this so you know that I have sympathy for the nightmare you found yourself in. I believe that you owe me for breaking you out from that gaol, but I will not insist that a debt is repaid. But I will ask that you come on a campaign with me, as you have proved yourself a good warrior and I require good warriors to accompany me. This will be the first step toward regaining my birth right."

What could I say, Olaf was a clever man, he gave you something and asked for nothing in return but you were made to feel you owed him and that debt remained unpaid.

"Of course Olaf, I will join you, as long as I can return to Iceland to regain my home."

He grabbed my arm and beamed a great smile at me, something he rarely did. I gathered my wits enough to request protection for my dear wife.

"My only worry would be my wife, Freyja, we have only just been reunited and I worry that with us both gone she will be unprotected here in Dyflin."

"Gunnar, I have already anticipated your concern, the Queen Gyda has taken to Freyja, as she is very likable, and will take her to Kirkham in the Fylde. It is garrisoned by my men and led by my oldest friend, Mort. I trust him with my wife so you can be assured that you can trust him with yours."

"Thank you Jarl, but please let me break the news to Freyja this time."

"Of course. I will see you after the feast, I plan to leave soon as there are some important men I must meet in Shetland and I need my best warriors with me there."

*

Erik sat on a bench watching the celebration. He had managed to achieve the perfect state of inebriation; he felt happy and knew with all certainty that one more drink would only improve his happiness, although it would probably, in truth, knock him over. Everything had worked out well recently, he had his old friend back and he had managed to have a proper fight too, even though his body seemed to ache all over now. The ale had dulled the aches and mutton filled his belly. A perfect evening, if only he could find a young maid to keep him warm tonight. As he thought this he laughed to himself, with any luck he could hope for a not so young widow.

Erik managed to get to his feet and went in search of more ale to ensure this night got even better.

*

There was laughing and fighting, just like any other celebration where too much drink was being consumed. A sail had been erected at one end of the field to protect the Queen in case of rain, which was common in Dyflin. Freyja was well dressed and enjoying it, between Gyda and Helga she had all that she needed, and more, although the only jewellery she wore was her jade necklace.

"You have come to us during interesting times, Freyja, there are many Jarls that would like to become kings, and many kings that wish to grow their empires. My husband has a claim to one of the greatest kingdoms in the north and plans to reclaim it. He will need loyal men, Gunnar is such a man."

"I know he is, and he believes strongly in repaying a debt. I only wish Njal was here to guide us as he has the gift of fore sight."

Helga looked up and the Queen went quiet, Freyja felt confused but was not sure what was wrong. Queen Gyda looked uncomfortable so Helga spoke up.

"Times are changing fast Freyja, and you will need to change with them. Ragnarok is upon us and the old gods will soon be no more. It is not good to talk of witch craft and such things. You are liked a lot but be careful how you speak in public."

Queen Gyda walked over to Freyja and held her hands, "Olaf is aware that there is a great division between followers of the old gods and the new Christian god. Helga is a Christian, but also a clever one. Olaf and I have tried to keep the peace between the religions without taking sides but eventually we will have to come down on one side. Anyway enough of politics, tell me how you came across that necklace?"

This was unusual; back in Iceland the old gods were still venerated. Yes, there were some Christians but they were mostly the subject of ridicule. Perhaps she should find Gunnar and warn him. He was not necessarily a religious man but he wore an iron hammer and looked for omens and messages from Grimnir and Thor.

"I would like to find my husband and warn him, as most of the people of Iceland follow tradition."

"Yes Freyja, Olaf talks highly of Gunnar and he must be protected too, but please tell me who gave you that little green figure?"

"It was the very first thing that Gunnar gave me, when I asked what it was he said it was a god from overseas and it is from the hot lands to the south."

"We must talk some more of these, as my husband has given me something very similar."

Gyda unwrapped a cloth parcel she was holding for Freyja to see the contents.

Freyja gasped as she saw the same figurine made of the strange green stone but at least four times the size of the little figure around her throat.

*

The fellow next to me stank like he had avoided a bath all his life and the front of his head was shaved. He sipped reluctantly at his warm ale and had the air of someone that wished to be anywhere but here. I raised my ale toward him and shouted a toast, "Skol."

His mouth tried to grin but his eyes looked at me with contempt.

"Friend, why do you not sink that ale quickly and get another one, it will raise your spirits."

"Thanks you for the advice, warrior, but I am in mourning for Prince Ragnal. I had hoped he would become a good Christian King and cleanse this foul land."

"Ah, you must be one of those Christians; well if Ragnal was one too you should rejoice as he must surely be in your heaven enjoying himself now."

The scrawny man sighed and took the demeanour of somebody trying to explain something simple to an idiot.

"Ragnal was a good man at heart but had not completed his confessions. This will mean he does not have a clear passage to be on the right hand of our lord. We must all pray for him to ensure that he enters the kingdom of heaven."

I looked around as my ripe friend returned to sipping his drink. I hoped to find some excuse to escape this dull man on this night of celebration. Luckily for me I saw my wife coming toward me so I stood and bade him goodbye. He just ignored me and scowled into his drink.

*

"Husband, do you have to leave so soon after we have repelled Ivar and my brother has just passed?"

"Wife, I do not want to part from you but my destiny is to reclaim the crown of Norway. I need allies and none come bigger than King Sweyn of Denmark. I need to meet his men and forge an alliance. Also it will mean weakening Aethelred so that we can keep the Fylde free from Saxon raids, for Sweyn will be looking to take back his lands around Jorvik."

"So we could have an ally on our border rather than an enemy. I understand husband but I will miss you."

"Dear Gyda, I always miss you when we are apart but please heed my worries about the defences of Dyflin while I am away. I think it is best if you travel to Kirkham with your house guard, for I know I can trust Mort to keep you safe."

"I will and I will take Freyja with me as we have become close."

"Follow what Mort says as with him and my trusted men I believe my precious wife will be safe."

Chapter 18

At this time, nothing went right for the nation,
Neither in the south or in the north

Aethelred was three and twenty years old and had been king for thirteen of them. Aethelwold had been dead for five years and when he died, so did the young king's guidance. He had got used to the double talk of the court now, but it frustrated him that he had no one to indulge his confidence and no one to trust.

Aethelred waited in the king's room for the arrival of Sigeric the Serious. Sigeric was a stern and holy man, who seemed to despise everything about the kingdom. The king was a little in awe of him and knew that he had favoured his own dead half-brother. But in his heart he knew Bishop Sigeric was not his enemy and when you took away the sharp tongue of Sigeric, he talked a lot of sense.

Aethelred needed to build his support across the kingdom as the threat from the heathen host was only going to get worse. His father had worked hard to unite the kingdom of the Angles and Aethelred was determined to leave a united England to his sons. The Norsemen were not his only problem; the Bishop of Rochester, Aelfstan, was growing wealthier every day and the king suspected the Bishop of Canterbury was his vassal. The king needed to halt Aelfstan's ambitions and it was common knowledge that Sigeric despised the Bishop of Rochester. Aethelred had decided to put Sigeric in Aelfstan's path and therefore slow his ambition. He would befriend Sigeric, as best he could, and eventually give the bloody minded bishop the seat of Canterbury.

There was a call from outside and Sigeric was shown into the king's chamber. The bishop was a stern looking man with mousey, grey hair. He was only a few years older than the king but he appeared much older. His gait was humble as he approached his Lord but his eyes held the king's and you knew he would bow to no man, only to his God. The look he gave the king said that he was a very busy man and he did not have time to waste at court.

"My Lord King," the slightest of bow was given to his master, Aethelred decided to be direct.

"My dear Bishop of Ramsey, I know you are a busy man but I also know you are very pious. England is under a great threat from pagans and heathens, and it needs your help." The bishop looked shocked and about to speak but Aethelred had not finished and held up his hand.

"Dear Sigeric, please speak when I have finished. I have heard only good things about you and I understand you were very loyal to my brother, whom I love and miss every day. I hope you can extend that love to me and aid me in these troubled times."

Sigeric looked stunned as he was sure he had no friends within the King's inner circle, and he still held the young King accountable for the death of his brother. However, you do not advance within the church without being good at politics so Sigeric composed himself and decided to see how this would pan out.

"My Lord King, I am honoured and confused, if you need spiritual guidance surely that should come from the Bishop of Canterbury?"

"But, I fear the advice given to me by Aethelgar will be misguided and will have come from the mouth of Aelfstan." The king saw what he had been hoping for, a brief glimpse of hatred crossed Sigeric's face when the Bishop of Rochester was mentioned.

A brief silence followed as the king awaited a response from Sigeric and the Bishop of Ramsey weighed up the consequences of addressing the king as directly as Aethelred had spoken to him.

"My lord you are quite direct in what you say, and it is not my place to criticise a holy brother. However if there is any way that I can help my king and country I would be happy to."

"Thank you Sigeric, you will know that I was close to Aethelwold and welcomed his advice. I would like to hope we could have the same relationship and eventually it would please the king to have a friend as Archbishop of Canterbury."

This time Aethelred saw a brief glimpse of avarice sweep across the face of the most holy Bishop of Ramsey.

"Now Sigeric, if you have time perhaps you could stay with me while I hold council and discuss the Dane problem."

*

"How do you put up with her, Soren? A few minutes in her company and I am undecided on whether to punch her in the face or ring her neck?"

Instead of answering, Soren picked up his ale and took a long draft. He wasn't particularly thirsty; he just wanted to block the words that wanted to come out. He did not trust anyone and although he got on well with Thorgils, he was not going to reveal any of his inner thoughts to him. Having washed down his dark thoughts he answered his drinking companion.

"She is my master's wife and I value my job, also I believe he pays better than anyone else in Iceland and I do not want to jeopardise that."

Thorgils just looked at him for a second and then shrugged his shoulders, if Soren wanted to give him a stale answer that was up to him.

"Well Soren, you are a better man than me, I have no time for her and her twisted ways. I actually feel sorry for Bjorn, or I did until I heard his latest scheme."

"What scheme is that?"

"Soren, do not act innocent, you well know all his business and you must be aware that I am friendly with Gunnar."

"Oh that business." Still Soren did not expand anymore so Thorgils pushed on.

"You are aware that a man should keep all his possessions until he is found guilty at the Althing? You cannot punish any man until he has been judged and as far as I can see, Gunnar has done no wrong until his peers decide he has done wrong."

Soren chose to remain silent, but he did not know for how long. The capture of Gunnar's possessions seemed to send a ripple right across Iceland and Soren had not heard one comment that supported his master. He regretted his suggestion now as it had been made in haste, a process totally against everything Soren stood for.

Thorgils was getting more frustrated with his silence and decided to fill the air with more accusations.

"And what about Freyja, she is very much loved in these parts and there is a rumour one of the Danes tried to rape her."

"Yes, that is true and let it be known that I threatened retaliation, but I faced armed men and I was alone. But did you know the rapist was gelded by our Freyja?"

"Really? Good girl, I am sure Gunnar knows about it now and I would not want him chasing me across the country."

187

"Is there any news of Gunnar, now the Danes have left?"

"Should I let you know all I hear at the quay Soren, so that you can go running to your master?"

"I am my own man Thorgils, and I have always respected Gunnar."

"Well Soren, I will tell you something that is common knowledge. Kolskegg has set sail in search of his brother and Njal is working hard to gather support against Bjorn. There are many lawyers in this part of Iceland but even the best ones do not want to take on Bjorn's cause against Njal in this case, they know it would be like receiving a blow from Mjolnir."

Soren took another draft of ale and swallowed the words of Thorgils. The master of the quay was a straight man who, like Soren, kept his own council. He was fond of Gunnar and like most in these parts was charmed by Freyja's kindness. What Soren did not know was that Freyja had nursed Thorgils' elderly mother, they had all expected her to die in pain but she lasted half a year and drifted away in her sleep at the end. Thorgils and his family knew that they owed a great debt to Freyja, but she would only take the smallest amount of silver and only then not to insult their kindness.

Thorgils liked Soren and thought his cautious ways were a result of working under Hild.

"Have you thought on what to do if Kolskegg finds his brother and they return? I am sure Gunnar will believe you to be as guilty as Bjorn."

"I have been thinking on that Thorgils, and though Bjorn is a good master he is not worth dying for."

*

We were sailing fast, northward through the Irish Sea. The skei we were aboard was about forty paces long with thirty rowing benches, not all of them occupied. King Jarn was visibly upset with Jarl Olaf, leaving Dyflin with significant men so soon after the failed invasion by Ivar. Olaf had been quiet since we boarded and nobody had dared approach him. It seemed to me that Olaf had an understanding that he could attend the gathering in Shetland with his core guard, but Jarn had felt this was no longer feasible. From the brief conversations I had with Olaf, the meeting in Shetland was his priority and the defence of Dyflin had gotten in the way of his main aim.

Jarl Olaf was scowling at the empty benches on the longship and it was obvious he had wanted a full skei. There was room for sixty rowers plus up to twenty eight passengers and cargo. But as a concession to Jarn we were only forty in total so the senior men, including myself, were expected to take an oar, while Olaf manned the rudder. I thanked Thor for the strong south westerly wind that eased the work of pulling this large vessel through the water.

Jarl Olaf had sent word to Mort and had arranged for him to send more men from the garrison at Kirkham. The ship was well stocked for a long journey but I knew this was a ship of war and nobody could say how long we would be at sea. I found Olaf to be an engaging man and a natural leader, although he could be stern and he was completely single minded. I wished Erik was with me but he had his own saga to write. Unfortunately I was seated beside that irritating fellow Ketil, who also claimed to be a Jomsviking and the closest friend of Berg. I was a little suspicious as Berg seemed to avoid any contact with him.

It is strange how you meet some people and they instantly rub you the wrong way. There was no stand out reason to dislike this man but he seemed to be a wild meadow full of irritants. He spoke about women using the base language when only men are together. It sounded like he had never known a woman and he had formed his opinion while only in the company of the coarsest men. I begrudgingly acknowledged his chatter with the merest grunts but I tired of him quickly.

*

Soren stood on the sharp slag, high up in the centre of Iceland. The wind whipped his hair and clothes and he could smell only the sulphur from the lair of Hel. How he got here he could not say, and why he stood in such a remote part of the country was another mystery. He knew that Gunnar had returned but could not remember being told and he felt it was wise to keep out of his way for now.

He looked up at the sky. It was dark grey with bubbles of white tinged clouds. Randomly the clouds lit up from inside but made no sound; the gods were busy but not interested in man.

The solid magma formed a small plain and at the end of it he could see a woman, Hild. She stood facing him, the wind striking her hard so that the purple silk vest stuck to her body making her look naked. He felt revulsion at the sight; some said she was a handsome woman, but only the folk that did not know her. To Soren all the jealousy, greed and bile generated from that woman negated anything positive. She had started to age and Soren had noticed. Perhaps every lie she told was reflected in the lines on her face, he smiled to himself when he recalled walking in on her while she was studying these. She acted as if she had been caught doing something she shouldn't and Soren still took pleasure from her embarrassment.

He looked to the left on instinct, although he heard no sound. There was a woman part climbing and part running up to the old lava plain. It was Freyja, she was too far away to call to and she seemed to be heading in the direction of Hild. Behind her Soren saw men on horseback following her. The lead rider was holding a bow but his ascent was too steep and he had to hold on tight to his horse. Soren was surprised that all the men were riding such magnificent horses, as the job was only suitable for the hardy Icelandic pony. The rider with the bow was upon a brilliant white mare and he wore a white tabard over his armour. On his head was a silver helmet with what looked like gilded gold around the crown. Soren shouted to Freyja, he put everything into that shout but it came out like a whisper. If she followed the plain toward Hild she would be disadvantaged, as it would surely favour the men on horseback. Between him and the horsemen was rough jagged ground, hard to cover and impossible for horses.

Freyja had reached the flat lands now, and flew forward in the direction of her nemesis. She was flight of foot and came close to a speed only gods could dream of; it was well known that the only person who could outrun Freyja was her husband. It was not too long before she approached the halfway distance to Hild and Soren could see the horsemen negotiating the last part of the climb. He looked over at Hild and she was laughing; it shocked him as he had become so used to her sarcasm he did not think she had any other expression.

He tried to raise his arms but the effort was too great and it seemed he had no control over his body. All Soren could do was watch the woman he secretly admired, as she was hunted like a common thrall.

Freyja had covered almost half the distance to Hild and she kept running at a fierce pace, but now the Horses were on fairly level ground and they broke into a fast trot. The lead horseman, him with the crown of gold, gripped his ride with his knees and raised his bow while on the move and loosed an arrow. To Soren, the watcher, time slowed down and he felt he could almost see the vibration of the twine as the feathered shaft flew across the gap between horse and woman. The arrow hit Freyja square in her back and she was thrown forward with the force, landing on the unforgiving pumice. Soren wanted to run to her, hold her and heal her but he could not move. As the horsemen approached Freyja the sulphur mist of Loki's world drifted across the plain obscuring his view. As Soren awoke all he could hear was the sound of Hild cursing the lifeless body of Gunnar's dead wife.

*

The Witan was gathered at King Aethelred's behest and he knew that this was a war council but he did not wish to address it as so. Most of his loyal Earls would understand given the constant coastal attacks from the Norsemen. However he had Sigeric to think of and he wanted an ally within the church and it did not pay to frighten him off at his first meeting. The King had asked Sigeric to attend and the Bishop had been happy to. Aethelred also asked him to speak if he needed a question asked or if he needed to make a statement. The Bishop of Ramsey would know most of the men at the meeting but as a formality he had been introduced to each in turn. Sigeric was not fazed at all, as the politics and in fighting of the church where not so very different from the king's court. Also there was an old ally of Sigeric in Ealdorman Brihtnoth, both had been loyal supporters of the king's dead brother and now found themselves at the young king's court. Godwin and Edgar of Kent were present, Thorod too and to everyone's surprise Earl Alfric. The man close to Aelfstan, Bishop of Rochester, Sigeric's nemesis.

Alfric had brought a substantial force with him under the pretence it was there in support of the king but in reality the Earl was expecting an ambush. He was a Wessex Earl but there were long held rumours of a Danish Jarl in his ancestry, this was underlined by the belief that Alfric would welcome the Danish King to rule England. He knew of the rumours and denied them in words only, never showing outward support of his king. Aethelred had him watched but knew he could not afford a civil war, so an uncomfortable stale mate held while the Danes raided the borders.

The Witan began with each Saxon lord swearing fealty to the King. Alfric and his men were last to swear and made a great sycophantic show which embarrassed the young king. Before the young prince could address the Witan Sigeric stood up and addressed the council.

"Honourable Earls, I am most pleased to be here at the side of our king and in the company of my old friend the Ealdorman of Essex. I am but a simple disciple of Christ and know nothing about how to administer a country as vast as all England. However, as a child of the church I am fully aware of the threat posed by the pagan forces of evil. Do not forget that it was the church that was attacked first by these pirates, and the heathens like to sniff around our coast looking for our most holy relics. I make this point clear as I do not want you to treat my presence with caution or hold back on details, while worrying about my delicate ears. Speak true in front of me and do not miss any details.

"Oh and one more thing, Ealdorman Alfric, please do not try and crawl up my arse also as you are not welcome there."

A great roar of laughter filled the hall as everyone sought to relieve the tension, everyone except Alfric and his entourage.

Chapter 19

The two Aesir, Vikings oath-bound
To the warrior's home, to Odin's,
As much great warriors they might be,
Waded hard through the swamp
Of swords flowing around them.

The ground was marshy and swamp like, hard tufts of grass were like islands among the sodden earth. The horses were skittish and showing signs of stress but the men on their backs had it easy when compared to the huscurls on foot. At some points the footmen would sink up to their knees and have to be pulled out of the sucking mud by their fellows.

"The next arsehole that gets stuck will be left to sink into the earth. I am not your lazy nurse mother and I could not give a skit who is left behind." Litta was angry at this delay, he had imagined riding to Ivar's aid and being welcomed by his king. Although he was pleased with himself, they had started out with only fifty men but travelling through the surrounding towns and villages he had been able to recruit another hundred. It had cost him a little silver but mostly he had threatened and warned of the wrath of their king. Ivar was known for his liking of combat and the common men in his kingdom imagined him wreaking vengeance on them personally.

Litta did not know how far it would be to Dyflin, as he was more used to being on a boat, but he did know that he needed a woman. There was talk of a settlement a few leagues ahead but it was taking an age to get through this marshy land. The movement of the horse did not help as it gave him an almost permanent erection, but a settlement meant women and all women had a kut tucked up at the top of their legs. Litta forgot about the marsh and moved onward thinking of a possible prize.

Eventually they started to travel up a slight incline that took them above the sodden ground on to something like dry land. Ahead of them was a large copse that the track circled around, and on the other side was the village. As they approached the copse Litta saw that it contained a large number of horses, probably tied to branches. His band of men approached more cautiously, knowing the horses must belong to another band of fighting men. He had his troop ready their spears and his leading men unsheathe their swords. As they came around the side of the copse they saw a group of about ten men standing there ready for battle. Litta stopped his men and hailed the group ahead of him. Instead of a hail coming back one man stepped out of the group and shouted, "Strike me, if it isn't that ugly groda Litta. Bring your men over to the camp and come with me to see your king." Litta relaxed, it was Tyr and he knew he had found Ivar, hoping his reward would be great.

*

King Ivar had already made some plans for a return to Dyflin, but he would need to build more longships and maybe recruit some Vikings from the Norse in the land of the Franks. He was angry at Baldr, but also himself for not making plans that were more solid. He had underestimated Jarl Olaf and he knew he would have to work harder to defeat his experienced foe.

He sat by the fire eating the meat that Kanin had cooked for him. She was bending over; turning a hare to ensure it was well cooked. The sight of her firm arse lifted his spirits and he knew that he wanted her again.

"Come here Kanin, your king needs comforting."

She turned and smiled at him but there was a guarded look in her eyes he had not seen before.

"What troubles you, I do not like to see the spark missing from your eye."

Becoming the king's lover had given her confidence but she still knew that she was a slave and he could bore of her quickly. Gwenhyvach stood in front of her seated king and decided to tell him how she felt in her broken Irish.

"I was scared, I thought you would be killed and then I would be raped and killed too."

"Come here and let me hold you, I will not bring you so close to the battle again. The next time I go into battle you can stay behind with the supplies and the injured men."

She sat between his legs, he held her and she felt safe again but she never wanted to see another battle field again.

Ivar held here tight and felt aroused but he knew this was no time for tupping, he had to inspire his men and let them know it was not a defeat, just a regrouping.

"King Ivar, may I interrupt, there is somebody to see you."

Ivar looked up as soon as he heard Tyr. Standing next to his captain was his ugly little friend from childhood.

"Odin's balls, I never thought I would be pleased to see your ugly face Litta. I thought you were worm food in Dyflin."

Litta beamed, he knew that his luck had changed and this would only go well for him.

"I escaped, and I managed to get back to Waterford trying to warn you. As you had left I managed to gather one hundred and fifty men, we were travelling to Dyflin to support your invasion."

"Well done Litta, sit down and eat with us, my Kanin will give you some of that hare, it should be cooked now."

Litta watched Kanin like a hawk, his eyes scanning her body. Ivar noticed and laughed, "you dirty bastard Litta, keep those disgusting hands off my woman or I will cut your other ear off. If you need to stick your orm somewhere, go and offer one of the women in the village a little silver. Although when I think about it, if she sees you it may need a lot of silver."

Litta took no offence and turned toward the township, as his cock had greater needs than his stomach.

"Do you trust him lord? I believe that all Litta thinks of are his own needs and would change sides in an instance."

"Tyr, if it had been Bjarni turning up here I would be suspicious, but Litta has a strange loyalty to me and anyway I think that if he spent any time with the men of Dyflin they would have killed him too. Don't forget what an irritating arsehole he is."

"Have you thought anymore on our next move? Do we return to Waterford and prepare for war with Dyflin?"

"Let us wait for Sihtric and see what he has found out."

*

Young Sihtric wanted to be of use to his father and to create something of a reputation as a warrior. He had not had much chance when they attacked Dyflin but he had been tasked with returning to the town as a spy. After hiding his horse in a small woodland to the south, he walked back toward Dyflin but kept off the main paths. He realised his sense of the distance on foot was wrong, as he seemed to be walking for an age with only

195

animal tracks to follow. Eventually he found his way close to the slave enclosure and settled down for the night. His temporary encampment was among the long grasses and nettles near the woodland scrub. He realised he had been a little naïve when choosing his camp, as a great celebration seemed to be happening not far away. This caused many people to wander close by his hide away and twice men came and pissed almost upon him. If it had not been dark he would surely have been found. Eventually the revelry ceased and Sihtric drifted into an uncomfortable sleep.

He awoke damp, covered in morning dew and desperate for a piss and a drink. The dampness crept into his bones and he thought he would never warm up again. He stood and stamped some feeling back into his feet. He had a few silver shards on him so he made his way through the thick, wet grass toward Wood Quay in the hope of buying some breakfast.

The Kingdom of Dyflin was a great crossing point in the northern world. Many folk from the north, south and east came to sell wares and trade in the markets. So a young man from the Irish Kingdom of Waterford did not sound out of place, especially as he spoke both of the two main languages of the kingdom.

He bought himself some weak ale and a fresh baked small loaf and sat down to watch the early work at the quay. Not much was happening apart from a longship being laden with provisions for a long sea voyage. After he finished his early meal he felt conspicuous and decided to wander back into town, when he saw something that would interest his father. A troop of about forty men were coming to the quay and made straight for the prepared longship. Sihtric stood aside for the men to pass and they all ignored him to a man. He felt the tickle of excitement in his stomach and a little afraid. He told his legs not to run and walk nonchalantly out of town and down the road, back to his waiting horse. King Ivar of Waterford, his father would be proud of him for he would bring news that Jarl Olaf and his huscurls were leaving Dyflin.

*

Litta was spent, and the old hag straightened and pulled her skirts down, not bothering to clean herself. She said something to Litta and grinned at him, showing just three teeth. For a man dominated by his libido, Litta was always a little confused in the moment after copulation and did not hear what she said. He was about to ask her to repeat herself when she shrugged and walked off tucking the silver coin into a fold in her skirt.

Litta walked back to his King and hoped he would be treated better by his lord.

"Litta, now you feel better come and tell me all you know about your time in Dyflin, do not forget the part where I was betrayed."

He knew he would have to be careful as it was obvious that Ivar was still upset about not being King of Dyflin and losing some good men. Litta was not sure how much Ivar knew so he chose to tell the truth while painting Bjarni and Baldr as less loyal than he thought they were.

*

After Litta had finished telling what had happened to him, embellishing the story with comments about Baldr being disloyal and Bjarni's greed, he sat down and helped himself to some cold meat.

"Well my ugly friend I expected you to come out with a trough of lies but you have surprised me and told something close to the truth. Perhaps a reward should come your way, what is it you want?"

Litta was taken aback and thanked all the gods he had not added more to the story.

"What I want King Ivar, is to be a respected freeman serving you and enough income to keep my own slave."

"Let me think on that for the moment, but you have pleased me and there will be silver coming your way soon."

Tyr did not look happy, as the smaller man was odious and repellent but he seemed to amuse Ivar in some way. As Tyr and Litta were pondering the small man's rise in the ranks a shout went up from one of the guards of the camp.

"Rider!"

King Ivar stood up and beamed as his son rode into the encampment shouting to his father.

"Slow down son, what have you found out."

"Sorry father, but Jarl Olaf has left Dyflin on a sea voyage, he has taken a longship full of warriors with him."

"Well done Sihtric, Tyr gather the men together. I think we should pay King Jarn another visit."

Chapter 20

But then the terrible one, the hard-reding Hymir,
came home heavy laden from hunting.
He strode into the hall with icicles a jangling,
the churl returned with a frozen beard.

We settled down in the great hall at Leirvik and Sigurd the Stout, Jarl of Orkney and Shetland, welcomed us all to his feast. It was the largest hall I had been in and at one end was a curtain covering the private area of the Jarl. In front of the curtain was a bench for all the important men and their seconds.

At one end sat Sigurd the Stout and his man, next to him was Jarl Olaf and Berg, then we were introduced to two Danish Jarls, Justin the Black and Guthmund Horadur, the skinny. There was space at the end for at least two more and Sigurd had indicated we wait for one more ally. Everyone had brought their warriors to show strength and the hall was full of the different groups all enjoying the ale of Shetland. Even among all the talking I could hear some commotion from outside. The big leather door was pulled aside and a giant of a man stepped in. He had to bend down to get inside but when he straightened up again you could not see the doorway. His hair and beard were the colour of the hot lava in Iceland and his fists were the size of a boy's head. Most of the hall was watching this giant arrive and I looked around and saw Jarl Olaf scowl at the new arrival. The big man stepped to one side and a man of normal height, although he looked much shorter now, entered the hall. He had black hair and a trimmed beard, plaited down the middle. His clothes looked freshly made and he had gold arm rings. He was followed into the hall by about fifty men and they were led to the few spare benches. The big red head and his Jarl made their way up to the main bench.

Before they got half way I saw Olaf stand up, he was obviously angry and he made it known to Sigurd. Sigurd's captain moved Olaf behind the curtain, all the while Sigurd was trying to appease him.

Ulf Rottskagg walked straight up to Berg and the older man stood up placing his hand on the pommel of his sword.

"I did not know they let weak old women in here."

"You haven't changed Ulf, go and bully somebody else before I teach you a lesson."

Ulf was ready to respond but his Jarl put a hand on his shoulder and asked him to be calm.

"Berg, how are you? Is 'Olaf the Unkempt' looking after you and Ketil?"

"I can only speak for myself and I have never been happier. I have a woman now and am missing her already. If you need to ask after Ketil you can find him over there."

"I will Berg, but let us be friends again as we were before. After this night we shall be allies against a common enemy so I hope we can forget old squabbles."

"I can Alfvine, but can Ulf?"

Alfvine tried a smile but it looked more like a grimace, they both knew that Ulf always struggled to forgive.

Sigurd and Olaf came back from behind the curtain and the husband of Queen Gyda approached Alfvine with his hand held out in greeting.

"My old adversary the well-dressed Jomsviking, I hear we shall be allies."

"Yes Jarl Olaf, and I hope you can forgive me for the way I acted in the past, but your wife is a beautiful and intelligent woman. I am afraid I was a little jealous but the best man won."

Olaf's jaw nearly hit the ground. He could not quite believe what he was hearing, but the proud man in front of him had apologised, a rare feat in these times.

"Please Jarl Alfvine, let us forget the past and look to future alliances."

Sigurd handed them both some ale and they sealed their friendship with a toast.

*

The big red head came over to our side of the hall and gestured to Ketil. They both left the hall and the smell of boar and mutton drifted in through the open doorway. Sigurd announced that a feast would happen and then there would be some entertainment. I was looking forward to some hot food as we had been eating dried and salted food on board the ship for some days now. On the table there were bowls of fruit and nuts and each of us had our own wooden bowl and spoon. Bread and cheese was brought in before the carved meat was distributed to the tables. There was plenty of ale to help wash down the feast and mead for those that enjoyed it. I looked over to the main bench and noticed that it was empty, and wondered where they had gone. This was only a fleeting thought as I was busy filling my belly.

*

Olaf and Berg followed the others around the curtain and through a smaller door at the back of the hall. Behind the hall was a small wooden hut similar to the kind of place a carpenter would own. It was a sturdy place with the lower part of the wall made from hardy, grey stone. Rising from this was a wall of wattle and daub reinforced with wood that looked like the pine of Norway. The roof had been made from wooden shingles held up with large iron nails. Inside was a large working area with a smaller living section at the back, away from the door. Sitting here was a man shrouded in darkness and Olaf recognised him from his brief meeting earlier.

Benches and a table had been set up in the main part of the cabin and they sat down before Sigurd and his man left. Food and ale was brought in before Justin spoke, "We will not talk business until our guest has arrived."

Jarl Olaf was confused; he thought that Alfvine had been the special guest. Ulf arrived and sat with Alfvine, his arrival broke the silence.

"Jarl, can I not sit with the men, they are singing and soon there will be entertainment, sagas will be told and there is a rumour that there will be women later."

"I need you here Ulf; you need to meet our new friends." Ulf took a look at the food laid out and beamed, "at least we are fed well here." There were four suckling pigs on the table, mutton stew, hard cheese and a choice of drinks.

"Ulf, you will remember me, Jarl Olaf. Will you drink with me to seal our new friendship?"

Ulf smirked at him and poured out two drinks, "Where is your slippery little man Olaf, I would like to drink with the only man that has defeated me."

"He is back in the Kingdom of Dyflin, protecting my Queen."

"Well you will have to do, let us drink to an eternity in Valholl."

Both men took a long draft of ale as the door to the cabin was opened. In walked a young man dressed as a warrior with an old bear skin over his shoulders. He was accompanied by six armed Saxons and of all things, a monk. They looked like an assassination party but behind them came Sigurd and his man.

"What, by Odin, is a Christian doing here?" Alfvine intervened again to calm down his hot headed friend.

"Ulf be quiet and listen, you are here to learn of our plans for the future."

The monk spoke up in accented Norse, "I am Brother Alfred the learned scribe of the Bishop of Rochester. I am here to translate for Ealdorman Elfgar and to offer our support to the King of Denmark against the usurper."

The Saxon Jarl had an armed guard but they would all surely die if things turned sour and they knew it. The only one who seemed to have any confidence was the monk, if he died he knew he was going to a better place.

Guthmund stood up and greeted the men who were instinctively the enemy of all Norsemen. The monk translated and had a small conversation with the young Jarl before giving his reply.

"Jarl Elfgar thanks you for the offer of food and drink and would gladly sit with you. He wishes all the men here to know this one thing. His father's mother, whom he knew as Farmor, was descended from a Danish Jarl from Jutland. Ealdorman Aelfric, Elfgar's father, believes his allegiance is to the Danish throne and not the English crown."

There was a loud harrumph from the direction of Ulf but all took the news at face value for now. After all, the boy's father would hopefully be a useful spy in the Saxon camp.

Guthmund and Justin both gave assurances of safe passage, direct from the King of Denmark. So Elfgar and Alfred sat at the table while Sigurd took the guard outside to get some food. Guthmund continued to lead the meeting although he always referred to Justin on important points.

"Jarl Elfgar, perhaps you can give us some news from Angle land?"

The young man stood up and his holy man stood with him to translate.

"I am Elfgar son of Aelfric and son of Denmark, my father attends the Witan and will have an ear close to the false King. The news I bring is Aethelred expects a direct attack on Wessex as his ancestral home is at Corfe Gate and at nearby Swanwich it is has a shallow sandy bay that is fodder for a longship. He has placed his most trusted warriors there and they are building many ships along the coast. My father passes this advice to you honourable men; approaching the estuary of the Temese, on the north side is the old burgh of Gipeswic. This town has left its defences to rot away and the local thegn is more interested in his market than maintaining his walls. It would be an easy target and it is accessed by the river Orwell known locally as Gipeswic water."

The young earl sat down at the bench and his monk continued with a closing statement of their loyalty to the King of Denmark. Guthmund stood again and thanked the Saxons for their support before offering them some ale.

"If you wish Jarl Elfgar, you may return to your camp but first we must confirm some points so that we may exchange messages after this night."

There were many people in the old area of Dane law that still held loyalties to their ancestors, so finding a route back to Jorvik would be easy. The man that built the cabin they were meeting in had a carpenters shop in the centre of Jorvik. He would be the central point of all messages as Guthmund and his allies would be constantly on the move. The Saxons left and returned to their camp but were given food and ale to enjoy. Even though a betrayal was afoot they still felt very nervous being in a Viking kingdom and being so heavily outnumbered.

*

"Do you trust the Saxon boy?" Jarl Olaf was very uncomfortable; the advice was leading them direct to a specific town in Angle land, very far from home.

"It is useful advice but we need not act on it, the fact that one of the men of the Witan has sent his son here tells us Aethelred has problems with loyalty. This means it may be easier than we thought to regain the area of Dane law and perhaps even the whole of Angle land."

Justin stood now and asked to speak, "also, dear friends, we have paid the Norsemen of the Franks to attack the south coast and reminded them of the rich pickings to be taken from the wealth of Wessex."

Chapter 21

What seekest thou here?
For what is thy search?
What, friendless one, fain wouldst thou know?
By ways so wet, must thou wander hence,
For, weakling, no home hast thou here.

Aelle stood on the grass hillock, above the bay of Swanwich. It was a perfect landing point for a Viking ship, being a long stretch of shallow sandy coast. The sea was fairly calm even though the sky was the same dirty grey as the water. Wind whipped around Aelle, lifting his old bear skin and cooling his skin. His instinct told him a storm was coming and he hoped it would be wild, long and treacherous to all ships.

The King had requested the Wincanceaster militia protect the coast near his birthplace of Corfe Gate. The local thegn, Alwin, had brought a few men along but not enough to make a difference, although all of them carried a bow. Aelle had half of the militia plus far too many new recruits. He was not happy, he had enough men to maybe deal with three longships and even then he would have to be lucky.

"Do you think they will come?" Alwin looked tense, reflecting how Aelle felt.

"They will come Alwin, the bastards always do. I was told that their land was in eternal winter and no crops could grow there. Although they seem to grow plenty of Norse and Dane; who swarm over our land like flies on a cow's skit."

They both stared out to sea and they could see nothing on the horizon. Eventually the sea seemed to blend in with the cold grey sky.

"Come on Alwin; let us send two of my new recruits to look out while we have some warm stew." Aelle patted Alwin on the back with his warriors hand and Alwin could feel that pat for a long time after. The pot of stew had been boiling for some days and contained mushrooms, wild garlic and roots plus a selection of animals, the primary ones being hare and gull.

Swanwich had a long strip of sand running south to north along the eastern coast of Purbeck. At the north it opened into Poole harbour with easy access to the walled town of Wareham. The other half of the Wincanceaster militia were stationed here in case the Norse raided the precious mint for silver. At the southern end of the beach the land turned west and rose to accommodate high cliffs. So if or when the Vikings came they would land at Swanwich or approach the River Frome to Wareham. Aelle had three men up on the cliff to raise the alarm if they saw an attack coming from the west. He hoped he had thought of everything, although he knew that his troops were spread very thin. Well there was nothing more for him to do but wait, so he ate the stew and welcomed the warmth of it inside him.

*

Relief washed over Bjorn Bjornsson; after much searching he had found a lawyer to represent him against the formidable Njal. Eyjolf Bolverksson was one of the most prominent lawyers in the south of Iceland. He was not necessarily an adversary of Njal but he had never challenged himself against the great lawyer and saw this as an opportunity to test his mettle. If Eyjolf could win this legal battle his reputation would be greatly enhanced.

There was a price to pay to employ one of the best lawyers around, but if Bjorn won the case he would have doubled his land and one harvest would more than pay for the lawyers' fees.

Life had become more difficult since Gunnar had left the country. Some of his best customers had gone elsewhere for their imported goods and he supposed it was caused by Gunnar in the long run. He had investigated each of his lost accounts and they fell into two categories; those that were close to Gunnar and those that objected to his underhand acquisition of Hlidarendi. He regretted obtaining the land now as it had caused nothing but trouble. Hild was obsessed with the place and spent most of her time there, which at least gave him a break from her vicious tongue. The worst outcome was that he felt Soren had become distant, he had challenged his farm manager last night and the conversation had surprised him.

"Master it was a mistake to take Hlidarendi, and I know it was me that encouraged it but I regret advising you so. My advice now is to go to Njal and try and resolve it by arbitration. Perhaps you can be reimbursed the blood geld you paid to Harald and Gustav?"

"Soren, are you drunk? After all the trouble I have gone through to acquire the land and secure legal representation? I will not give it up and I cannot believe you have changed your mind on it!"

"But master we should look at all the facts; perhaps looking at how you can profit from this purchase. Imagine the farm was owned by a third party and not Gunnar Hamundsson, would you have bought it off the Danes, knowing Kolskegg could come and seize it at any time?"

"But Soren, Gunnar and Freyja are gone; Kolskegg is overseas searching for his brother. It could be more than a year before we see Kolskegg again."

"What of Hjort or his sister Arnguda and her kin? You must not forget Njal, he is openly gathering support for Gunnar, while reminding everyone that the law rules Iceland, not any King."

"I am close to securing an equally skilled lawyer and I am confident in my pursuit. You will not advise me again on this matter Soren. Remember I am your master and you will do as I say."

Bjorn recalled Soren standing there far too long before leaving his hall and going to do whatever his farm manager did at these times.

*

Soren was furious with himself at breaking one of his golden rules. He had spoken on impulse seeing only the profit, and only realising the error when it was too late. At the time he had not thought of Kolskegg or the rest of Gunnar's family, but the facts were obvious. Either Gunnar would return and forcibly wrench back his land or his brother would do the same. Soren knew in these cases it was the lesser important allies that could end up dead. He would ensure that he did not become a small debt of blood geld.

He was a freeman now and it would take Bjorn a few days to realise that Soren had left his employment. He would recover his hidden horde and retire to the mountains until this all blew over. But first he would put some insurance in place to confirm that he was not on Bjorn and Hild's side.

He waited in sight of the buildings but far enough away so that he would not be noticed unless somebody was looking for a wayward traveller. Eventually he saw a man come out and receive a pony before riding his way.

Njal had seen him but kept up a pretence that he hadn't, although Soren could see he had dropped one hand to his sword.

"Well met Njal Thorgeirsson, I hope you have had a pleasant morning."

"Soren Guldhuvud, forgive my suspicion but have you come here to kill me? For if you look back to my home you will see armed men heading this way."

Soren glanced back to the farm and saw three men already on horseback heading toward them.

"I am not here to kill you; I wanted to speak to you without witnesses as I have left the employ of the fat fool and his evil wife."

Njal turned in his saddle and called back to the men to wait at a distance.

"Well Soren, speak, as I am a busy man."

"I have already told you that I no longer work for Bjorn but I need to tell you that he has ignored my council to end this matter of Gunnar's property.

"I advised him to come to you and return the farm and land in exchange of the blood geld but he will hear nothing of it. Furthermore he has employed Eyjolf Bolverksson and believes he can win this case."

Njal smirked at the mention of Eyjolf and then started to ride on.

"Ride a little with me Soren and explain why you have come and told me this. Have you changed sides or are you on the side of Soren Guldhuvud as always?"

"It has been hard working there these last few months, Bjorn is melancholy and jealous of all others and his bitch of a wife is too much to take. I cannot suffer to be in the same place as her, she fills me with hatred and I could easily plunge a knife in her guts."

"What will you do now; have you come to me for employment?"

"No, I have enough money to survive, but I will hide away and watch what happens. I will not return to the world until this episode is over."

At this Soren turned his horse away and rode north, Njal guessed he would hide in the mountains with only Loki for company.

*

Alwin walked over and woke Aelle from his doze.

"Time for fighting, the Vikings have been spotted at sea."

Aelle had felt comfortable after his meal and rested a little on the hill side.

"Where are they Alwin?" he asked this as he stood and concentrated on the sea.

"The men on the cliff have spotted them and are running down to join us with more detail, but I suspect they have come from the west."

"Ok Alwin we will wait, but I want the men hidden from the sea. It is better if the enemy land here and face a fight than if they sail straight up to the walls of Wareham."

Alwin resented being ordered around by Aelle, especially as he was a thegn and Aelle was only a captain. But Aelle commanded obedience, was an experienced fighter, and a formidable looking foe.

They lay atop the small hill above the strand and saw the first of the six longships come round the rocks at Handfast Point. All they could do was wait and it was a strange feeling for Alwin, if they landed here he would have to face Vikings intent on killing him but if they sailed past they would cause destruction in his own neighbourhood, and maybe set up camp on Brownsea Island.

"Right Alwin, we will let the bastards approach the beach but when they are in the water we will attack. We can start with your bowmen and then launch our spears at them, and when they have got used to that we will have to cut down the arseholes."

Aelle spoke with the confidence of a seasoned soldier but in his heart he was concerned. There were over three hundred Norsemen in those boats and his Saxons numbered only two hundred.

Now they could see all six longships and they seemed to be struggling to get round Handfast Point. Aelle could see flecks of white on the wave tops and he noticed the wind was blowing harder into his face. The pagans were trying to pull down their sails as the wind blew in off the German sea. The Viking war ships, dragons of the sea, were deploying their oars but the last one was close to the devil and his wife, the two tall chalk monoliths standing out in the cold salty water. As the Wincanceaster militia watched the waves were being whipped up against their foe and the last longship was driven against the devils rock and Aelle could see men being tipped into the ocean. He hoped they were wearing chainmail, axes and swords, metal to drag them down to a watery hell.

Whether the Danes wished to land at Swanwich or had planned to sail to Wareham, the weather ensured they made for the sandy beach and the comfort of dry land.

"Alwin, if they land do you think your bowmen could hit them from here?"

"Almost, but it would be better to stand a little closer, then we could kill more Vikings."

Aelle noticed that Alwin was smiling at last; maybe this would be easier than he thought.

"Get them ready but do not show yourself, we do not want to scare them away just yet."

It looked as if the leading five ships were intent on getting into Poole harbour but now turned and headed for the safety of Swanwich sands. The waves were coming in quite rough now and the oars of the longships spent half the time rowing in the air. Alwin was glad that he was on dry land and not in those boats, as another longship tilted too far and was taking on water. Soon it was spilling more Danes into a cold salty death. Some of the sister ships tried pulling on survivors but it was so rough and most were too far away. The surviving ships headed for land and Aelle could almost see the determination etched on the faces of the sailors.

The first longship scraped across the shingle and sand, soon enough the Danes leapt out and started to pull the boat up the beach.

"Ok Alwin, let them get a second boat ashore and then let fly with your arrows."

The warriors in the first ship got it safely on dry land and then they went back into the surf to help their comrades. They managed to get two more longships on land while the last surviving ship was struggling to straighten and come ashore. As the second and third ships were half way out of the surf Alwin gave the order and his bowmen ran half way down the hill but stayed on the high ground and let loose their first volley. From the bottom of the hill to the sea was only about thirty paces; no real distance for even a poor bowman. There were twenty archers and now there were twenty dead Vikings. The invaders tried to reach into their ships to collect shields and weapons but another eighteen where dead before they were fully armed. A few men were still stuck in the longships and tried to use the ship for protection. Still out at sea the final longship was being spun round, its occupants could see their colleagues were under attack. The Vikings on the shore looked up at the twenty archers, and then saw them joined by ten times as many warriors. At the front was a big man with long brown hair and a bushy brown beard. Across his shoulders was the hide of a great bear and in his hand was a double headed axe. If any of the invading Vikings said they were not scared that day they would have been lying. Ahead of them was a Saxon army and behind them was the angry sea.

Aelle called a halt to the arrows; he could see that they were low anyway. On another order his front row ran toward the bottom of the hill and launched their spears at the enemy. As soon as they were in the air his second line ran forward and launched their spears. When the spears hit their targets the Wincanceaster militia ran screaming across the sand. The Vikings had suffered even more casualties under the onslaught of arrow and spear, and it was only the difficulty of running through sand that gave them time to form a simple shield wall.

Aelle was on the right flank and Alwin took the left and they ran hard at the hastily formed shield wall.

Aelle hit it hard with his broad axe and he felt joy as his great weapon cut through the birch shield disabling, the Viking holding it. He pulled his axe toward him and opened up a gap in the thin wall. His men poured into the gap, cutting and slashing, causing panic among the pirates. Aelle dropped his faithful axe to the ground and pulled out his sword, laughing as he entered the fray.

Alwin was glad of Aelle's militia around him; they knew what to do in a shield wall. They were all well drilled and knew how to break down the enemy. He felt pleased with himself that he kept his bowmen well trained. The arrows and spears had cut the Viking numbers on the beach in half. Now they had to face twice as many Saxons, all well fed and well rested. Alwin was sure that the trial of rowing through the storm would have sapped their strength, and Aelle's men knew it too.

Aelle thrust his sword deep into the belly of a Norseman and was sprayed in his vomit of blood. He withdrew his sword and hacked at the man to his left, but he was already falling under the blow of one of his men. Aelle stood and watched as his men finished off the Vikings, killing everyone. The sea was coming in to wash away the blood, but there was so much soaked into the sand it would take a high tide to remove it all. Aelle looked out to sea and saw the last longship had gained control and was now rowing away to the south as the storm finished. Godwin would be pleased with his captain, as they had repelled another invasion, albeit a small one.

Chapter 22

There, weary of ocean, the wall along they set their bucklers, their broad shields and bowed them to bench:

The breastplates clanged, war gear of men;

Their weapons stacked, spears of seafarers stood together, grey tipped ash:

That iron band was worthily weaponed!

Erik was at Wood Quay early, he had not been able to sleep for fear of missing his transport this morning. He was so early that even the food sellers had not finished setting up yet. His boat to Iceland was only just showing signs of life so he waited by the baker unloading his ware. He gave the man a silver coin and gathered what he hoped would be enough fresh bread for the crew. He was due to meet the captain of the boat at dawn and they would load and set off for Iceland, but there was no sign of Kjar. Erik set the bread down in a wicker basket and waited. The crew had told them Kjar liked a little female company before sailing, he said it was for good luck but Erik suspected he needed a little comfort before spending a week at sea.

While waiting a medium sized boat pulled into the quay and men started to gingerly disembark. Erik glanced over nonchalantly and was surprised to see Gustav helping to secure the boat.

"Gustav, as I live and breathe, what are you doing in Dyflin?"

"Well Erik, we have come to find you."

The two friends embraced and realised how much they missed the other's company.

"Gustav, have you told Erik the news about the fugitive?" Harald had crept toward, them still suffering some pain.

Erik was struck dumb at the arrival of Harald, of course he would be close by if Gustav was here, but he was not welcome since Erik had learned the truth. Before he could gather himself Gustav spoke up.

"We found Gunnar, he was in Iceland and we believe he could have come to Dyflin."

"Gustav, I need to talk to you in private."

"Hey Erik, if you want to come to Iceland we need to leave now." Kjar called over from his boat interrupting the old friends.

"Gustav, wait a moment I was just leaving but I will postpone my trip as I need to speak with you now."

Erik went over to Kjar and cancelled his plans, paying the captain in silver for his trouble. Kjar was a practical man and was happy that he had earned a little coin for doing almost nothing.

Erik returned to the brothers and noticed Harald was using a stick to hold himself up.

"What happened to you?"

Gustav stepped in and answered for his brother, "Gunnar's wife almost gelded him for putting his hands in the wrong place."

"Get to Hel Gustav, and show your brother some respect."

This reaction only caused Erik and Gustav to laugh.

"Harald, you can find somewhere to sleep tonight, I will go with Erik to find food and supplies." Harald started to object but Erik and Gustav walked away, ignoring his protests.

"Gustav, we will only talk when we are alone, so follow me."

Erik walked to the king's quarters and made his way to the armoury store. The King's guard recognised him and let him use the store with the help of a silver coin. Erik pulled the wooden door closed and stood facing his old friend in the cramped storage.

"Gustav, Gunnar did not kill your brother Gull."

"What, no you must be mistaken; he was found next to Gull and covered in his blood."

Then Erik told Gustav all he knew about Harald, Gull and Gunnar. Gustav sat on the floor and put his head in his hands. Erik stood in silence and waited for his friend.

"Erik, I do not want to believe it but it is a convincing argument. We all knew that Gull was attracted to married women, but Harald's wife Greta!"

"That is not all I know my friend. Gunnar was here in Dyflin until very recently and his wife is still here with the queen. Perhaps we should go and meet her so you can hear from her what she has to say about Gunnar."

The two men left the storage and made their way to the queen's quarters. As they crossed to the royal buildings there was a little commotion as some warriors arrived and went ahead of them to the same destination. A slim, black haired warrior was at the front of the party, Erik and Gustav heard him address the guard.

"You know who I am; I am here to take the queen to the safety of Kirkham under orders of Jarl Olaf."

The guard let them through and Erik recognised him as one of King Jarn's men from the battle field.

"Well met, my friend and I need to speak with the lady Freyja."

"I am sorry friend but I am to let nobody but the king and his family in."

"Why is that, surely a friend who fought alongside you is no threat."

The guard looked embarrassed as he recognised Erik as one of the men who came to the rescue of the huscurls.

"My heart tells me to let you through but I have orders and I have to follow them. But take some advice friend, wait outside a while as I believe the lady Freyja will stay with the queen and she is leaving soon. You should be able to speak to her on the way to Wood Quay."

*

Harald was in a foul mood. He knew that Gustav was getting more distant and he feared catching up with Gunnar. If he found him he would have to kill him and then return to Scania and that whore of a wife. His groin still ached and his damaged testicle was nothing more than a tiny pebble in his sack. However, he was getting stronger every day and he felt he needed to build his fitness up so he decided to practise his sword work with Glum.

"Are you sure Jarl Harald, you are still limping and in battle I would want to finish off a wounded man quickly."

"The limp is going away and I need to build up my sword arm. We should all practise every day for when we meet the outlaw."

They clashed swords a few times and already Harald could feel the weight of his weapon becoming uncomfortable. He imagined he was knocking some sense into Gustav and found some extra reserves to carry on.

"Why are my brothers such arseholes, Glum?"

Glum looked shocked and he noticed the other men look away. Harald was a difficult master but usually made sure there was a good supply of silver. Although since they had heard about Gunnar being in Iceland he had become more and more difficult. Glum, Helgi, Flosi and Hrut were all new recruits to Harald's band and did not know Gunnar or Erik. In fact, after the death of Gull the group had drifted apart as most were left distraught by the murder of the most likeable brother and the loss of his friend Gunnar.

"Gustav is a good man Harald; he just misses his wife and her lovely arse."

The joke did not raise a smile with Harald; he just dropped his sword and looked exhausted.

"I need to eat and drink now."

*

Mort and his guard waited for Queen Gyda to come out of her private room. He recognised Helga but there was another woman offering him and his men some ale. She had shoulder length hair plaited down the back. Her hair looked both brown and blond and mesmerised him. But her hair was nothing compared to her eyes, she had long lashes, eyes of pale green with a hazel ring at the centre. She spoke to Mort but his throat was dry and his tongue felt too big in his mouth. He mumbled something to her and felt himself go red in the face.

"I am sorry, is that Irish? Do you speak Danish, and would you like some ale?"

"Yes, sorry my throat is very dry, what is your name, I am Mort."

"Well Mort I am Freyja and the Queen is taking care of me while our husbands are away."

Mort was crestfallen, he had only known this woman seconds but he was devastated that he could not have her.

The Queen came out from behind her curtain with Helga close behind.

"Is it time Mort, I will need to take some things?"

"From the message I got, Olaf is very concerned for you and would like you safely behind the walls of Kirkham until he returns. If I were you, Queen Gyda, I would take everything you would miss if you were away for a year or more."

"Thank you Mort, but I would prefer it if you looked at me rather than Freyja." Gyda had a smile on her face when he glanced back at her and he felt like a fool. Could women read a man's thoughts so easily? "We will wait outside; it feels hot in here to me." As Mort left he could hear the stifled laughter of the women and he knew he was blushing again. He was distracted by a blond man with untidy hair addressing him.

213

"Is the lady Freyja in there with the Queen?"

"Yes she is, and what is your name, friend?"

"I am Erik and this is Gustav, he has just arrived in Dyflin but I fought alongside your Jarl Olaf when Ivar attacked."

"Well then I owe you thanks for your support."

"Why do you need to speak to Freyja?"

"We just need to pass on a message from her husband."

*

Harald was sleeping in the sunshine while his men made camp. They were busy and only noticed Erik and Gustav arrive at the last moment.

"Boys you have done a good job, why don't you go and find yourself some ale and I will wake my brother."

Gustav gave the men some shards of silver and they left for the nearest brewer.

Gustav walked over to his brother and took out his sword. He touched the tip of it on his brother's cheek and poked until he awoke.

Harald felt the sharp point push into his skin and opened his eyes. He looked along the length of the sword and thought he would be a dead man until he noticed Gustav at the other end.

"By the gods, what are you doing, get this thing out of my face," he tried to push it away but Gustav held it firm, cutting his cheek.

"Tell me the truth big brother? What happened the night that Gull died?"

Erik saw a brief expression cross Harald's face but as soon as he saw it, it was gone.

"You know what I know, brother, we found Gunnar with our dead brother, ask Erik he was with me when the outlaw was caught."

"There is something I would like to say about that Harald," Erik stepped forward and took out his sword too.

"I had drunk a belly full of ale the night before and felt terrible when you woke me but I remember you said you had something to show me. Tell me how you knew you would find Gunnar with Gull dead?"

"Your memory fails you Erik, I did not say that."

214

"I am Erik Ericsson and I know I can be a little slow when it comes to thinking but I have a good memory and I know what happened and I remember what you said. Now tell Gustav why and when you killed Gull."

"I know I should have killed him Erik, but I have lost one brother and I could not have Harald's death haunting me." Gustav looked broken, all the old pain of Gull's death was opened again and he wept as his brother admitted what Erik had strongly suspected. They had told Harald that when they returned to Scania he would be declared outlaw. At this point Harald's men had returned and Gustav told them the news. Helgi, Flosi and Hrut joined Gustav and Erik while Glum decided to stay with Harald, perhaps out of pity. Gustav told Glum that he would be welcome back to Scania if he changed his mind, as long as he did not return with Harald, otherwise Glum would share the charge for helping Harald.

They had bought some supplies for the journey and planned to stop in the Hebrides on their way back to Iceland. The plan was to go straight to Njal and tell him of Gunnar's innocence and buy back his land.

They were only five so they hoped for a good wind to carry them to Iceland, they sent a few prayers to Aegir, as they were travelling on his realm, and a request to Thor for that strong wind.

Chapter 23

An ash I know there stands,
Yggdrasill is its name,
A tall tree, showered with shining loam.
From there come the dews that drop in the valleys.
It stands forever green over Urth's well.

It was early in the morning and the sun was just coming up on this late spring day. At the front of the army a hand went up and they started moving toward the Poddle Valley. Leading were the majority of the horsemen with a few bringing up the rear. The lead horse was a large grey mare carrying the King and his slave lover. Behind them came the bulk of the army on foot, and at the very rear some carts carrying supplies. The Norns at the foot of Yggdrasill would not be watching as they had already woven the future of every man here.

On the right side of the King rode Litta, in a position of power and influence. In his life he had not been so elevated and he would work hard to stay at the King's side. He would drop back a little at times to get a better look at Kanin and wished he had a little Knulla to call his own.

Kanin had recognised him as soon as he had met up with King Ivar's troops. She remembered his torn ear and the look in his eyes. She did not fear him now as she was the property of the King, but she did not want to be alone with him again.

Tyr hoped that this battle for Dyflin would go smoother and he hoped he could forget the wrath that Baldr had bestowed upon him. If he was lucky the disgusting Litta might just get himself killed. The death of Litta would be something to celebrate.

Sihtric was excited, his father had been very pleased with his report and as a reward he could fight at his side. He felt taller and bigger on his horse and the men must see him as a man now. If he was lucky he would be able to kill somebody today and he was looking forward to the enemy's death.

*

The army made its way along the north side of the Poddle and a spring mist drifted across the river and blocked the view of the town. King Ivar was beaming as he could not hope for such luck. If they could not see the town the defenders would not see his army until it was too late.

"Sihtric, take my Kanin to the back to the supplies, and tell the guard that she is very precious to the king."

"Yes father, but do not start without me, I wish to kill a few men too."

"I can look after her for you, King Ivar."

"Litta, you are the last man I wish to look after Kanin, you dirty bastard."

The king waited for his troops to all gather two hundred paces from the town and rode along their line addressing his men.

"Ok boys, this will be easier than the last time. King Jarn thinks he has seen the last of Waterford and his general has left Dyflin in a longship with all his warriors. Remember in that town is gold, silver, ale and women. Kill the men and stay alive and you will get your share of it all."

*

Kent had not been punished for allowing the young prince to die, but he was always guarding the town through the sleeping hours and it was exhausting him. His hair was getting whiter by the day and his body ached all the time. All his old war injuries had their own specific cold ache and none of them where ever quiet. He was a light sleeper so he struggled to rest when the sun was up and he was surviving on about three hours of sleep a day. It had been two weeks now and there was no sign that he would be relieved of this nightmare. He leaned against the wooden post, looked out to the dark west and rested his head on his arms. He was asleep as soon as his eyes closed.

*

"Old man, do you need a young prince to fight by your side again?"

"Prince Ragnal, can you forgive me for not protecting you. Your brother is angry with me for not keeping you alive."

"It was a battle Kent, men are trying to kill men, somebody will die, and it was my fate that day."

"But I was given one task and that task was to protect you with my life. Now I am still living and you have become a spirit."

"Kent, you are very tired and you are sleeping now, for this is only a dream and not the realm of men. You must wake up and fulfil your duty to your king. You should be awake now and defending the kingdom. For the wealth of Dyflin is coveted across Ireland and there is no time to sleep. Wake, Kent and watch to the west."

Kent lifted his head and opened his eyes into the new dawn. Facing west the sky was still black on the horizon but the dim light of dawn was flooding around him. He was exhausted and just wanted to lie down and sleep from one full moon to the next. To the west was a light morning mist and it was moving with a small breeze. His tired mind must be playing tricks on him as it seemed the mist became a horde of men holding swords and running at the walls of Dyflin.

*

The mercenaries went first, running toward the town looking for a weak point to break through. Tyr held back with half the cavalry ready to ride into Dyflin as soon as there was a way through. Behind Tyr were the huscarls of King Ivar, with the king, Sihtric and the rest of the cavalry bringing up the rear.

The mercenaries were a mixture of desperate men and outlaws, outcasts hoping for a way back into civilisation. One possible way back for them was wealth and Dyflin held the key to unlock their own personal nightmare. King Ivar welcomed them to his side but they had to fight for him and be at the fore front of any battle. These men that lived their life on the edge had to be able to adapt or die. The survivors were resourceful and it was not too long before the gate of Dyflin was opened and the horsemen poured in.

"Ride with me son, and let us kill the King together."

Sihtric beamed as his horse galloped behind his father, for today he would become a man.

*

His head was full of the fog of exhaustion as he ran to the gate. Before his brain had fully woken up invaders were at the walls and there was only a light guard to defend the town. The men attacking the walls quickly started moving toward the gate and on instinct Kent ran there too. As he got close he could see men and horses pouring through the opening so he veered off to his left between two dwellings. He pulled back the door to his right and shouted inside, "Invasion, grab your weapons and defend your families." He turned on his heel and shouted into the door on his left. A man and his son came out the first door, thankfully already dressed and ready for the day.

"Get weapons, we are being attacked and they are already in the town. Hurry and follow me."

While waiting for his two allies another man came out of the door on his left.

"Wake as many as you can and meet me near the King's hall. I will have spears and shields for everyone."

Kent ran with Igor and his son Einar to the weapon store. They ran parallel to the main street between the small wooden dwellings. To their right they could see glimpses of the invaders but kept going as it was not far to the king's hall.

*

Harald and Glum awoke to the sound of men shouting. They were sleeping outside in their war gear so were up and ready with swords drawn. Between the dwellings of Dyflin they could see horses carrying warriors chasing men and women down.

"Glum, let us go to the king's hall and see if there is a defence of this kingdom we can join. For two men alone can be cut down by either side."

"Do you want to fight for the King of Dyflin Harald?"

"Well I see it like this, Dyflin is a Norse kingdom and we do not know who is attacking it but the likelihood is one of the Irish kingdoms. I am Norse, not Irish."

The two men jogged toward the king's hall hoping to find some allies in this surprise fight.

*

King Ivar rode into Dyflin with his sword held high. This was more like it, the mercenaries had done a good job breaking into the town and now it would be his. He saw a man running away from his attack and could not resist hacking into his back with his long sword. The blow was not fatal and the man stumbled before trying to get up and continue his escape.

"Son, finish him off, kill your first man."

Sihtric caught up with his father and ran at the wounded man with his sword held out straight. He was so excited that he would finally kill a man and become a warrior like his father. He caught the running man up and stabbed the back of his neck with his sword.

His weapon got stuck in the man's neck and he lost hold of it. The poor undefended peasant hit the floor hard, his face taking the responsibility of halting him.

"Sihtric, you have lost your sword, it is still stuck in that fellow's neck."

"Don't worry father I will retrieve it." Sihtric reined his horse in and jumped down to get his lost weapon. King Ivar and a few of his huscurls stayed close to the prince to ensure his safety. Sihtric approached the dead man who was laying on his front with the sword stuck in the vertebrae of his neck. The prince grabbed his sword and pulled but it stayed stuck and all he achieved was to lift the corpse up a little. He put his foot on the dead man's back and pulled with both hands. After a few seconds the neck gave way and he stumbled back as his sword was released. A thick syrup of red gore oozed from the wound and Sihtric stared at it, realising he had taken a life. His head swam and he leaned forward, dropping his weapon, before throwing up on his boots.

*

Kent arrived near the king's hall with five men in tow. Two warriors arrived at the same time and as he did not recognise them, he spoke only in Norse to test if they were with the Irish invaders or not.

"Tell me your loyalty or we will kill you here."

"I am Harald and this is Glum, we are from Scania so we will fight with the kingdom rather than the Irish."

Hearing a strong Danish accent Kent relaxed.

"I am Kent and this is Igor and his son, I have not had time to ask the names of the other three men."

"I am Leif and this is Hakon and Harald."

"Right everyone, I am a captain of the King's guard, stay together and we may live through this."

They were a little distance from the king's area but things did not look good, as there was the chaos of battle all around them with horsemen riding down anyone on foot.

"We need to get to the weapon store, as there are many spears inside and they will help us defend against a man on a horse. So wait for my signal and we will cross to it together."

They stayed in a tight group and waited for the right moment. There was a small lull in the fighting between them and the store so they ran quickly toward their goal.

The wooden door of the storage hut was closed; Kent made straight for it and pulled it open. There were two broken shields on the floor and a spear head. The hut had been ransacked and there was nothing left of any use inside.

"Skit!"

"Kent, forget that and tell me who is approaching."

From the direction of Wood Quay a troop of about four hundred warriors were approaching at walking pace toward the seven warriors.

*

Litta stayed near his king under the pretence that he was protecting the young prince. But Litta felt safer with King Ivar's huscurls nearby. He was an accomplished fighter but he did not feel happy on the horse. Most of the men around him had swords drawn, but Litta's small sword stayed in its scabbard. To give him extra reach he had a long handled broad axe. He was making the best of his time and enjoyed chopping down on the panicked residence of Dyflin.

Litta had spent a lot of time in Dyflin but it did not feel like home. He was a short, ugly man and used to ridicule. On top of that he was a slaver and looked down on by the residence of Dyflin, the very people that profited from his activity. These bastards were happy to let him do the dirty work for them but they did not want to socialise with Litta, or even Bjarni, when he was alive.

Usually when Litta was in a new town or village the older children would try and tease him or call him names. It would only stop after he had caught one and beaten them sufficiently to warn off their friends.

As they rode along at a slow trot, chasing some more merchants and their families, he noticed Ivar's men rode around a boy of twelve, running for his life. Litta took great pleasure in swinging his axe into the back of the small bastard's head. The axe struck hard and made a beautiful crunch as he took that young life.

"One less little skit to throw scorn at the great Litta."

*

King Ivar pulled his grey mare to a stop and his huscurls stopped around him, including Litta and a sick covered Sihtric.

"Havelock, find Tyr and gather the troops together inside the gate, make sure you leave enough men to keep the new slaves we have acquired."

221

"Ok Litta, this seems too easy so let us assume we have not met the main force yet. I think we better prepare for a battle."

King Ivar took his men back to the town gate and wondered what had happened to Jarn Cuaran. If he was dead Tyr should know as Ivar had not seen any sight of him.

"Kent, is this all there is? Where are the rest of the guard?"

"My Lord King, I believe most of the guard are dead and I have seen at least thirty fit men lying in their own blood. It is only us seven left to join you in defending the town."

"Take one side Kent, I am short of experienced men."

King Jarn stood on a small wooden stool and addressed his men.

"We do not have time for long speeches and false hopes. The future of Dyflin hangs by a thread. Waterford are not only at the gate, they are within the town causing destruction. I have men loading all the ships at Wood Quay with the wealth of the nation and therefore I have left enough men to guard that. We need to engage Ivar and his troops and do our best to repel him. If it is an impossible fight we will move back and defend the Longport. If Ivar has the upper hand we can find sanctuary at the Fylde."

Kent was shocked by the speech, it sounded to him that the King had given up on Dyflin already. Although he estimated that the invaders had at least twice as many warriors as his king. He dropped to the right side of the troop and recognised quite a few old comrades. His seven new friends joined him there.

"We will have to be in the second row at least, as none of us has a shield. But have more faith than the king, we need to defend our homes and family from rape and slaughter."

The words touched the men close by and Kent hoped they would find extra courage knowing their wives and children faced a terrible threat. King Jarn had sent a few men to locate the bulk of King Ivar's force and they now returned; all telling of an advance through the town. King Jarn had already decided on his course of action and they retreated to Wood Quay and set up a defence there. The loading of the ships was complete and the guards at the port were a welcome addition to the Dyflin defence.

Igor had stayed close with his son and now spoke up, voicing his greatest fear.

"Kent, we live near the town gate, my wife and daughter were still in our home when we left. I told them to stay there as I would return and protect them. What do I do? I am

222

defending the Longport with my son and our choice is die or leave Dyflin. One question remains in my head at this time, what is happening to my wife and daughter right now?"

Kent grimaced at the emotional speech from Igor, the father and husband, for he shared the same dilemma, Kent's wife and son were somewhere in the part of town now controlled by King Ivar.

Chapter 24

Forward he went on the midmost way,
He came to a dwelling, a door on its posts;
In did he fare, on the floor was a fire,
Two beauties, by the hearth there sat,
Hfran in olden dress.

Litta was pleased with himself. While King Ivar was gathering the main force to strike hard at King Jarn and ensure victory for Waterford, he was tasked with going through each building and taking prisoners. He had thirty warriors and they would check each hut with three men. Kill any resistance, arrest possible warriors and have fun. The last point was added by Litta for his own pleasure.

He was getting annoyed as half the dwellings were empty and any containing inhabitants usually had old women and children. But now Litta struck lucky, he pushed through the leather door and found a woman of about thirty three summers with a young woman half her age. A mother and daughter, and they were a pair of beauties. He licked his lips and knew he would be searching no more today.

The woman was pure Scandinavian with plaited blond hair and a lovely full figure, the girl a younger version of her mother. The older woman held a seax in her hand and the girl defended herself with a small axe. Litta looked into the pale blue eyes of the mother and saw fear. She feared rape and murder but that was secondary compared to her fears for her child.

"Ladies, that is no way to welcome a guest into your home, you should be more hospitable than that."

"IGOR!" The older woman shouted out and looked around for emancipation, but none came.

Litta turned to the two soldiers accompanying him, "boys, let's disarm these lovely ladies before they hurt themselves. When we have them tied up you can go and root out some more thralls."

"Kent, we cannot stay here and face slaughter. The King has given up on Dyflin. Why don't we swim up the Liffey and come back into town and at least try and save our families?"

"Igor you speak sense but I am torn as I owe my allegiance to the king. I am a captain of his troops, my job is to fight and die for the king."

"Is it your job to stand by and let your wife be raped and murdered? And what of your son?"

Kent knew he was right but to leave the defenders here, at their last stand, would be an obvious act of betrayal. He thought of his wife and son then, making his decision easier.

Kent surveyed the area, they were close to the bank of the Liffey and the water lapped at the coast a pace behind them. He knew what he had to do, his boy may have joined in the defence of the town but his wife Unn would be vulnerable. Her need was greater than King Jarn. He looked at Igor and the other man patiently waited for him to choose his family over his honour.

*

The two other men had left and that was some relief as they had looked at her daughter, Hrafn, with much lust. But it still meant they were both tied up and left with the little ugly one. Thorhild had made a decision and it was not taken lightly. She would sacrifice herself to protect her beautiful daughter. It might buy her enough time for Igor to return and kill this ugly little man.

"What a lovely feast I have here, I just cannot decide who to have first." Litta came up with an idea he liked, he would strip them both and have the mother while feeling the daughter.

Thorhild had pleaded with him to take her and leave her daughter but the vile beast ignored her and started to strip Hrafn. He cut her clothes away with his seax and Thorhild could see his orm pushing to be released. Hrafn was weeping uncontrollably and he left her lying naked with her hands bound, before starting to cut away her mother's clothes.

Thorhild looked at her daughter and told her to be brave. She told her little girl that her father would come and rescue them soon but in her heart she feared that Igor was already dead, as they would be soon. The vile rapist approached her now and his orm was long,

225

thick and ugly. He was dribbling with excitement and when he climbed on top of her she could not hold back the tears.

*

Kent, Igor and Einar had slipped into the water as soon as the invaders attacked the defenders of Dyflin. A couple of men turned and looked at them but they were soon busy fighting King Ivar's men. They moved out a little way, half swimming and half walking on the muddy silt of the Liffey. Their intention was to get far enough away from the fighting so they could not be seen coming ashore and heading back to their homes.

*

Glum and Harald found themselves at the front of the shield wall. It was a force of desperation and the best equipped warriors took the front and centre of the defence.

Glum had been following Harald for over three years and had a fair amount of silver to show for his service. Harald was a cantankerous man but usually made the right decisions when it came to making gold and silver. He had felt a strange loyalty to the older man and knew he was still not recovered from his injury. Glum could not imagine what pain he went through, having a knife in the bulle. So against his better judgement he had stayed to look after Harald and now he was in a shield wall facing twice as many men and four times as many warriors.

"Harald, today we are going to die defending a town we do not care about and a king who appears weak."

"Glum, we have no choice, perhaps Odin is making me pay for killing my brother or for letting my enemy take the blame. But think this, if we had met the army from Waterford as two men, they would have cut us down any way. This is a fjord full of skit and if we fight well we may get out of it. Remember there are boats behind us, so pray to any god you like and hope they are looking down on Glum and Harald this day."

"Well if I must die this day I mean to take a few with me to Valholl."

*

King Ivar was enjoying this battle; he had his distant cousin King Jarn with his back to the sea and at least twice the troops to attack him. The defenders of Dyflin were proving a hard nut to crack but they could not stay where they were forever. Ivar could see they had a few boats ready to make their escape but only half of them could fit on board. King Ivar

226

would do them a favour, he would kill the other half and then there would be space for the survivors.

*

Kent helped the two men climb up the bank and they started to make their way back toward the town. The plan was poorly thought out as there was the tail end of King Ivar's train making its way into the town. The three comrades kept low in the long grass so they were not seen, but it made for slow progress. Kent watched the coming and going into the town, the men leaving were obviously taking away the spoils of glory. Although he saw a young woman and her ugly brother riding away too, it was a strange sight among all the warriors.

"Kent, we cannot skulk along like this while our wives are being abused. Let's just get a move on as I have a daughter to protect as well."

"I have been thinking Igor; we can get to your place quicker. We should stay together as the town is overrun with Waterford militia."

"All help is welcome, and when we have made my girls safe I will come and help you find your wife."

*

The Waterford troops hit the Dyflin wall hard, so hard the men at the back found the back of their feet in the Liffey. The Dyflin warriors had a few swords, many broad axes, and a few only had the belt knife, the seax. The biggest problem for the defenders was they only had enough shields to cover the first few rows. Much of the fighting gear of Dyflin had been left at home, everyone expecting a peaceful day at the market, and not this. The invaders were well armed and had many axe and sword to fight with.

The shields were pushed hard together with the iron pommels scraping against their enemies shield. Harald and Glum were experienced fighters and they had iron strips in their leggings to protect against a sharp stab at the shins. The enemies were so close you could smell the breath of the men on the other side of the shield wall. Both sides were locked in a vicious scrum to the death. The second row kept their shields held above the front row to defend their colleagues. Although if they saw an opening in the opposite wall they would throw their axe over and try and hook the opposing shield down. The pushing and shoving was only beginning but Harald felt himself weakening, he knew he could not do this for too long.

227

Tyr had left his horse tied up behind and now joined his men in the shield wall. His men held the advantage, as this time the men of Waterford had really caught Dyflin by surprise. The front line of defenders had shields and some in the second line, but Tyr suspected they were a little thin at the back. It gave him an idea and he made his way out of the pack to go and speak with his King.

"Tyr, what shall we do, push the bastards into the Liffey or make a pile of corpses at the Longport?"

"I have an idea King Ivar; I think you really caught them by surprise this time. I believe they are a little light in shields. I think we should pull back from the shield wall and launch a few volleys of spear on their heads."

"Give the order Tyr, and when the spears have fallen we will ride our horses into them."

The men of Dyflin thought there was a reprieve as the Waterford warriors pulled their shields away. The invaders moved back ten paces and formed a strong line. The tired men of Dyflin held their weapons close and waited for the next move. King Jarn remained quiet, not giving any proud speeches to his men, for what could he say, they knew they were all doomed.

A shout went up from the Waterford ranks and the sky darkened as spears flew over the front rows of Waterford and rained death down on the men of Dyflin. The front two rows held up their shields to defend and the few men that had a shield behind. A well thrown spear will bring a great weight down upon a shield and will most likely pierce the wood. Many of the men with shields suffered injury but they were the lucky ones. The men without shields were devastated. Many crouched down to hopefully escape the wave of death. Some were killed instantly and a few survived with crippling injuries. King Jarn lost nearly eighty men in that one volley of spears. Glum had crouched down and felt the hard blow of a spear on his shield. He opened his eyes and saw the tip of the spear between his nose and fist.

"Thank you Odin, for sparing me this day." He looked over to his left to see how Harald was. His Jarl was still crouched with a spear held aloft from his shield also.

"Harald, are you hurt, we have to rise and face the enemy attack." Glum pushed at his friends arm and Harald rolled over. Glum saw the tip of the spear coming out of Harald's back. He looked like a baby curled up on a skewer.

*

King Ivar rode around his troops with his horsemen ready for battle and he saw a beaten opponent. King Jarn stepped forward holding his sword aloft. When King Ivar got close Jarn threw his sword to the ground and left his hands in the air. King Ivar pulled his beautiful grey mare up in front of his cousin and smiled with triumph.

"Well Jarn I was enjoying that, can we not fight some more?"

"Ivar, you have won Dyflin, there is no need for further bloodshed."

"But what shall I do with you cousin? I think I should take you as my prisoner for now, while I enjoy the moment."

Jarn was taken away by two warriors, but he was not bound at the hand to reflect his status. The front two rows of the defenders of Dyflin were butchered at the long port while all the men that were badly armed were set free. All free men of Dyflin had to swear fealty to King Ivar first. When this was finished the new King of Dyflin stepped down from his horse and welcomed his slave queen. Kanin rode in on a pony, but on seeing Ivar jumped down and ran to her king.

*

Kent stood in the doorway of Igor's home and watched the man he hardly knew cradle his dead wife. The younger man, Einar, had his arms round his parents and was weeping too. The dead woman was naked and Kent felt ashamed that he could see blood between her legs. She had been raped and her throat had been cut but in which order they would never know. It was still obvious that she had been a handsome woman and no doubt Igor had been very proud of her.

There was no sign of the daughter.

"Igor and Einar I am sorry for your loss, stay here while I check my home but I will return to help you bury your wife and mother."

Kent's home was a few narrow streets away near Cooper Gatan. He approached his home with a feeling of trepidation and dread. He saw the back of their small home at first and all looked normal. When he came round to the front his heart sank as he saw the leather door was hanging off. He looked inside and there was nobody there. It was obvious there had been a struggle but he saw no blood. Perhaps Unn and Bjorn were still alive; he hoped so and sent a prayer to Jord to protect his family. He stood outside his home and listened to the celebrations of the invaders and the screams of the defeated.

*

Litta rode to the camp outside the town; it had been an excellent day for him. What he had wanted since his balls grew was his own Knulla and now he had one. Her hands had been bound and she was dressed before she was placed upon the horse.

Hrafn was in a daze, it was like a bad dream and she still could not believe her mother was dead. Any moment now her mother and father would come and take her away from the odjur that held her prisoner on his horse. She could feel his horrible thing pressing against her back and her kut still felt sore from the invasion it had suffered. Her blond hair hung over her face and through the tears she could see they were leaving the town. She felt the panic rising again not knowing where the odjur was taking her. They were following a few horses and carts leaving the town, probably to the invader's camp. She looked over toward the Liffey River and saw a few men crouched on the bank and wonder what they were doing there. She closed her wet eyes, crying for her mother and her freedom.

Epilogue

The cold wind blew at us from Norway, across the great, grey northern sea. It gave a little respite from the rowing as it was strong enough to take us southward. We had met some more of Jarl Olaf's men at Orkney and they joined us in travelling to the meeting point at the Saxon sheep island of Sceapige.

I had never seen or heard of such a great army of Danes, although when I spoke to him about it Jarl Olaf told me that the great Roman Emperor of Germania could call on a force as great. I have been told there are up to seventy longships converging on Sceapige Island and none of these take less than sixty men. The money was coming from King Sweyn of Danemark, but he hoped to gain a nation and extend his empire.

I had received a promise of great wealth from Jarl Olaf and held an elevated position among his men. Berg had stayed by my side and also the odious Ketil but I still missed having Erik here. The only problem with this adventure was being so far from my Freyja and I hoped we could engage the Saxons quickly and then return home to Iceland. But I have the feeling that Jarl Olaf wants me to stay with him until he has taken the crown of Norway. Deep in my heart I am sorely tempted.

Historical Note

Gunnar, his kin, Njal and Bergþorar are all characters from the Icelandic Saga 'Njal's Saga' sometimes called 'The Saga of Burning Njal'. There has been much debate among historians whether the characters from the Icelandic Saga's are real or pure fiction. The generally accepted conclusion is that they are somewhere in between. Possible real people who have been embellished and slightly fictionalised over all the years their stories have been told.

I read and enjoyed Njal's Saga but wanted to know more about the hero Gunnar Hamundsson, unfortunately there was little known about him so I decided to give him a history.

I have tried to write my own version of an Icelandic Saga but in a more modern form. I hope I have come close to that and you have enjoyed reading this first instalment in Gunnar's Saga.

In the late eighth century Scania (Scania), the southernmost Swedish county was part of Denmark. It stayed Danish until 1658 and would not officially becoming Swedish until 1719. Even now the local dialect in that region is littered with Danish words. By the way my favourite Danish/Scania word is Elbow.

Iceland at the time of this saga was an independent republic and would remain so until 1262, coming under the rule of Norway and then Denmark, not gaining its independence again until 1918.

Cornwell was deemed part of the English nation under King Aethelred but was not finally subdued until well into his reign. It finally succumbed to Saxon rule slowly but I have dramatised this and bootlegged the battle of Liddyford for the sake of my story, the battle was actually between the Saxons and Vikings. Therefore King Cadoc and his son Prince Tristan are fictional; however the seer Mawgan is based on an actual seer who looked into Olaf Tryggvason's future. The last recorded King of Cornwall was Dumgarth who apparently drowned in 875.

Olaf is a real historical character who was born the grandson to the former King of Norway. At this time his grandfather had been deposed and his mother tried to escape persecution but ended up being captured and sold into slavery. He was bought out of slavery by a kindly Swedish merchant and taken to the court of King Valdemar, in Russia. Eventually he became a captain under the King and fought with the Holy Roman Emperor against King Harald Bluetooth of Denmark. After his wife Geira died he left her homeland and began raiding Gotland and Scania as a Viking. He is driven to reclaim his birth right, the crown of Norway.

The events around the Althing called by Queen Gyda of Dublin are all based on the story from the saga Heimskringla, although there are two further sagas written about Olaf. Effectively the records recount that there was an Althing called by Queen Gyda and the two best candidates were Olaf and Alfvine. Although Olaf was in his bad weather clothes the Queen chose him over Alfvine, Alfvine was devastated and challenged Olaf to 'holmgang'. There is no record that Alfvine was part of the mythical Jomsviking but I thought the story would be enhanced with their inclusion.

Dublin literally means Black Pool as the town was built beside the small lake formed at the seaward end of the River Poddle. I believe there was a settlement there before the Vikings arrived but they made it into a great trading town. At the time of Gunnar and Olaf it was the only true Norse kingdom across all of Ireland. There are records that the Kingdom of Dublin extended over to the British mainland but I could not find where this part of the kingdom was located. I decided to give the peninsula of The Fylde to Dublin as it has been known by its Scandinavian name for a thousand years. Kirkham was a small town at the time and 'Kirk' is the Scandinavian word for church although 'Ham' is Saxon.

The main trade in Dublin was the slave trade and the one nation that was commonly enslaved was the Picts. Nobody truly knows why the Picts disappeared from the east of Scotland but perhaps it was something like the devastation of the Native Americans by European settlers. Perhaps they were easy fodder for the slavers and the remaining small populations of Picts were absorbed into the Scottish/Viking majority.

The Invasion of Dublin is a real event and King Ivar of Waterford was repelled initially before re-grouping and seizing the Kingdom from King Jarn. The records show that Jarl Olaf was probably instrumental in repelling the first attack before leaving in pursuit of his birth right.

Nearly all the King's, Prince's, Bishops, Jarl's and Ealdorman mentioned in this book are historical characters, apart from the men of Cornwall, Harald Sveinsson and his kin.

The characters in this story have more journeys to travel and battles to fight. Gunnar needs to make his fortune back so he can return home and clear his name. He also needs to reunite with his wife and make sure they both stay alive. Olaf needs allies in his quest to become King of Norway and Njal needs to win the case against Gunnar at the Althing.

The Battle of Maldoon

Gunnar's Saga 2

Chapter 1

The battle raged around him but he was ignored by friend and foe alike. He could smell the smoke of a fire but the sound of the battle was muffled to him. The battle meant nothing to him, the outcome was irrelevant. The death of one man was important; this was about revenge for the man he loved above all others. His feet squelched in the marsh grass as he walked between individual bouts, the men around, fighting for their life, meaningless to him.

Ahead he could see his Jarl, a tall slim man, expertly deploying his sword, causing genocide among the Saxon warriors about him. Beside his overlord were a group of the best fighters who would surely cut him down eventually. He came close to his Jarl and the man still had his back to him, the warrior to his right glanced back, seeing it was him, an ally, the man turned away and continued to cut into Saxon flesh.

Now he was only a pace behind his Jarl and stuck his long knife into the man's back, hoping to cut into his kidney and guts. He had wiped the blade in some animal dung and hoped this would guarantee death.

His Jarl crumpled to the ground and the man to the right turned and saw it was him who had dealt the fatal blow. His adversary screamed at him and swung his long blade. He watched the arch of the black iron sweep through the air and wondered what it would be like to die. He had his hand on his pommel so he should make it to Valholl and be reunited with the man he loved above all others. The blade cut hard into the place where his neck met his shoulder and it was like being punched by Ulf. The force knocked him to one side but he felt no pain as he hit the cool, damp grass. Many blades came at him now as if they were jabbing for pork at a feast but again pain did not accompany the strikes. He drifted away and knew when he woke he would see Alfvine again, never to leave his side.

Printed in Great Britain
by Amazon